The One That Got Away

The One That Got Away

by
Chris Ryan

POTOMAC BOOKS

An imprint of the University of Nebraska Press

First Memories of War edition published 2006
First Brassey's Edition 1998

Copyright © 1995 by Chris Ryan

First published in 1995 in the United Kingdom by Century,
20 Vauxhall Bridge Road, London SW1V 25A.

Library of Congress Cataloging-in-Publication Data

Ryan, Chris, 1961
    The one that got away / Chris Ryan.
      p. cm.
    Originally published: U.K. : Century, 1995
    1. Ryan, Chris, 1961– 2. Persian Gulf War, 1991—Personal narratives, British.
  3. Great Britain. Army. Special Air Service Regiment, 22nd—Biography. I. Title.
  DS79.74R93   1998
  956.7044'2—dc21   97-40358
  ISBN-10: 1-59797-008-5   CIP
  ISBN-13: 978- 1-59797-008-2
A CIP catalog record for this book is available from the British Library.

First Edition

Acknowledgements

I wish to thank the following:

Duff Hart-Davis for all his encouragement, patience and
valuable time that he spent on this project.
All my family and friends for the patience and understanding
they showed me throughout this whole adventure.
My editor Mark Booth and his team at Random House for their
help and hard work.
Jeff Pope and Paul Greengrass at LWT for the initial debrief.
Last but not least Barbara Levy my agent for pointing me in the
right direction.

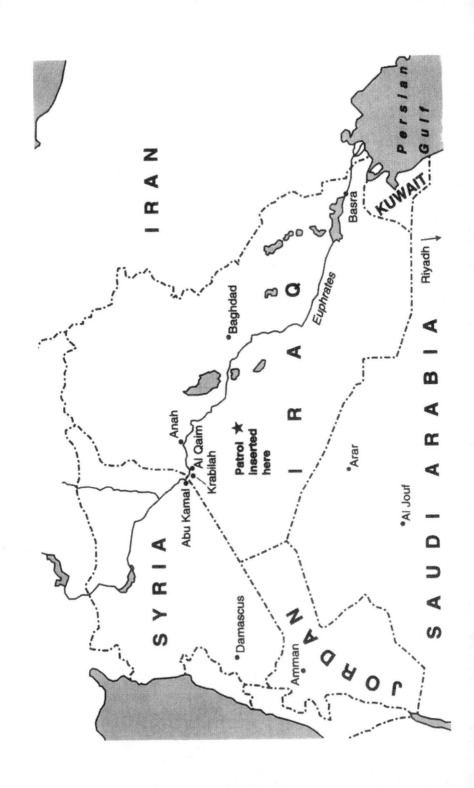

Contents

In The Beginning

I believed,
But found the time for doubting.
He made no sound,
I heard the Devil Shouting.

I wanted peace,
I did not want the glory.
I walked in Hell,
And now I tell my story.

I sing sad song,
I did not write the music.
I find sad words
Waiting – just inside my mind.

I played my part,
But seldom did I choose it.
I held a gun,
I did not want to use it.

Call it fate or destiny –
By either name, it troubles me.

And now,

If you should look into my eyes,
By chance you might just see
A sad, sad soul that sheds its tears,
Yet lets the heart go free.

And in between the two of them
If you should read my mind,
You'll know the soul still sheds its tears,
For deeds left far behind.

But if you see the eagle there,
Then don't ignore the dove,
For now that all the killing's done
There's nothing left but love.

J. Miles

Glossary

AWACS	Airborne warning and control system aircraft
Basha	Sleeping shelter
BCR	Battle casualty replacement
Bergen	Haversack
BG	Bodyguard (noun or verb)
Casevac	Casualty evacuation
CO	Commanding officer of the regiment
Comms	Communications
DF	Direction finding (equipment)
Director, The	Officer commanding Special Forces, generally a brigadier
DPM	Disruptive pattern material camouflage clothes
E & E	Escape and evasion
ERV	Emergency rendezvous
FMB	Forward mounting base
FOB	Forward operating base
GPS	Global positioning system (navigation aid)
GPMG	General-purpose machine gun (Gympi)
Head-Shed	Headquarters
Int	Intelligence
Loadie	Crewman on RAF military flight
LUP	Lying-up position
Magellan	Brand name of GPS
MSR	Main supply route
NBC	Nuclear, biological and chemical
OC	Officer commanding the squadron
OP	Observation post
PNG	Passive night goggles
PSI	Permanent staff instructor
REME	Royal Electrical Mechanical Engineers

Rupert	Officer
RTU	Return to unit
RV	Rendezvous
SAM	Surface-to-air missile
Sangar	Fortified enclosure
Satcom	Telephone using satellite transmission
Shamag	Shawl used by Arabs as head-dress
Shreddies	Army-issue underpants
SOP	Standard operating procedure
SP Team	Special Projects or counter-terrorist team
SQMS	Squadron Quartermaster Sergeant
SSM	Squadron Sergeant Major
Stag	Sentry duty
TACBE	Tactical rescue beacon
TEL	Transporter-erector-launcher vehicle
U/S	Unserviceable
VCP	Vehicle control point

Weapons

203	Combination of 5.56 calibre automatic rifle (top barrel) and 40mm. grenade launcher below
.50	Heavy machine gun
66	Disposable rocker-launcher
GPMG	7.62 medium-calibre general purpose machine gun
Minimi	5.56 calibre machine gun
M19	Rapid-fire grenade launcher

Chapter One

Stand By . . . Stand By . . . Go!

Our target was a disused mental hospital – a large, red-brick, Victorian building, once handsome but now derelict, standing in spacious grounds that had gone to seed. According to the exercise scenario, the five Middle Eastern terrorists who had gone to ground inside were holding nine hostages captive, and after a three-day siege matters were moving swiftly to a head.

As commander of the Sniper Team, I was in charge of eight men, pre-positioned with their rifles at observation points in outhouses, trees and on the ground. Two men were watching each face of the hospital and sending back running commentaries over their throat-mike radios to the Command Centre, which had been established in a separate building some two hundred metres from the front door. Each face of the hospital had been accorded a special code for instant recognition.

From the Command Centre the police negotiator was talking to the chief terrorist, but the man's patience appeared to be running out. He was demanding safe conduct to Heathrow for himself and his colleagues, threatening that if transport were not provided immediately he would shoot one of the hostages. Meanwhile, the officer commanding the SP (Special Projects, or counter-terrorist) team was continuously refining his plan for a deliberate assault on the building.

One sniper had just reported, 'There's a terrorist moving in a particular window,' when a shot cracked out from within the hospital. The negotiator established that a hostage had been executed. The terrorists called for a stretcher party to take the body away. The front door opened briefly, and a limp figure was bundled out. A four-man team ran in to collect it. Then the chief terrorist threatened to kill another hostage in half an hour if his demands were not met.

The moment had come for the police to hand over to the military. The police chief signed a written order passing command to OC 'B' Squadron, the senior SAS officer present, who gave his assault team orders for a deliberate option. The moment he had finished, the assault groups moved to their entry points. Now it was just a question of waiting for my snipers to get as many terrorists in their sights as possible. Listening to their commentaries on the radio net, the OC suddenly called out the order we'd all been waiting for: 'I have control. STAND BY . . . STAND BY . . . GO!'

For the past two days an eerie silence had prevailed in the grounds of the old hospital. Now a volley of rounds went down and the whole place erupted into action. Two vehicles screamed up to the building and disgorged a swarm of black-clad assaulters. Explosive charges blew in the windows. Within seconds a Chinook helicopter was poised above the roof and more black figures were fast-roping out of it, to abseil down to the windows or enter through the skylights. Stun grenades blasted off; smoke poured out. The radio carried a babble of shots, shouts, explosions and orders.

In a matter of minutes the building had been cleared, the terrorists theoretically killed and the hostages rescued. The assault commander reported that he had control, and command was formally handed back to the police. Then the OC went in to start taking statements, and the exercise wound down. The guys were pouring with sweat inside their black kit, but elated that things had gone well. As always, the assault had been realistic in every detail, and had been excellent training.

'Well done, everybody,' said the OC at his preliminary debrief. 'That was pretty good.' Because we'd had three tough days in a row, and were now facing a five-hour run back to base, he didn't go into detail. Rather, he set 11.00 on Friday morning as the time for the main wash-up in the squadron office.

'Thin out, guys,' said the Sergeant Major. 'On your bikes.'

So we packed our kit into the vehicles and set out for Hereford. But on the way events took an unexpected turn. It was 2 August 1990, and on the news we heard that Saddam Hussein had ordered the Iraqi army to invade Kuwait.

'So what?' said one of the guys scornfully. 'He's just a wanker.'

'Don't be too sure of it,' said someone else. 'It'll make big trouble, and the odds are we'll find ourselves in there. Maybe some of the guys have gone already.'

Speculation about Iraq and the possibility of war in the Gulf helped speed our journey home – but I don't think any of us realised just how Saddam's aggression against his neighbours was going to change our existence.

For the rest of that year our lives were dominated by uncertainty. Two squadrons – 'A' and 'D' – soon went out to the Gulf for build-up training; but until the last minute, we in 'B' Squadron were assured that we would not be going, as it was our turn to take over what are known in the SAS as team tasks – assignments for which small teams of men are needed in various parts of the world. Rumours began flying. As the likelihood of war increased, it was said that 'G' Squadron would go out to the Middle East as BCRs – battle casualty replacements – and since the commanding officer at Regimental Headquarters was ex-'G' Squadron, the story gained credence.

Different options were frequently discussed, one of them being that we might become sky-marshals on civilian flights to the Middle East – travelling ostensibly as normal fare-paying passengers, but in fact carrying weapons – to deal with any terrorist who might attempt a hijack. The idea seemed quite plausible; on the SP team we'd done any number of assaults on and inside aircraft, so that we were thoroughly familiar with the possibilities. But then the rumour died a natural death.

Throughout November and December, men were being selected for team tasks, and it was my luck to be chosen for an Everest expedition which a friend of mine, Harry Taylor, was planning. When I joined the Regiment six years earlier, he and I had found ourselves in the same troop. We partnered off together, and had formed a good rapport. He left the SAS in 1986, and by the autumn of 1990 he was preparing for his second attempt on Everest. On his first he had tried to ascend the unconquered North-East Ridge, but had been driven off by bad weather. Now his aim once again was to climb the North-East Ridge – Alpine-style, with a partner, Russell Bryce – but this time I would be coming up the North Ridge with Sherpas, bringing lightweight parachutes.

3

The plan was that I should meet the other two at the North Col; we would then climb to the summit together, jump off, and paraglide back down to basecamp. Everything was geared to breaking records: if I could reach the summit without oxygen, it would be a personal record for me; if the others came up via the North-East Ridge, they too would establish a first – as would we all by parachuting from the top. I was quite well qualified for the role, having done plenty of parachute jumps, and because I had spent eighteen months in the Alps on a German Army mountain guide course, during which time I became proficient at climbing in snow and ice.

In October the adjutant gave me permission to join the Everest party. Once my stint on the SP team was finished, he said, I could take three months off. I went to an exhibition in Harrogate where Berghaus, the mountain specialists, fitted me up with equipment. Already I had my mind focused on the Himalayas, and I was planning to start build-up training with hard walking in the Brecon Beacons early in the New Year.

Preparations for the Gulf were playing havoc with the annual rugby knockout competition between six squadron teams. Perhaps it was just as well, because so much needle develops during those matches that things become vicious, and guys are sometimes written off due to injuries for as long as six months. One of the players was a good friend of the England skipper, Will Carling, and invited him to bring the national team to train. The players could stay in the officers' or sergeants' mess, he said, and they would be saved the usual hassle of fans clamouring for autographs whenever they showed their noses out of doors. He also suggested that England might take on the regiment in a friendly game. Carling came up with a couple of colleagues for a check round, but one look at a match between squadrons was enough. 'Not a chance!' they said. 'We'll not play this lot. There'd be guys left crippled all over the field.' So that little plan never came to fruition.

A week before Christmas, we were dragged into the Briefing Room at Hereford and told that half of 'B' Squadron was going to deploy to the Middle East after all. 'G' Squadron would take over the SP team. Everyone who had been detailed to go began laughing and joking, and saying, 'Great!' The guys still allocated for team tasks were seriously disappointed, and angled to join the Gulf party. But I think that privately most people were concerned that the conflict could develop into a big and nasty war. We reckoned that if Israel came in, Syria and Jordan might side with Saddam Hussein; things could easily get out of hand, and half the Middle East would go up in flames. There was also the threat that Saddam would use chemical or nuclear weapons.

I was excited by the prospect of war, but I hoped that if the deployment did come off it would be a quick one, so that I could return to the team training for Everest.

When I heard the news, I went home and said to Janet, my wife: 'Listen – we're heading out.' Being a calm, level-headed woman, she took it well. Normally, SAS guys say nothing to their wives and families about what they're doing, but in this case it was obvious where we were going: after Saddam's invasion of Kuwait, there had been so much coverage on television and in the newspapers – our destination could only have been the Gulf.

Christmas was not a relaxed time. The Regiment was stood-to throughout the holiday period, and we were busy getting our green kit ready. (In SAS terms, 'green' refers to normal military operations as opposed to 'black' work, like that on the SP team, for which you wear black gear from head to foot.) When you've been out of the system – that is, away from military duties – for a while, as I had, your kit's not as it should be, and it takes a couple of weeks of hard graft to get everything sorted out.

On the Alpine guides' course in France, Italy and Germany I had learnt German, skiing, climbing, mountain rescue work, weather prediction and how to clear avalanches with explosives, but no real soldiering. Before that, I'd done nine months on the SP team as an assaulter – so again there was no military work involved. After Germany, I returned to the SP team for another nine months, this time as Sniper Commander. So altogether I'd been in black roles for at least three years, and had not worried too much about having the right equipment at hand, all sorted into the correct places.

Now I brought my webbing and bergen home to paint them in desert camouflage colours. We were having an extension built on to our house, and a labourer called John was digging the footings. Seeing me at work outside, he came up and asked what I was doing.

5

'Just painting my webbing.'

'Those colours are a bit light, aren't they?'

'Well,' I said carefully, 'you'd be surprised. It works quite well.'

In fact he was right: I had the colours too light and sandy, as I was to find out to my cost.

One of the rules within the Regiment is that all married men should have life insurance. Jan and I had a policy already, so we were all right; but as soon as the deployment was announced, pressure to take out policies fell on those who weren't already covered. Naturally the insurance companies put up the shutters, having heard where we were going, and those who did get policies had to pay high premiums. The result was a minor panic: in normal times the guys try to get away without paying premiums, but now, with a war in prospect, the future suddenly looked very different.

On New Year's Eve, with my departure imminent, Jan and I got a friend to babysit our daughter Sarah, who was just over two, and went downtown to a bar. But after one drink we looked at each other, returned home, and sat at the dining-room table, discussing painful questions – What would happen if I didn't come back? Should she marry again? Where would Sarah go to school? – and so on. We stayed up until three or four o'clock, and became very emotional. I wasn't concerned about myself or about Jan, who I knew would be able to look after herself. The person I worried about was Sarah; if I went, what sort of a life would she have?

If the Gulf conflict were to escalate into a major war, the SAS would become a small cog in a huge machine. Until then – during my service, at any rate – we'd always been the ones who called the shots, who had responded to particular threats. Even in Northern Ireland, we could to some extent choose our own ground. Another advantage was that our physical appearance was always much the same as that of the natives. In Iraq we would be operating among Arabs, immediately recognisable as aliens, without any friendly forces or civilians to back us up. On top of these worries was the threat of chemical warfare. It was impossible to say how dangerous things might become, but the uncertainty alone was enough to put the wind up even seasoned operators.

Next evening Sarah's godfather, John, a friend of mine in 'A' Squadron who'd been my best man, came round to the house and wrote out an unofficial will – a letter saying that if he was killed, I (or Janet) was to make sure that his house was sold; £10,000 would go to Sarah, the rest of the money to his mother, his stereo to his brother, and so on.

Packing our kit took some time. All our weapons were bundled together and went separately, rolled up in canvas sleeves. When I asked the SQMS if he'd included pistols, he said, 'Yeah – twenty of them,' and that reassured me, since pistols were essential back-up weapons, which we would need in case our own weapons failed or if we were caught in a confined space like a vehicle or an observation post. Most of us would be carrying M16 203s – a combination of 5.56 calibre automatic rifle in the top barrel and grenade launcher below – or Minimi machine guns. Both are over a metre long and awkward to handle or conceal at close quarters.

Personal equipment was our own affair. As I was sorting mine, I asked the SQMS if I could draw some cold-weather mountaineering gear.

'Nah,' he replied. 'You're going to the fucking desert, yer dick! It won't be cold there.' He laughed at my request as if he was the regimental expert on desert warfare. Little did he know what the winter in Iraq would be like. In spite of his brush-off, I kept thinking that we might end up at high altitudes, in the mountains of northern Iraq on the Turkish border, where snow might be lying. It was as if I had some premonition. But I did nothing about it, and most of us didn't take any cold-weather gear at all.

At a briefing early in January the OC came up with a statement to the effect that if war broke out we might find ourselves 300 miles inside Iraq, taking out various installations. We thought that could mean somewhere round Baghdad. Back at home, on an atlas, I drew a circle with a radius of 300 miles from Kuwait and the Iraqi border. Jan and I talked about the Euphrates, which runs out of Syria and right through Iraq until it joins the Tigris at Basra. From school Jan remembered that ancient civilisations had flourished in the fertile land along the two big rivers: they had been among the most important waterways then, and the land between them, known as Mesopotamia, had been called the cradle of civilisation. I wondered idly what the Euphrates would look like now.

That evening I telephoned my parents. I always did this before going somewhere. I'd just say, 'I'm off,' and normally they'd reply, 'All right. See you, then. Take care.' But this time things were different. There was a feeling that the war might last a long time, and that it would turn nasty. Mum and Dad did their best not to sound upset, but when my younger brother Keith came on the phone he started crying, and it cracked everybody else off. I said, 'Eh – stop that. Everything's going to be fine.' But the conversation brought home to me the fact that we weren't playing any more.

At last we heard that we were to fly on the night of Saturday 5 January. Being one of the senior guys in the party, I went into camp to make sure that everyone was ready. One of the lads said, 'Bob and Rich are in the club, and they're shitfaced.'

'Jesus! Where's their kit?'

'They haven't packed it yet.'

I got one man to go to Bob's room and one to Rich's, telling them to pack everything they could see, and bring it up to the guardroom. Then I and another lad went down to the club and dragged the two boozers out. Both very short men, they were propping up the bar, pissed out of their brains and giggling like schoolgirls. The rest of us walked them slowly to the coach, laughing and joking to keep them quiet. They gibbered away happily to each other as we got them aboard and sat them down at the back – and away we went to RAF Brize Norton, everyone else very quiet, just chatting to each other, shooting the shit.

The Tristar landed at Cyprus to refuel, then flew on to the Gulf, where it taxied up behind a hangar. Getting off into the warm night, we found the OC, SSM and SQMS lined up waiting for us at the bottom of the steps, all wearing desert kit with shamags, or Arab shawls, wrapped round their necks like scarves. It was our first sight of anyone dressed like that, and it rammed home to us where we were.

A Hercules was parked alongside and we jumped into the back. Normally RAF crewmen are sticklers for the rules, and every time you board an aircraft they make you sit down and buckle up. But now, on operations, there were no seats or straps, so we pleased ourselves and sat on the metal deck for the short flight up to our Forward Mounting Base, known as Victor. The head loadie (loadmaster) said, 'Hold tight, because we're going to do an operational take-off.' The pilot revved his engines until they were screaming and the whole aircraft began to judder; then he let go his brakes and we were hurled forward and heaved into the air. Fifteen minutes later he went diving in and landed with a couple of heavy thumps and violent deceleration. At Victor a hangar became our temporary home. A heap of bergens, weapons piled in big rolls, a stack of American cots, boxes of radios, medical kit, demolition equipment – everything looked as though it had arrived just that minute. We gathered round for a quick briefing from the SSM: 'No walking around in your shreddies when the RSM's about . . . There's a couple of you need haircuts . . . Don't go into the Int hangar unless you're invited . . . Let's have the hangar tidy, fellers . . . Keep your kit up together round your bed space . . . I want the place swept out periodically . . .'

Then the SQMS talked about the stores. 'OK,' he said, 'the stores are there. There's rations there, but I don't want you going into them. If you need any kit, come to me . . . the ammo bunker is next to the cookhouse . . . Cookhouse timings: six to seven breakfast, twelve to one lunch, six to seven dinner . . . Grab yourself a bed, get a space . . . We'll start training tomorrow morning.'

The OC also gave us a brief, which amounted to his personal perception of how the build-up to war was going. He said that plans for Special Forces were still fluid. 'A' and 'D' Squadrons were already well advanced with their build-up training for deployment far behind Iraqi lines, and were out in the desert doing a squadron range package – that is, putting in squadron attacks which use all weapons, including .50 browning heavy machine guns, mortars, LAW 90 rocket launchers, Milan anti-tank missile launchers, and – most effective of all – M19s, high-speed grenade-launchers, in effect machine guns firing bombs.

As for 'B' Squadron – the OC said he hoped to get us a few vehicles, which we would have to convert for desert operations. He promised to keep us updated on the way things were looking, then told us to get our heads down before we started training next day. We each found a cot and set it up against the wall of the hangar, with a six-foot table across the foot of the bed and mosquito nets rigged on poles above – and that was to be our home for the next ten days.

Morning revealed that we were well out in the desert, at one of several different camps dotted about a vast training area. Most of the desert was a flat plain of hard, beige-coloured sand, but every now and then runs of low dunes broke the monotony; on these ridges, which were maybe thirty feet high, a few tufts of dry grass and the odd tree were growing, and the sand was very soft, so that vehicles often got stuck. The wind had sculpted the sand into waves, which gave the landscape an attractive appearance.

Approaching Victor you came over a rise, and there was a high chain-link fence surrounding the large hangars and a runway, with sand-dunes lapping the perimeter wire. The base had been built as a parachute school; the hangars were for storage of chutes and other equipment and there were tall towers for hanging chutes to dry. At night the perimeter was brightly illuminated.

We began build-up training, and there was plenty to organise: radios, satellite communications, TACBEs, NBC drills. As a trained medic, I set up some medical instruction, teaching guys how to put drips in, how to pack gunshot wounds to stop bleeding, how to treat heat exhaustion. To demonstrate intravenous techniques, I grabbed a 'volunteer' from the front row, choosing someone lean, because he had prominent veins; tough though the SAS may be, some of them were also pretty squeamish, and it's not unknown for them to faint when it comes to injections.

Most of our training took place inside our hangar, but we also went on the ranges to zero our weapons, which included 203s, Minimi machine guns (also 5.56 calibre), and the more potent general-purpose machine guns (GMPGs, known as gympis), which fire 7.62 rounds, have a greater range and are harder-hitting than the Minimis. There was one set of ranges only a couple of hundred yards away, and a larger complex three hours out into the desert. We'd fired the weapons already on a gallery range in Hereford, but because they'd all been packed up, loaded and unloaded several times, we needed to zero them again.

The trouble was, we were short of ammunition. For our contact drills on foot – practising reaction when you bump into enemy – we had only thirty or forty rounds per man. In a full practice for a single contact – contact front, contact left or right, contact rear – you can easily fire a couple of hundred rounds. We drilled in groups of four or six, as if we were patrolling along. Cardboard targets would appear ahead, somebody would shout, 'CONTACT FRONT!' and we'd split into pairs to fight our way back, each pair covering the others as they moved. The SOP, or standard operating procedure, was never to go forward after a contact, always to move back. For one thing, we never knew the size of the force opposing us, and in a reconnaissance patrol there were too few of us to take on any major enemy unit. For another, we couldn't carry enough ammunition for a prolonged engagement. Working in small groups, our immediate aim was to shoot our way clear of trouble, which gave us a better chance of escaping uninjured. But now in training, with our severely limited ammunition, all we could do when someone called 'Contact!' was to go to ground and put in one bound each; then we were out of rounds – and doing it dry is never the same.

At that stage we had no 203 grenades, and we badly needed some to zero our sexton sights – pieces of auxiliary kit that you can bolt on to the side of the weapon to improve accuracy. We hadn't been issued with these sights, but I'd had one for years and had brought it with me, so now I fitted it myself.

We seemed to be short of everything, not least proper desert vehicles. What we needed were purpose-built, long-wheel-base 110 Land-Rovers, known as 'Pinkies' ever since they'd been painted pink for the Oman campaign of the 1970s. 'A' and 'D' Squadrons both had Pinkies, which they had brought out with them; the vehicles had mounts for heavy machine guns and posts for Milan anti-tank missile launchers. All we could get were short-wheel-base 90 Land-Rovers, which had no seat-belts or gun-mountings, and were derisively known as 'Dinkies'. We also had one bigger truck, a Unimog, to act as a mother craft, carrying ammunition.

Under the guidance of a sergeant from Mobility Troop, we got stuck in and stripped down the Land-Rovers, taking off the doors, tailgates, wing-mirrors and canvas tops, removing windscreens, fixing hessian over the lights and mirrors to prevent any reflection at night, and welding baskets for jerricans on to the sides. Somebody said that when the war was over, we would have to put the vehicles back together again, and we looked at each other, thinking, 'You bet!' But we kept all the pieces and piled them in a corner of the hangar. We also had three trials motorbikes, but only a handful of us had been trained to ride them. With bikes of our own at home, we had plenty of experience, and we took the Armstrongs out and practised throwing them around in the desert.

Even as we worked, we were looking at our Dinkies and thinking, 'Bollocks! This is crap!' When we practised navigation and drove about the sand-dunes, we wasted a tremendous amount of time getting bogged down and having to dig the Land-Rovers out. When we had a day doing vehicle contact drills, everything became farcical: we tried to fire the gympis off sandbags piled on the bonnet, which was hopeless, and when the drivers reversed hard into a J-turn, guys started being thrown out. With the whole squadron watching the range-work, a big Australian called Stan was flung out at high speed and cartwheeled half-way across the desert with his gympi attached to him, so that he was burnt by the hot barrel.

We laughed at the time, but underneath we were alarmed by the thought that we might be sent across the border in these vehicles and might have to use them for real: what looked funny now might easily be disastrous later. We also experimented with six of us standing in the back of the Unimog and firing from there: it was like the chuck wagon in a cowboy film, with the good guys popping off at the Indians. But we soon found that it was impossible to hit anything, because at any speed the vehicle bounced up and down outrageously.

In general, it was pathetic trying to operate with the wrong equipment, and altogether our training was poor. The other two squadrons had far better facilities. The reason for this was simple: they were the ones who were supposed to be going into Iraq; at that stage we were no more than BCRs. Nevertheless, we were still hoping that we'd be deployed.

Wild ideas started coming up. There was talk of 'B' Squadron parachuting into Kuwait City, which had been occupied by Iraqi forces. The idea was that we would capture a big block of flats and direct mortar and artillery fire on to Iraqi positions. Also, being snipers, we could fire from the building and take individuals out that way. The originator of this plan – whoever he was – didn't seem to have realised that once the Iraqis saw where we were, they would simply blow the shit out of the place – and we would have no means of escape. The RAF planners actively considered throwing us out of a Hercules at 400 or 600 feet (the usual height is between 800 and 1,000), and insisted that we made a practice jump at that height.

One suicide mission had been proposed for 'B' Squadron during the Falklands war, and now here was another. Half the guys were going to be knackered by the jump alone. On the SP team, I had been on one practice jump in which sixteen out of thirty men were injured – not killed, but put out of action. This time we had drawn and fitted the parachutes, and we were about to walk out of the hangar for the training jump when our own OC cancelled the option.

Immediately, another rumour came up, even crazier – we were to jump into Baghdad and take out essential installations such as power-stations. But soon it was found that Cruise missiles could do the job from a distance of several hundred miles.

The desert around the base was exactly as I'd expected it to be – hot and sandy, with plenty of dunes and undulations to give cover. In spite of the limitations imposed by our lack of equipment it was good for training, and we were working long hours: up at six, train all day, have dinner, sit down for a couple of hours, and then, once it was fully dark, do a night navigation exercise, before going to bed at ten or eleven. Several of the guys had radios, and when the six o'clock news came on the BBC World Service, everyone would crowd round to listen. High-level diplomatic negotiations were going on in Geneva and elsewhere as world leaders struggled to avoid a confrontation, and from one night to the next the chances of war went up and down. For recreation, there was a school of card-players, and some people would read – anything from Shakespeare to *Viz* comics. I'd taken a load of paperbacks by Tom Sharpe, who always makes me laugh. On the whole, though, we were too tired to read or play, and we began to suffer from sleep-deprivation.

Then suddenly another job came up, for a team to go down and put extra security on the British Embassy in Abu Dhabi during a visit by Douglas Hurd, the Foreign Secretary. They picked five of us who had done the bodyguards' course and ferried us down there. In Abu Dhabi we had a look round the

Embassy, and settled into a flat-roofed bungalow within the grounds, which were maybe a hundred yards square, and beautifully kept – a huge garden with irrigated lawns, shrubs, flowerbeds and trees. The main Embassy building was two storeys high and quite large, and several other staff bungalows were dotted about. Local security was operating outside the walls of the compound, and we were to patrol inside.

Up at Victor we were banned from going into town, but here there was nobody to keep an eye on us. Hurd was not due to arrive until 6p.m., and we had a couple of hours spare. Also, we were dressed inconspicuously in casual civilian clothes – polo shirts and corduroys – so we took our chance and went into town for a look round.

It was strange, walking round the streets of a prosperous, gleaming new town, to find that everything seemed normal, with not a hint that a major war was about to erupt. It felt good to have a break from training, see a different culture, and eat different food. After a meal we did some shopping, and bought little radios, miniature binoculars and a camera. I also bought a couple of shamags for myself, and another four or five for the guys still at Victor. Then we slipped back to the Embassy in time for the arrival of our star guest.

When he came in, we saw him get out of the car and go into the building, so that we knew he was our responsibility for the time being. The situation, in the run-up to war, was enough to make anyone jumpy. We'd been getting reports which suggested that the Iraqis were capable of parachuting a special forces team into Abu Dhabi to take Hurd out – and at the time we had to treat them seriously. We thought they might have kamikaze types trained either to drop from the air or to come in by boat, because the Embassy was only about a hundred metres from the sea.

After dark the perimeter wall was illuminated by lights that cast deep shadows, so that it would have been difficult to spot anyone hanging about. In the middle of the night one pair of our guys was on patrol in the compound and the other three of us were asleep in the bungalow, when somebody suddenly began screaming 'CONTACT! CONTACT!' at the top of his voice. Still half asleep, we leapt up and cocked our weapons, bumping into each other as we rushed about trying to make out where the enemy was. Just as we were about to burst out and sweep the compound, we realised that the person yelling was Paul, who'd been having a nightmare and had dreamt up the whole confrontation.

Somehow we settled down again, and in the morning, after Hurd had made an early departure, we whipped into Abu Dhabi again for breakfast of coffee and croissants. A couple of the guys bought telephone cards, so that they could call home. Back at Victor, nobody mentioned anything about having been in the town, and when I handed out the spare shamags, I said to the lads, 'Just don't tell anyone where they came from.'

That little episode left us even more exhausted, and we told the OC we needed a day off because we were knackered. He made a compromise and let us off a navigation exercise, so that we were able to get our heads down for an extra four-hour stretch.

The Regiment had established a Forward Operating Base at Al Jouf, an airfield in the north-west of Saudi Arabia, and we knew that if we were deployed across the border it was from there that we would go in. When the air war began, on the night of 16/17 January, with Coalition aircraft bombing targets in Iraq, we expected to be deployed at any moment.

Although we didn't know it at the time, the Commander of British Forces in the Gulf, Lieutenant General Peter de la Billière – himself an outstanding SAS officer who had served in numerous earlier campaigns, from Korea to Malaya, Borneo, Oman and Dhofar – had been trying his hardest to persuade the American Commander-in-Chief, General Norman Schwarzkopf, to send us in. But Stormin' Norman had a hang-up about using Special Forces; he had seen the American Special Forces make a hash of things in Vietnam, and now he preferred to use conventional methods – to soften up the Iraqis with bombs, and then overrun their positions with tanks, without wasting highly-trained special troops. Besides, he could get all the intelligence he needed from satellites and reconnaissance aircraft.

In the end, however, DLB persuaded him that SAS patrols would glean useful intelligence if they were inserted deep inside enemy territory, and the C-in-C agreed to our deployment. Hardly had he done so when Saddam Hussein started putting Scud missiles down on Israel, and neither satellites nor aircraft could find the mobile launchers. Suddenly – and quite by chance – the regiment had a vital role to perform: to find the mobile launchers, put an end to the bombardment of Israel, and so prevent Israel entering the war with potentially disastrous consequences to the coalition.

Suddenly our future became more clearly defined. No longer mere BCRs, we were assigned a proper task. The big Special Forces punch was to come from 'A' and 'D' squadrons, who would go in as substantial motorised patrols, each heavily armed and half a squadron strong, tasked with finding the Scud TELs (transporter-erector launchers) and calling in Allied aircraft to take them out. But the plan was that before the heavy mob was deployed, three eight-man patrols from 'B' Squadron, designated Bravo One Zero, Bravo Two Zero and Bravo Three Zero, would infiltrate deep into Iraqi territory and lie up in OPs (observation posts) to report enemy movement, especially that of Scuds. De la Billière believed that if we could establish OPs first, and start passing back useful intelligence, it would strengthen his hand in bargaining with Schwarzkopf and increase the chances of the big patrols being deployed. Naturally our own CO was as eager as anyone to get people in there.

For our patrol, Bravo Two Zero, members were selected from a nominal roll, and according to their particular skills: besides fighting power, we needed a demolitionist, a signaller and a medic (myself). Our main task would be to gather intelligence; our aim was to find a good LUP (lying-up position) and set up an OP. From there we would maintain surveillance on the MSR (main supply route) which ran westwards from the town of Al Hadithah to three airfields known as H1, H2 and H3, and along which it was thought the Iraqis were moving Scud launchers. Once established, we would remain in the OP for up to ten days, reporting enemy movements by radio or Satcom telephone, and calling in fighter-bombers to attack any worthwhile target. A subsidiary task was to blow up any fibre-optic communications links we could find. After ten days, we would either get a re-supply by helicopter, or move to a new location, also by chopper. Besides all our personal equipment, we would take kit for building the OP: 120 empty sandbags per man, vehicle camouflage nets, poles, and thermal sheets to put over the top of our structures, so that if Iraqis flew over with thermal-imaging kit they wouldn't be able to pick up the heat rising from our bodies.

To practise the task we'd been assigned, we went out into some sandhills and dug in OPs. Now it so happened that I was pretty good at this, having done a lot of it with the Territorial Regiment in Germany, where one of our main roles had been to construct OPs and man them for three weeks at a time. After the earth and rock of Europe, the sand of Arabia was a doddle. We began by digging a pit three metres by two. The sand kept sliding in, but once we were down to a reasonable depth we built walls of bags filled with sand, then laid poles across the top and covered them with thermal sheeting and sand-spattered hessian. At the front we left a slot for observation, camouflaged with strips of hessian like a net curtain, and a small aperture at the back, concealed by a flap of hessian covered in sand and glue.

The main object of the exercise was to work out what we would need to go to ground in Iraq, and the answer seemed to be plenty of sandbags and plenty of water. At the end of the day we all went round each others' OPs, and I am glad to say that ours was by far the best. Encouraged by the nature of the desert in the south of the Gulf, we decided that to build an OP in Iraq would be a viable proposition, and that we should be able to get away with it.

Each patrol's plan, in fact, was to put in two OPs, one covering the other, 50 or 100 metres apart and linked by telephone line. One would have an observation opening facing forward on to the MSR, and the other would be in front of it with the opening facing backwards, so that the guys there could watch the ground behind their colleagues.

It was when we started getting our kit together that the scale of the shortages finally emerged. 'Right,' we said to the SQMS, 'we need 203 rounds.'

'Well,' he replied, 'we haven't got any.'

'Why the hell not?'

'There are just none here.'

In that case, I decided, I wasn't going to carry the grenade-launching part of my weapon across the border, because it made the whole thing so heavy. The launcher, or lower barrel, is easily detached, and without it the rifle becomes considerably lighter and a joy to handle – but in that mode it needs a replacement stock, since the main stock comes away with the lower barrel. The SQMS told me I couldn't split my weapon, because he had forgotten to bring out the extra stocks.

In fact there were plenty of 203 rounds – but other people had them. One day I went across to see two friends in 'A' Squadron and found them sitting in their Pinkie. They were just about to move up to Al Jouf, within striking distance of the border. I said, 'Listen – we're flying up tomorrow, just after you. Is there any chance of you giving us some bombs?' John – Sarah's godfather – lifted up the seat, and underneath were boxes of 203 rounds. They brought out twelve and said, 'Here, take these.' So I went with both parts of my weapon fitted after all.

It was the same with claymore mines, which we wanted as a deterrent to put the brakes on anyone trying to come after us in the desert. (If you're being followed, you can put down a mine with a timer, and crack it off after maybe five minutes. Even if it doesn't do any damage it slows people down, because they wonder if there are more mines in front of them.) When we asked for claymores, the answer was that there weren't any, and someone told us to make our own out of ammunition boxes packed with plastic explosives and gympi link – the metal belt that holds machine-gun rounds together.

This was ridiculous: home-made devices like that are crude, large and heavy, and we hadn't got the capacity to carry them. Later we did make a single claymore out of plastic ice-cream cartons, and one of us took it in his bergen. In fact there was a whole tent full of claymores, but through lack of communication at various levels, they remained hidden away. In the end we were given a mixed load of stuff by the Special Boat Squadron: five claymores, a box of L2 grenades, one of white phosphorous grenades and some 66 rockets. We shared out some of this with the other two patrols, and I myself finished up with one L2 grenade and two white phos.

Yet another sore point was pistols. The twenty pistols packed and shipped for our own use simply disappeared, nicked for the other squadrons. The result was that the only guy in our unit with one was Vince, who had brought it with him from 'A' Squadron. We also asked for silenced pistols, and in particular for the make invented during the Second World War for Special

Operations Executive. Although fairly primitive, these have never been surpassed for sheer quietness. They come in two parts – the silenced barrel (a fat tube) and the pistol grip, which is also the magazine – and part of their secret is that they have so few working parts. They fire single shots only, and have to be reloaded manually, by undoing and pulling back a screw, which lifts the next round into the breach; but the quietness of the report is uncanny – no more than a *pffft* – and at close range the 9mm. slug is deadly. The other two squadrons had such weapons and as things turned out, there were several moments during my escape when I could have done with one; but again, we were told that none were available.

People started getting a bit pissed off with all these shortages, and one day in the hangar someone challenged the OC about them, saying, 'Look – we've got no pistols, we've got no grenades, we've got no claymores. You're expecting us to make claymores out of ammunition boxes, and it's bloody stupid, because they're not effective.'

The OC, who was doing the best he could blew his top, and said, 'Listen, you're about to go to war. You'll take whatever you can get. You're not in Northern Ireland, where you can ask for any kind of asset. You've got to improvise. That's what makes the Regiment so good – improvisation.'

In fact the things we were missing were basic equipment which we should have had. Take the maps, for instance. The only maps we had were really poor and designed for air-crews; their scale (1:250,000) was so small that they showed few details, and although they might have helped navigators they were no good to people on the ground. To back them up, we badly needed satellite-derived information – but again, we were told that no satellite imagery was available. Our first escape-maps were also as old as the hills. Incredibly, they had first been printed in 1928, then updated for the Second World War; but at the last minute we were issued with newer ones, printed on silk, which we worked into the waistbands of our trousers.

Each of us was given a photostatted indemnity note, in Arabic and English, promising £5,000 to anyone who handed over a co-alition serviceman to a friendly power. Deciding the document was rubbish, I threw mine away. Later, however, I changed my mind; because I couldn't speak Arabic, I thought I'd better have a note after all. So I got another member of the patrol, Bob Consiglio, to photostat a copy of his (with the serial number 075 in the top right-hand corner), and took that with me. We also signed for twenty gold sovereigns apiece, in case we had to bribe somebody or buy our way out of trouble. Of course we were supposed to return these after the conflict, but not everybody did.

At Christmas, back in Hereford, we'd had what was known as Cross-brief Studies, the formal review of what the Regiment had done during the past year, and a forecast of what it would be doing the next. Proceedings had finished with an address from the CO, who asked everybody except 'A' and 'D' Squadron to leave, and then made some pretty sombre comments. 'Look, guys,' he'd said. 'There's a good chance we're going to be at war, and it may escalate into something big. But if any of you look like getting caught, you certainly want to consider saving the last round for yourself.' Basically he'd been saying: 'Shoot yourself rather than get caught.'

Now, out at Victor, those words began to spread around. The Regiment didn't want anyone else to know that the SAS had been deployed, and we were supposed to be in isolation – not only within the camp as a whole, but also within squadrons. As soon as we were tasked, we should have been separated from everyone else and put into our own isolation pen. Our briefing room – in this case a tent inside the hangar – should have been secured by the Headquarter unit, and nobody should have been allowed in there except members of the patrol – because, if you're captured, the less you know the better. As it was, maps and papers were left lying about the floor, and everybody knew what everybody else was doing. Inevitably, people talked to each other, and the CO's advice leaked out to us as well.

For years people had reckoned that you'd be better off shooting yourself if the IRA got hold of you, and that black Africans would probably skin you alive. Now the same seemed to apply to the Iraqis. Guys went around saying, 'These people will carve you up if they get you. They'll have your bollocks off, for a start.' We were not to know that most of this was pure hype. The military capabilities of the Iraqis were also becoming wildly exaggerated, but our intelligence about the true situation was so sketchy that rumours kept building up.

While we were still at Victor, we were given jabs against anthrax, which made everyone feel like shit for three or four days, with bad bruising in the arm that had been injected. One man's arm remained black and blue for six weeks, and some people had muscle around the puncture actually go rotten three or four weeks after the jab. Several guys from 'A' Squadron had to be dragged back out of the field for minor surgery. I was lucky, and got nothing worse than a cold and a burning throat; I kept waking up in the night, coughing up lumps of phlegm the size of golf balls.

The patrol's principal task would be to man the OP, but there was also the possibility that we might be tasked to blow fibre-optic communication lines, one of which was thought to run alongside the MSR. Luckily one of our lads had done some moonlighting for a contractor laying fibre-optic cables, and he told he us that we needed a particular device, like a metal detector, for tracing them – so we indented for one immediately. He also knew that if a cable is cut, the operators can send out a pulse of light which bounces back along it, giving them a precise indication of where the break is, so that repairs are fairly simple. We therefore worked out that, if we did blow a line, we would put anti-personnel mines around the break, so that when engineers came to repair it they would be taken out. We would also lay another, delayed-action device to blow the line again later. But the main aim of the exercise would be to kill as many skilled personnel as possible. Western technicians had poured out of Iraq during the past few weeks, and we knew that there must be a shortage of engineers; if we managed to kill the first wave coming out to make repairs, it was a good bet that the next lot, in true Arab fashion, would say they couldn't find the break, and the line would remain cut.

When I heard the code-word for our patrol – Turbo – I couldn't help laughing, because Turbo was the name of the best dog I'd ever owned. A black Staffordshire bull terrier of incredible strength, he was the most engaging character you could imagine: a desperate fighter and randy as a billy-goat, but deeply affectionate with humans, with a look in his eyes that would melt any heart. When I thought of all the scrapes he'd got me into, a warm feeling came over me, and I almost felt he'd become a member of the patrol.

The One That Got Away

At first we heard that Bravo Two Zero would be commanded by Bob Shepherd, an exceptionally level-headed Scotsman, always cheerful and smiling, who had been my instructor on selection. He had come out to Saudi with 'A' Squadron, but had recently been brought into 'B' Squadron to strengthen its middle management. The news of his appointment delighted us. By our standards Bob was quite old – thirty-six – but he was always closely in touch with the younger guys, and someone we could look up to and trust absolutely. Tall and strong, with swept-back dark-brown hair, he'd always been outstandingly fit. On the selection course he was probably the fittest instructor of all, but also one of the nicest; you could be sure he would never stitch you up, but would spent time helping you.

Unfortunately his command lasted literally a few minutes. Partly because of personality clashes, partly because he'd had experience with heavy weapons, so he was kept back to work with the other squadrons – and his place was taken by Sergeant Andy McNab. Andy was then about thirty-two, a Cockney Jack-the-Lad with such a gift of the gab that he could talk his way out of any situation and tie you in a knot. Dark-haired, with a moustache, he'd done a lot of work in the Regiment and was a good demolitionist – but words came out of him so fast that you never quite knew where you were.

Paired off with Andy – sharing bed-spaces, vehicles, cooking equipment and so on – was Dinger, a lance-corporal of twenty-eight who'd been in the Parachute Regiment. A bit of a wild character, Dinger drank like a fish, smoked like a chimney, couldn't give a flying monkey's, and was always game for a fight. If you described anyone as mad, or as a joker, it would be him. Yet he was also a good family man, married with two daughters. Just before we left, one of his mates did him a really short crew-cut, which gave him an extra-youthful appearance.

The other sergeant was Vince, an older man, about thirty-five, a medic like myself, who tended to be a bit nervous and twitchy in his movements. He was tall and slim, with an athletic build; he had fuzzy, dark-gingery hair and a drooping, Mexican-type moustache. He came from Swindon, and was married with three children. He was putting a bold front on things, but I knew his heart wasn't in this operation. Only a few days before, we'd sat on his camp-bed and he'd said to me, 'I don't want to be doing

22

this.' We discussed things a bit, and I said to him, 'Well – now that we're here, we'd better just get on with it, and hope we'll come out OK at the end.' I got the impression that he wanted to finish his time in the army and be done with the whole business. A closer friend of mine was Trooper Bob Consiglio. Twenty-four years old, the son of a Sicilian father and an English mother, he was dark as any Italian and very small (only 5' 5") but incredibly strong, with a heart like a lion. He was the only guy ever known to have spent six months in Hereford without trapping a woman. He used to try like mad, every night, all night long, but he never made it. It seemed that his lack of height was against him. Girls somehow didn't realise what a good sense of humour he had; if ever someone was going to say something really daft, it would be him. He was a really nice lad, and would do anything you told him to; a hard worker, and a cheerful character. If you thought of Bob as a dog, he'd be a terrier.

Bob was endlessly good-natured, and, when he was the newest member of the troop, had taken a lot of stick from the rest of us. He didn't exactly look at us in awe, but he went all out to impress us, trying his hardest not to appear the dummy. The result was that we kept playing jokes on him. Once, when the staff sergeant was away and I was running the troop, we went climbing in Pembrokeshire, on the Welsh coast. I went into Bob's bag and took out one shoe. When we reached the foot of the hills he started to hunt about, and although he wouldn't say anything I could see him getting worried, thinking he'd left the shoe behind. I deliberately started to hustle him: 'Get your kit on. Let's go.'

'Can I climb in my big boots?'

'No – get your stickies on.'

He began muttering and hesitating, playing for time, but in the end he had to say, 'Listen – I forgot to put one of my stickies in.'

I pretended to blow my top at him, and he began to apologise. 'I'm sorry,' he said, 'I'll run back and get it.'

'Go on, then,' I told him. 'And make it fast.'

Away he went – and when he'd gone a few yards I shouted after him to come back.

No matter how much we used to pull the piss, when it came

to fighting, Bob wasn't frightened of anything. At Al Jouf he and I lived under the same vehicle cam net, and I said to him one day, 'Bob, if anything happens when we're in there, make sure you stick with me. Get on my arse when we're leaving.' And he said, 'Yeah – I will.' It wasn't that I didn't trust him to do anything by himself – though I did want to protect him, almost as if he were a brother. Rather, also because he was such a brave little sod, it would be to my own advantage to have him close.

Twice Bob's size was Stan – a different character entirely. A Rhodesian who'd moved to Australia, he was over six foot tall, not that obviously muscular, but very, very strong, well-spoken, and a gentleman. Down under, he'd been at university, rowing in the university boat team, and then became a dentist, with a practice of his own in Sydney. But all he'd wanted to do was join the SAS, and gradually he had worked his way there. In Hereford he again had a dental practice, while at the same time serving in the Regiment. A single man, and very good looking, he became known in the camp as 'Dr Sex', such havoc did he create among the local girls. Nothing ever seemed to bother him; whatever happened, his voice kept the same tone, and he just got on with things. If he had a fault, it was that he was too nice, too placid and, for all his intelligence, perhaps a bit naive. He was another good mate of mine – and I wouldn't have liked to see him get angry, because he could be a formidable fighter.

The other two members of the patrol were Legs Lane – so called because he was tall and thin – and Mark, a keen New Zealander who had joined the squadron only a month before. Both were very quiet – Legs particularly so – and it was difficult to get much out of them; but both were good men, and Mark especially was always one to start straight in, game for anything. Legs was a key man in the patrol as he was carrying the 319, the main radio set.

Finally there was myself: a Geordie from near Newcastle, aged twenty-eight, and a corporal. During six years in the regular SAS I'd gained a good deal of useful experience in many countries, and at the beginning of 1991 I was physically the strongest I'd ever been, because during my last tour with the SP team I'd hit the weights and built up a lot of muscle on my upper body. The extra strength had been useful, because much of what you do on the SP team is bodywork – you're forever going up ropes or sliding down them, climbing into buildings, carrying guys, jumping off vehicles, pushing people away or restraining them. In all this, you're handling a lot of weight. In your black kit, you have your body armour, kevlar helmet and waistcoat loaded with ammunition, stun-grenades and axes, besides your machine-gun and pistol. With all the hours on the bench, and practical work, my weight had gone up from 11 to 12½ stone. Little did I know that the extra muscle was going to save my life.

In our last days at Victor we were busier than ever. Andy was getting the demolition kit sorted. I saw to the medical packs, Legs Lane to the radio. Everyone scrounged ammunition. We were told that when we moved up to Al Jouf we would go more or less straight in, so that everything had to be ready before we left. We were also told to leave all our non-essential kit behind.

We flew up on the evening of 18 January in three Hercules, staggered. On board were all the squadron vehicles and stores. The air war was then at its height, raging for the third night, and there was quite a high risk of being shot at en route. Through the headsets dangling from the walls in the back we tuned in to an American AWACS controller directing a US pilot with an Iraqi on his tail. The pilot was highly excited, and kept yelling, 'He's got us! He's locked on!' but the controller remained completely cool and talked him calmly through the turns: 'OK. Steady. I have you on radar. Steady. Bank left. Just bank left . . .' The American ended up taking the Iraqi out, and it was great to listen in; the pilot's excitement and fear and the controller's laconic replies brought home to us the fact that the war was going on in earnest. The sky was full of armed warplanes, all trying to blow the opposition out of the air. During the flight the SSM went round telling everyone to start taking their NAPs tablets, to combat the effects of nuclear or biological contamination. We were all saying, 'Yeah, yeah. OK.' But somebody muttered, 'These fucking things make you sterile,' so although a couple of the guys took the pills, the rest didn't risk it.

When we felt the wind at Al Jouf, somebody gasped, 'Jesus! It's a hell of a lot colder up here.' Because we'd been told we were going to deploy immediately, we'd left most of our warm kit behind.

The moment we landed, we began to unload our equipment

and pile it in a grassed area like a garden, about thirty metres by twenty, next to one of the hangars. Helping us was an officer who had been commissioned from the ranks, and had a fearsome reputation of being a real bastard. Everyone was in dread of him, even the majors. Now he was the quartermaster, but he got stuck straight in, and was carrying the long cardboard boxes of rations off the aircraft with us. He laid three boxes down parallel to each other in one layer, and three across them in the next tier. When Bob Consiglio started the third layer with a box lying in line with the one below, instead of across all three, the quartermaster took one look at him and said in a menacing voice, 'Get it right, cunt.'

Bob, not knowing the man from Adam, was about to say something, or even to grab hold of him. I looked at him and shook my head, silently praying, '*Please!* Don't say a thing, or he'll kill you.'

Someone told us we'd be sleeping that night in the grassy area; so we sorted out bivvy bags and sleeping bags, made a brew, and got our heads down in the open. The night sky was clear, and as we lay there we watched streams of B-52s crossing high above us, with fighters skimming like minnows alongside. The sight sent my mind straight back to the time when, as a boy, I'd watched television pictures of B-52s going over in streams to bomb Vietnam. Now, as the aircraft reached the Iraqi border, their flashing lights were suddenly extinguished, but we heard the roar of massed jet engines rumble away into the distance. It was comforting to know that our aircraft were bombing the shit out of the enemy, and we hoped they would do enough damage to make Saddam capitulate before we were even deployed.

Morning showed that the airfield was surrounded by security wire and primitive, flat-roofed wooden towers with glass windows, which reminded us of the German concentration camps we'd seen in World War Two films. Eight A-10 pilots were stationed on the base, flying their tank-buster aircraft in and out all the time. There were also a couple of small Saudi jets coming and going.

There was one main terminal, quite small, with a few other buildings attached to it. Our regimental head-shed and all our stores were there, but we were billeted on the other side of the airfield, where there was a cement building with a single washbasin and a hole in the ground to act as a toilet, which inevitably became blocked. The SSM had been told to bring the squadron tents, but he had decided that, because we were in the desert and the weather would be hot, we wouldn't need them. In fact it wasn't hot at all. It was bloody cold, and the dust was phenomenal. All we could do was sling cam nets from our vehicles for a bit of shelter, and we lived on the ground like pigs, huddled round the Land-Rovers. We had no tables or chairs, so we ate our meals sitting on the deck, with the dust blowing around everywhere, covering us, our kit and our food.

We'd hardly got our bearings when the RSM came across for a chat. He was a bit deaf, and as he was talking to one of the lads, a clerk from the HQ building came past and made some remark. The RSM thought he heard 'Good morning', so he politely said, 'Aye, good morning' back. In fact what the clerk had said was, 'Scud warning'. Suddenly, through the hedge, we saw groups of people running like hell, and one of the last of them yelled, 'There's a Scud coming in!' Some of the squadron stayed where they were, drinking their tea on the grass, not bothering. Others ran left and right for the shelters, some struggling to pull respirators on, others to don NBC suits.

Soon afterwards the all-clear came. We rapidly learned the drill: the operators in Riyadh were monitoring every launch and putting out general alerts, then a few seconds later, as soon as they had determined the missile's track, they began to call 'Stand down here, stand down there' to the areas not under threat. Every now and then the SSM would tell us to dig slit-trenches, but the guys just said, 'Ah, bollocks!' The airfield was remote and unimportant, and the possibility of a Scud landing on it was infinitesimal. When warnings came in the middle of the night, we soon decided to ignore them. The OC would run round all our positions shouting, 'Scud warning!' and he himself would run for the shelter. At first some of the guys did the same, but it soon reached the point at which we all just zipped up our sleeping bags and stayed where we were. In the end the OC went berserk and gave us all a bollocking – but then we deployed across the border, and that was the end of it.

We had no time for detailed planning – but that hardly seemed to matter, because we knew what we wanted to do, and the task seemed fairly simple. The site we had chosen for our LUP was opposite a slight bend in the MSR, at a spot where it looked from the map as though we could dig into the bank of a wadi and have a view straight up the gully to the big road. If we saw a Scud on the move, we were to report it immediately by voice over the Satcom telephone, and follow up with a message on the 319, so that the sighting was doubly confirmed. Then aircraft would be launched or vectored to take the missile out. A brief on the missiles gave us an idea of what big beasts they were. Nearly forty feet long and three feet in diameter, they would look a bit like fuel-tankers when in the horizontal position on their trailers. Apparently the Iraqis' habit was to park them alongside embankments or under road bridges so that they were all but invisible from the air. When on the move, a TEL would always be accompanied by several other vehicles in a little convoy.

Privately, we agreed that if we did find a convoy we would allow a few minutes to elapse after it had gone past us – otherwise the Iraqis might pinpoint the source of the intelligence which had brought an attack down on their heads. There was also anxiety about what the Scud warheads might contain: if they were nuclear, or full of gas or biological agents, we didn't want to be around when they came apart. We were also nervous of using satellite communications, because they give a hell of a splash-off, and a good direction-finding station can locate a transmitter within twenty seconds. So we practised getting on the phone and putting over the bare essentials of a Scud sighting in as few seconds as possible.

Bravo One Zero and Bravo Three Zero had decided to take vehicles in with them, but at the last minute we opted to go without. Over the past few days the matter had been the subject of intense debate. Obviously vehicles would give the patrol far greater mobility and enable us to drive out of trouble and back over the border if things went wrong. On the other hand, they would be hard to conceal, and might easily give away our presence. At one point we were positively ordered to take them, but the order was rescinded, and in the end we elected to go in on foot. In Bravo One Zero and Three Zero the decision went the other way, and they took Dinkies with them. (The vehicles that we had prepared for ourselves were eventually used by 'A' and 'D' Squadrons.)

In our patrol, as usual, the matter was decided by Chinese parliament, with every man having his say. Opinion was evenly divided, and nobody insisted that vehicles were essential. Looking back, I realise that I had a strong influence on the decision. I had built countless OPs in Europe. In the Territorial Army I'd made more OPs than all the rest of the guys in the patrol put together, and I'd specialised in what we called hasty hides – we'd dig in, put logs across the top of the hole, and bury them. Altogether, I considered myself something of an expert at the job; but I had never operated in the desert, and just couldn't see a small patrol like ours escaping detection if we were saddled with vehicles. Looking back, I realise it was a cardinal mistake to go without. What we should have done was to drive in, install an OP with a couple of men, change them over every night, and pull off to a safe distance during the days, hiding the vehicles under cam nets in the bottom of some deep wadi. Mobility apart, the advantage of vehicles would have been that we could fit them up with powerful armaments, including heavy machine guns.

The penalty of leaving our Dinkies behind was that we were saddled with huge individual loads. The average weight of a bergen was 60 kilos, or 150 lbs: with that lot on, you had to walk with your head down like a donkey, so that you'd be useless in a contact, and if you fell over you'd be knackered. No wonder straps were breaking and stitches starting to pull out.

But that wasn't all. Apart from the bergens, each of us had a belt kit of pouches weighing 20 kilos, and a whole load more gear that wouldn't fit in anywhere else: seven days' rations in one sandbag, two NBC suits in another, an extra bandolier of ammunition, extra grenades for the 203 launchers, and a jerrican of water. Altogether we had nearly 120 kilos of kit apiece.

Talking to the RAF helicopter pilots who were going to fly us, we heard how they planned their routes into Iraq to avoid known anti-aircraft positions, and with their help we identified the precise spot at which we wanted to be dropped. At first we chose a point five kilometres short of our LUP, but later, because of the phenomenal weight of our kit, we changed our minds and asked to be put down only two or three kilometres short.

Arrangements for evacuation seemed straightforward enough. If we had not come on the air within forty-eight hours of being dropped off, a chopper would come back to pick us up. If we needed casevac, a heli would come within twenty-four hours of any call. If we had a contact and needed assistance, half the squadron would be on board the helicopter to pull us out.

The OC tried to reassure us. 'Don't worry,' he said. 'You've got your 319. You've got your Satcom. You've got your TACBEs. "A" and "D" Squadrons are going to be in your area. Also you've got your forty-eight-hour Lost Comms procedure, and your twenty-four-hour Casevac.' That all sounded fine – but, as will become apparent, things didn't turn out as we hoped.

One detail to which we should have paid more attention was our cover-story. We agreed that if we were captured, we would claim to be members of a medical team, sent in to recover downed aircrew – or possibly members of a team sent to provide security for medics, and that our chopper had been forced down. The general idea was to stick as close to the truth as possible, but to say that we were reservists or ordinary infantrymen, and that we'd been brought into the war because we worked in a medical centre. Yet we never had time to work things out in any depth – for instance, about which fictitious regiment we belonged to.

We went off in such a rush, in fact, that when we boarded the Chinook on the evening of 19 January, Andy went on getting his final briefing on the ramp at the back of the helicopter. (Bravo One Zero and Three Zero were to go in the next night.)

Guys from 'B' Squadron threw our kit into vehicles and came with us to the helicopter. Among them was Bob Shepherd, and as he helped me with my equipment I said, only half joking, 'Bob, I wish you'd fucking well failed me during selection!'

'Yes,' he said. 'So do I!'

I sensed a peculiar atmosphere. Nobody had much to say. As we were going on board, our mates were all around us, but I got the feeling that they thought this was a one-way ticket. Somebody said to me, 'This is bloody ridiculous – it's not on, to carry loads like this.' But by then it was too late to change things.

Off we went into the dusk, and after half an hour we landed at Arar, an airfield just inside the border, to refuel. When the pilot shut down his engines, we stayed where we were, in the back. Then came an incredible let-down. The engines started turning and burning again, we lifted off and were almost over the frontier when the pilot radioed for permission to cross – and it was denied. He came on the intercom to announce, 'Sorry, guys – mission aborted.' Because the Americans were saturation-bombing targets on our route, he had to deconflict and keep out of the way.

Having psyched ourselves up to a high level of preparedness, we somehow had to come down. Although everyone pretended to be disappointed, in fact the guys were immensely relieved. We all looked at each other, and grins spread over our faces as we headed back to Al Jouf.

Chapter Two

Contact!

As soon as we landed back, the guys started stripping their kit in an all-out effort to save weight. Until the final moment all eight of us went on sorting and repacking, throwing out anything that didn't seem essential as we tried to lighten our loads. Out went luxuries like sleeping bags and most of our warm clothes. We realised that the weather was much colder than at Victor, but we simply had to cut down on our weights, which had reached ridiculous proportions: our bergens were so heavy that the only way we could get them on was to sit down, settle the straps over our shoulders, and have a couple of the other guys pull us to our feet, as if they were hoisting knights in armour on to their chargers.

I became obsessed with the need for ammunition. Pressured by the thought that we were going to be on our own behind enemy lines, I left food out of my belt-kit in favour of more rounds. Normally I carried 24 hours' worth of rations in a belt-pouch – enough to spread over four days at a pinch – but now I reckoned that if we did get compromised, I could reach the Syrian border in two nights. All I would need on me in that case would be two packets of AB (army issue) biscuits; so I put the rest of the food into my bergen and filled my belt kit with extra ammunition. Altogether I had 12 magazines of 28 rounds each, and also about 90 loose rounds, including a few armour-piercing, which I'd brought from Hereford.

One of the items I threw out was my brew-kit: tea-bags, sachets of coffee, orange powder, sugar and inflammable hexiblocks. Since were were going in on hard routine – which meant no cooking, no fires and no smoking – I thought I would have no chance to use anything like that. Another serious omission was puritabs, for sterilising water. If we'd been going into the jungle, where you use local water all the time, I'd certainly have taken some – but I thought that in the desert we'd be drinking out of jerricans; it never occurred to me that I might have to rely on the Euphrates. Certainly we wouldn't risk drinking from wells: in the light of how Saddam had treated his own people, especially the Kurds in the north, there seemed a good chance that wells might have been deliberately poisoned.

Gradually more guys from Hereford floated in, building up the squadron's numbers, and at the last minute a British Telecom fibre-optic detector turned up, looking rather like one of the metal-detectors that treasure-hunters use to sweep the fields. We also got one Magellan GPS (global positioning system) – a hand-held navigation aid, not much bigger than a mobile telephone, which locks on to satellites as they pass overhead and gives you your position to within a few feet: altogether an excellent device.

The atmosphere in the patrol remained tense but cheerful. If the guys bitched, it was at the lack of equipment. Until the last moment we kept demanding satellite pictures of the area for which we were heading, and in the end some did arrive. They were of poor quality, but they appeared to confirm our decision to leave vehicles behind, since they showed that the desert was extremely flat and open. What we failed to realise, through lack of proper instruction, was that we were reading the imagery upside-down, mistaking low ground for high ground, wadis for ridges and so on.

As time ran out, I was thinking a good deal about escape and evasion. At one Int briefing I asked the officer if he had any information about enemy movement or positions along the border with Syria.

'No,' he said, 'as far as I know, there are no defences along it.'

'Can you tell us what the border looks like?'

'Sorry – I just don't know.'

When we discussed crossing this border among ourselves, the guys began joking. 'Aye,' said someone from another patrol, 'if we get compromised, we'll all meet up at the Pudding Club in Istanbul (the café where, in *Midnight Express*, the guy says you can always leave a message). For someone like myself with a sweet tooth, that seemed a good enough rendezvous.

The second time, our departure was set for the evening of Tuesday 22 January 1991. Just as we heard we were to fly that night, the mail came in. I thought, 'Christ – I don't want this.' I'd been waiting for the post, and normally I looked forward to getting a letter from Jan; but for the past couple of days I'd been trying not to think about home, because it upset me. So I read the letter quickly, and glanced at the new photos of Sarah, who was walking well and stringing quite a few words together. Then I put the letter and the snaps into the bag of equipment I was leaving behind in the SQMS's tent. Just seeing the pictures made me realise what I was missing, and what I might be throwing away.

Before we left, we had a big meal of fresh food, which we ate sitting on the ground – there still being no tables or chairs. Then came last-minute checks as we went through all our pockets to sterilise ourselves, and make sure that we were carrying no scrap of paper that would give away who we were or where we came from. The only identification I had on me was the pair of metal discs slung on a chain round my neck, bearing my name, army number, blood group and religion (Church of England). To stop them clinking, I'd covered them in black masking tape, and on each I'd taped a good-luck talisman. One was a new five-pence piece given to me by my mother-in-law, to accompany her Christmas present of a Samurai sword – for the Japanese reckon it's bad luck to give a sword without a coin. The other was a big old British penny which I'd found lying head-up in the sand of the training area near the camp at Victor. It must have been dropped there by a Brit many years earlier – and if that didn't bring luck, what would? I'm not really superstitious but thought I might as well give myself any advantage I could.

Again, our mates in 'B' Squadron came to see us off, and the atmosphere became fairly emotional. This time all three Bravo patrols were deploying simultaneously, in two Chinooks. Because we were sharing our aircraft with half of Bravo Three Zero, and they were due to drop off first, we hauled our own gear to the front of the fuselage, leaving room for four guys, their kit and two Dinkies at the back. On the tailgate one of the lads said, 'Hey – I'm getting a picture of you lot,' and he took the patrol photograph which appears in the illustrations.

Earlier, we'd been joking with the loadies, saying, 'Can't you damage this fucking chopper so that it won't take off?' Unfortunately, there was nothing wrong with it – but it was so heavily laden that the pilot had to taxi it like a fixed-wing aircraft in order to get it off the ground. Then, as he had it rolling, the tail came up a bit and we lifted away.

The noise in the back was horrendous: the roar of the engines, backed by the thudding *boop, boop, boop* of the rotors, made normal conversation impossible. But a few headsets, plugged into the intercom system, hung down from the sides of the cabin and made it possible to listen to the pilots talking. When we landed to refuel at Arar, the pilot shut down his engines, and I sat there thinking, 'I hope this damn thing doesn't start up again!'

Once again we waited where we were, and no one had much to say. My mind wandered back to the occasion when, on a training exercise with the SP team, we were aboard a Puma, going in to attack a runaway coach. In the back of the heli we were all dressed up in black kit with respirators on; two guys were sitting at the open door with the fast ropes bundled up under their legs. In front of me was a young Scots fellow, and when we went into a hard turn, I put a hand on the back of his equipment, to keep him steady. He shook his shoulder to show he didn't need holding. All of a sudden the noise changed to a high-pitched screech and the padding inside the roof started to fall off. The pilot had banked round so steeply that we were looking straight down at the ground through the open door. The Scots lad began yelling, 'Get a fucking grip of me!' In a couple of seconds it was clear that the aircraft didn't have the power to pull out of its turn, and we went crashing down on to a bankside, bounced, narrowly missed some telephone lines and smashed down into a field. On the bounce, one of the fast ropes fell out and wrapped itself round a fence; it could easily have dragged the chopper back down, but as the aircraft was rising, the rope slowly uncoiled itself.

After the final impact we all jumped off and began running after the coach, continuing the exercise. But we'd only gone about twenty metres when someone stopped, threw his respirator off and shouted, 'What the fuck are we doing? For Christ's sake, bin the training!' We all stood round laughing, partly out of relief: having narrowly escaped death, we'd still been hell-bent on chasing the target. The Puma was written off, with its whole tail section cracked away. By a miracle, when it hit the bank, the rotor blades still had room to turn, because there was a ditch at the foot of the bank. If the ditch hadn't been there, the blades would have been ripped off, and we'd probably have gone in upside down.

This time there were no such dramas. With the refuelling complete, the Chinook's engines re-started faultlessly and off we went. By then darkness had fallen, and we'd flown for only a few minutes when the pilot came on the intercom to announce, 'Congratulations, guys, we've just crossed the border. You're now in Iraq.' I thought, 'Great! This is cool, flying three hundred kilometres into enemy territory. Nobody else is doing this. Nobody else knows we're going in.' But at the same time I was thinking, 'Jesus! This is real! This is bloody dangerous.' During my time in the SAS I'd been in some hairy situations on exercises in various parts of the world, and on operations in Northern Ireland, but nothing as dramatic as this. This was the first time I'd been to war.

To keep under the radar, we were flying only ten or twenty metres off the ground. I took my hat off to the pilots, who were prepared to go into hostile airspace so lightly armed; apart from our own weapons, the only armaments on board were the two SA 80 automatic rifles which the loadies could fire through the portholes. SA 80s are poor-quality, unreliable weapons at the best of times, prone to stoppages, and it seemed pretty tough to have to rely on them. We'd told the pilots that if we were attacked when we landed, we would handle the firefight, and bring the aircrew back with us on our escape and evasion, so all they had to do was stick with us.

The red canvas sling-seats along each wall had been pushed back to make room for the vehicles, and we sat on our bergens, squashed into any space available, each man busy with his own thoughts. A good deal of room was taken up by the extra fuel tanks – two fat black cylinders, like propane gas containers. I had my back to one of them, with one of the Land-Rovers in front of me, chained down to D-rings in the floor to stop it shifting during the flight.

In the dim light I watched my mates' faces, all preoccupied with their own thoughts. Then in my headphones I heard the pilot start shouting. A SAM site had locked on to us. With such a heavy load, no violent evasive tactics were possible; what he did was to go right down and hover only a foot or two above the desert. He had chaff, which he could fire off if necessary, to confuse incoming missiles, but I felt quite scared by the realisation that someone else was in the driving seat, and I wasn't in charge of my own destiny.

Time slowed to a crawl. We seemed to hover for an eternity, and when I looked out through one of the portholes, I was appalled to see how bright the moonlight was. The desert looked totally flat, without cover anywhere. Then after a minute or two we lifted again and carried on.

In my head I ran over the rations that I'd chosen and stowed in a sandbag. Deciding what you're going to eat for ten days ahead isn't easy. We'd done it by breaking down standard army ration packs and laying out our selection for each day on the ground – Monday, Tuesday, Wednesday and so on. I knew from experience that when you're sitting around in an OP, boredom makes you want to eat; for most of the time there's nothing else to do. But I'd resisted the temptation to overload, and restricted myself to a daily ration of one main meal, two packets of biscuits, and some fruit like pineapple or pears in syrup. The main meals were boil-in-the-bag – things like beef stew, chicken and pasta, pasta and meat balls, bacon and beans – pre-cooked and sealed in tough silver foil sachets, which you could roll up and squash down. Because we would be on hard routine, I'd gone mainly for lighter meals like pasta, which are easier to eat cold than solid meat. We'd also done some swaps with the Americans on the base, and I had one MRE (meal ready to eat) of corned beef hash to make a change. But our own boil-in-the-bag stuff was good – tasty and satisfying.

I thought wistfully of the brew-kit I'd left behind. Most of the other guys had brought theirs, because for them brewing-up is an ingrained habit; they do it automatically whenever they stop for a break, as much for social reasons as the need for refreshment. But I, not being a great tea or coffee drinker, had decided to go without.

As for personal kit, I was dressed, like the rest of the guys, in regular DPMs (disruptive pattern material combat fatigues). We'd also been issued with lightweight, sand-coloured desert smocks which – unbelievably – dated from the Second World War. I had worked my silk escape map into the waistband that held the draw-string of my trousers, and taped the twenty gold sovereigns given each of us for E & E purposes on to the inside of my belt. On my head I was wearing a German Army cap – a souvenir of my Alpine guide course – and on my feet a pair of brown Raichle Goretex-lined walking boots, with well insulated uppers and soles, which I'd also acquired in Bavaria at a cost of more than £100. On my hands I had a pair of green aviator's gloves, made of fine leather. As useful extras I had the two shamags I'd bought in Abu Dhabi. One was very light coloured, like a biscuit, and I'd made vain efforts to darken it by dyeing it in tea. The other was thicker and altogether more suitable, being oatmeal and purple, with the design favoured by the special forces of Oman.

In my right arm I was cradling my chosen weapon, a 203, which I'd fitted with a makeshift sling made of nylon para-cord. Four of the patrol had 203s, and the rest Minimis, the allocation being determined largely by the other burdens that each of us was carrying. Since the 203 weighs 10 lbs and the Minimi 16 lbs, those with less to carry had the machine guns. I, being the patrol medic and saddled with the 12-lb medical pack, had a 203, as did Legs Lane, who had the 30-lb radio. Stan, on the other hand, who was exceptionally strong, had a Minimi. On board the Chinook we kept the rifles loaded, with bullets up the spout and safety catches on, in case of sudden action.

Each of us also had a 66 rocket launcher – a brilliantly simple, disposable American device, which you throw away after firing. In its folded state it looks like a simple tube, with the rocket pre-packed inside it; you can carry it either slung over your shoulder on a strap, or, as I had mine, laid across the top of my bergen, under the flap. When the time comes to fire, all you have to do is pull out the second half of the tube to make a longer barrel, flip up the sight and pull the trigger.

As the chopper clattered on through the night, I was trying to think ahead, mainly about E & E. We should have had written orders, and a definite plan, but all that seemed to have been bypassed in the rush, and in the end everything had been word of mouth. The regiment's official line was that if the patrol was compromised, we should head back towards Saudi Arabia. But since Saudi would be nearly 300 kilometres off, and the Syrian border was only 130 kilometres to the west, we had already decided that if things went tits-up, we'd leg it for Syria (Stan had asked the pilots to measure the distance on their map, so that we knew exactly). That would make obvious sense – especially as the Syrians had publicly shown their defiance of Saddam Hussein by announcing that if they picked up downed air-crew from any of the allied nations, they would hand them back to the coalition forces.

Talking it over at Al Jouf, we reckoned that if we went all-out in light order, jogging and running, jogging and running, we could make the border in two nights. I'd even considered packing a set of shorts, in case we had to go for it. What we had failed to take into consideration was the lack of water; you can't jog carrying full jerricans, and there was no other source around. Nor had we bargained for the cold.

Five minutes out from Bravo One Zero's location, the loadie gave a thumbs-up signal. I unshackled the chain nearest to me, and smelt rather than heard the Land-Rover engine start up. One member of the other patrol, Paul, was wearing a single glove – for a special reason. Two days earlier he'd burnt the palm of his hand on a metal mug while making tea, raising a blister the size of a fried egg. The only treatment possible was to take the fluid out, apply some Flammazine ointment, and keep the wound clean. Paul wouldn't let the OC or the SSM see it, because if he had, he'd have been taken off the patrol. I found him holding his hand in a bucket of cold water, and as I dressed the burn for him, I said, 'Paul, you're an idiot. Just step down and let someone else go.' 'Not a chance,' he replied. 'I'm going.'

With two Land-Rover engines running, the back of the Chinook filled with choking diesel fumes. I began to think, 'I wish to hell they'd get out of here.' Then two fingers from the loadie indicated 'Two minutes to landing.' Then one minute. We felt the helicopter decelerate and settle into a landing attitude. All at once, with a bump, we were on the ground. The tailgate went down, the vehicles rolled, and the guys hustled out into the night. That was a tense moment, because it was perfectly possible that enemy were waiting to receive us. The rest of us were at the ready: we had our webbing on and weapons in hand. If the chopper had come under fire, we'd have burst out and gone to ground. But nothing happened. The tailgate came up. With some of the weight gone, the heli made a normal take-off, and we were away again.

Twenty minutes later it was our turn. We grabbed our own kit and dragged it to the edge of the tailgate. Soon the loadie gave us five fingers, then two. We pulled on goggles to keep flying sand and grit out of our eyes. As the chopper hit the deck, the tailgate went down. Cold air and dust came screaming in; particles bombarded my face, but thanks to the goggles I could still see. We tumbled out, dragging our kit. Above us was a horrendous sight. Two enormous blue fluorescent lights seemed to be blazing above the aircraft. For a moment I couldn't think what the hell was happening. Had we been caught by an Iraqi searchlight? I felt appalled that the illumination must be showing up for miles around. Then I realised that the downdraught from the rotors was raising a storm of grit, and as the grains hit the whirling blades they lit up with a bright blue glow. I thought, 'Bloody hell! Somebody's bound to see this.' The noise was terrible, too: the Chinook makes a dreadfully distinctive clatter – a *doo, doo, doo, doo* from the blades, backed by the piercing whistle of the engine exhaust.

While the racket still covered us, the guys with machine guns snapped their belted magazines into place. Then in a few more seconds the heli lifted away into the night and was gone.

The contrast was extraordinary. For the last couple of hours we'd been in deafening noise. Now suddenly we were thrown into silence. The air was still, the night clear. We lay facing outwards in a circle on the desert floor; as the sound of the engines died into the distance, we heard dogs barking not far off to the east. Obviously they were round some building – and *they'd* heard us if nobody else had.

After the stink of exhaust in the back of the chopper, the air smelt incredibly fresh and sterile. There was no trace of any plant or animal scent. That clarity alone told us we were in the middle of a barren wilderness. With our goggles off, we had all too good a view of our surroundings. We'd landed in the middle of a dry wadi or river bed, maybe 200 metres wide. Scattered clouds were sailing across the moon, and in the clear intervals its light was very bright. It was brighter than I'd expected – altogether too bright. As our eyes adjusted, we could see that the wadi had walls five or ten metres high, apparently with a level plain above them on either side.

The MSR was somewhere up ahead of us, to the north, running roughly east and west across our front. The ground beneath us was dead flat, and consisted of hard-baked clay, but we found we were lying right between a set of tracks made by a vehicle whose tyres had sunk into the dry mud. I realised that the mud was only an inch or two deep, and that under it lay solid rock. There was no loose material with which to fill our sand bags.

For what seemed an age Andy just lay there, doing nothing. It's always essential to spend time letting your eyes adjust to night vision, but this was getting ridiculous. It had immediately occurred to me that if any Arabs had seen the chopper, they'd already be running or driving across the flats towards the lip of the wadi without us being able to see them. I had visions of people coming from all directions and suddenly appearing on the rim, against the stars.

Looking at Andy, I thought he seemed semi-stunned. 'For fuck's sake,' I whispered, 'let's get some guns on to the high ground.' So we sent out two lads, one on either side, to go up the wadi walls and keep a lookout.

Gradually the barking of dogs died away and left us in total silence. Our most urgent need was to get our kit out of sight, and we began dragging or humping it across into the shadow of the moonlight cast by the right-hand or eastern wall. Everything was black and grey, like in an old film. From the middle of the wadi that shadow looked solid and deep – a good place in which to hide. But when we reached it, we found it was an illusion. There was no cover of any kind, and in the daylight the whole river bed would be dangerously open.

In heaving and dragging our kit, we were inevitably leaving marks in the baked mud of the wadi floor. But it wasn't long before we realised we were much deeper in the shit than that. From our study of satellite imagery, we had expected the sides of the wadi to be made of sand. Far from it. They were slabs of rock, some smooth, some crumbling, with a jumble of loose lumps at the bottom. There was hardly a grain of sand in the whole area. We were on bedrock. Training in the dunes of the Gulf, we had built beautiful OPs with the greatest of ease, digging into the sand and filling as many bags as we needed. Here, without sand, our bags were useless, and we couldn't dig an inch.

One urgent necessity was to find out exactly where we were. So Mark got out the Magellan and plotted our position to within a few yards. Then we pulled in our two flanking guys, who reported that the desert on either side of the wadi ran away level in flat plains, without a stitch of cover.

Andy went forward with Mark to recce the ground ahead. As the rest of us lay waiting for them to return, we began to realise how cold it was. The wind bit through our DPMs and smocks, which were far too light for the job, in both weight and colour. They gave very little protection against the cold, and were such a pale sandy colour that they shone like beacons in the moonlight. Under mine I was also wearing a dark-green Helly Hansen sweater, but the combination was nothing like enough for the temperature, which can't have been more than a degree or two above freezing. Besides, the wind was producing a high chill-factor. Way down at Victor, several hundred miles further south, a good deal further south, the nights had been warm and the days hot enough to make us sweat. Nobody had thought to warn us that things would be different up here.

The dogs started barking again. It was hard to tell what had set them off this time – could they hear us, or was our scent carrying on the wind? We reckoned they were no more than four or five hundred metres away. That figured, because the satellite photos had shown irrigated fields and habitations within about that distance of our drop-off point. We just hoped they didn't come across to suss out what was disturbing them.

In twenty minutes Andy and Mark were back. 'Right,' Andy whispered, 'We'll head up here. Get forward up the wadi.'

Four of the guys struggled into their bergens and walked forward about 300 metres, then went to ground. We watched them lumber off like pale-coloured bears, their smocks glowing in the moonlight. As soon as they were settled, the rest of us moved up to join them. Then the first four went back and picked up the rest of their kit, including the jerricans, which were tied together in pairs with tape. Once they'd joined us, we went back – and so it continued for most of the night: shuttling forward, back, forward, back. It was knackering work, but I remember at one point seeing Stan stand up with his bergen on, belt kit and all, and put two of the jerricans on his shoulders. Off he went, walking upright, with his Minimi held correctly in front of him – an amazing sight. I knew he was a strong guy, but this was incredible.

By 0500 we had moved about two kilometres to the north, and

were in the area selected for the OP. The sky in the east was already beginning to lighten. We were still in the wadi, and the walls were still bare rock, so that there was no chance of digging it. We sat around for a minute or two, discussing what to do. We couldn't stay where we were, because the ground was far too open. Then Andy went on round a corner with Stan and found that the wadi came to a dead end in a cul-de-sac no bigger than a good-sized room. The walls were fairly steep, but on the left-hand side, as we faced north, one massive slab of rock had fallen off the side of the ravine. The detached lump was about seven feet high, and lay a couple of feet clear of the wall, with a second, smaller rock near its foot, making some natural shelter. A few feet farther to the south there was an overhang going back under the wall. The floor was of hard-baked clay, with loose rocks and some stunted thorn bushes scattered about.

It wasn't a great hiding place, but it was the best we could find. So we went in and packed away all the kit for the OP, the poles and nets, because they were no use to us in this rock desert. We put the jerricans at the bottom, with the thermal sheets, cam nets and empty sandbags on top, to deaden any noise. Some of us sat on the cans, a couple tucked in underneath the overhang, and the rest settled around the rocks at various places. If we wanted to shift about, we went at a crouch or on hands and knees, but all movement was kept to a minimum.

The end of the wadi covered us from the north – the direction of the MSR – and we were reasonably well protected by the sides; but to our rear we were dangerously exposed. If anyone came up the river bed, following our tracks, they'd be bound to walk or drive right on top of us. 'This is no bloody good,' somebody muttered. 'If it looks bad in the daylight, we'll have to consider getting on the phone and getting relocated.'

Before dawn, we put out two claymore mines, about 50 metres down the wadi, with wires running back to our position, so that we could blow up anybody who approached along the foot of the eastern wall.

Within the patrol, Vince had been nominated as second-in-command, so if anything happened to Andy, he should in theory take over. Once we were on the ground, however, I found that I was emerging as more positive than him, and keener to take decisions. Apart from this, there was no definite command structure.

At first light Andy and I crept carefully up a small channel and lay at the top of the bank for a look around. Daybreak revealed that flat, grey-brown plains stretched away into the distance to the east and west. But there, straight ahead, only a couple of hundred metres away, was the MSR, running right and left across our front on a big embankment, like a long ridge. To the left, one harmless-looking civilian truck was parked on the edge of the highway; it had an open back and slatted sides, as if it was used for carrying animals. One or two other lorries rumbled along the road, but on the high ground to our right, another couple of hundred metres away, was something much more sinister: an anti-aircraft position. Through our binoculars we could see the twin barrels of guns, which we identified from our manual as SA 60s, poking up above the emplacement, and at least two Iraqis moving about.

The sight gave us a nasty jolt: to see those guns so close to us was bloody frightening, because they could only have been placed there to protect some installation from air-attack, and they showed that we were right on the edge of an enemy position. We knew we were going to have to be extremely careful.

We came back down and let the rest of the guys know that there were enemy within 400 metres of us. In the shelter of the wadi we heard the occasional vehicle go along the road, but we kept our heads down while we conferred in whispers about what to do. Clearly it was too dangerous to spend any length of time where we were, and the vital necessity was to get a message through to base, asking for a relocation or a return.

The trouble was, the 319 radio did not seem to be working. It should have been possible for us to communicate instantly with Forest Hero, the base station in Cyprus, and from there messages should have been back in Al Jouf within a couple of minutes. Any message from us would be passed straight to the CO or the Ops officer, whatever the time of day or night. But although Legs patiently tried different frequencies and experimented with various aerial arrays, he could not evoke any response. What we didn't realise till much later was that we'd been given the wrong frequencies – so Legs sat there, trying and trying to get through, assuming that this was one of those days (which you often get) when atmosphere conditions are bad, and radios just don't work. For the moment there was no serious worry, because we knew that as a fall-back we had the Lost Comms procedure whereby, if we had not come on air within forty-eight hours, a helicopter would automatically return, either bringing us a new radio set or armed with a plan to shift us elsewhere.

We took turns to go on stag, while the others had a meal or a sleep. We did an hour's guard-duty each, holding the clackers for detonating the claymores and watching the wadi. The rest of the guys, having had a sleepless night, were glad to get their heads down. It was so cold that several of them struggled into their NBC suits and lay around in them. We were all more or less hidden, and there was a good chance that if we kept still, even a man looking up the wadi from a distance would not have seen us.

Then, late in the afternoon, we heard voices. A boy of twelve or thirteen, his voice just breaking, began calling out, and a man answered him. Peering cautiously over the western rim, we saw the boy and the man – maybe his father – driving a herd of goats. They were walking across the plain, nearly parallel to the course of the wadi, but heading in towards us as they moved northwards, and calling the goats on as they went. The truck with slatted sides was still parked the far side of the MSR, so it looked as if the goatherds had come out to check their flock, or were about to load the animals up.

Either way, they were too close to us for comfort. We grabbed our weapons and lay like stones, hardly breathing, every man with a round up the spout. From the jingling of the goat bells and the voices, we reckoned the flock passed within fifty metres of our hiding place. As the sounds faded into the distance, we kept still, listening. Half an hour later, we crept to the top of the bank again to check what was happening: the truck had disappeared, and there was no sign of the goats – but where they had gone, we couldn't tell.

This place was decidedly bad news. There was so much activity in the area that it could only be a matter of time before we were compromised. Legs, cool as ever and lying in a hollow, redoubled his efforts to get through on the radio. Mark went over to help him, and the pair of them worked on the set, switching frequencies and rigging different aerials. Once you get through to base, you always feel better – at least you have contact. But now there was no response, and people began to grow apprehensive.

We were also getting frozen. At one point Andy came up to me and said banteringly, 'I hope your feet are cold.'

'Like fucking ice,' I told him.

'Good,' he said, 'I'm pleased to hear that – with those bloody boots on.'

I had the best boots of anyone in the patrol. One of the guys had ordinary army boots, and a couple were wearing jungle boots. Whatever we had, our feet were numb. Oddly enough, I didn't feel hungry, and all I ate during the day was a bar of chocolate and a packet of biscuits.

As soon as it got dark, we put out a recce party; Andy, Mark, Stan and Dinger decided to take a look round.

'We'll leave in this direction,' Andy briefed the rest of us in whispers, 'and we'll come back in the same way. The pass number's the sum of nine. We shouldn't be more than three or four hours. As we come in, the first man will walk down with his arms extended and his weapon held out sideways in his right hand.'

If the rest of us heard a contact, he went on, we were to stand-to, wait five or six minutes for the recce group to come through our position, and put fire down on anyone following them. If our own four guys didn't appear, we were to make for the drop-off point, and they would join us there.

They left at 2300, hoping that by then all the natives would have got their heads down. With the recce party gone, the rest of us took turns to do an hour's stag. Not a sound broke the silence; the night was utterly still, but not nearly so light as the one before, because the sky was full of clouds.

In the event, the recce party returned safely at 0330. They came back to the wadi from the agreed direction, but they were never challenged, because Vince, who was on stag, had fallen asleep. I happened to be awake and saw their black figures appear on top of the bank, against the sky. A moment later Andy was bollocking Vince for not being alert.

The recce group had found that the MSR was not a metalled road but a series of dirt tracks running parallel through the desert, and spread out across nearly a kilometre. They'd also discovered a single white post standing in the ground, about 300 metres from the LUP, but they could not make out what it was marking. Then they'd checked out a little tented encampment beyond the spot on which the lorry had been parked. It was a second AA position, with a few vehicles parked round it. When dogs started barking, they pulled off and moved round to see if they could find mounds or ditches or anything marking a fibre-optic line, but there was no sign of one. They also looked for a better position for us to move into – but, again, with no luck.

For what was left of the night they got their heads down, and the rest of us stagged on again. In the morning we at least felt confident that we had got in without anyone knowing we were there, but we had decided that it was too dicey to stay; there were too many people about, and we were too close to the site that the AA guns were guarding.

When I crawled round to where Andy and Dinger were sitting, I found them composing a message.

'What are we going to do?' I asked.

'We're asking for permission to attack the AA position.'

'What the hell's the use of that?'

'We might as well do something while we're here. Half of us'll sneak up the back and take the position out while the rest of you guard the kit here. Once it goes noisy, you get on the radio and call in the chopper to lift us out.'

As I listened, I was thinking, 'This isn't our mission. If we start messing around, they'll get annoyed back at RHQ.' In fact they'd get infuriated; to do something as reckless as that, outside our remit, would constitute a serious offence in regimental terms. It was pretty obvious that the installation which the AA positions were guarding must be manned by a fair-sized force of regular army or militia. Whatever the outcome of an attack, we would have to hustle back to the drop-off point wearing our bergens. With the sandbags and OP kit removed, their weight had come down to about 100 lbs each, so that they were more manageable – but a sudden pull-out such as Andy had outlined would mean leaving all the OP gear behind and giving way what we'd been up to. Until that moment we'd taken great trouble to leave no trace of our presence, pissing into a jerrican and shitting into plastic bags which, in an orderly withdrawal, we would take with us.

Another serious objection to the plan was the erratic behaviour of our radio. As far as we could tell, there was nothing wrong with it, but if we couldn't get through to base within the next few hours, we would have serious problems.

For the moment I didn't say anything. Instead, I went back and sat down beside Vince. When I told him what the others were planning, his eyes bugged out like a frog's.

Then, after half an hour, I decided, 'Ah, bollocks. We can't do this.' So I went back round the corner and told Andy it wasn't on. 'If there's something big there,' I told him, 'we're going to end up in the shit. Especially if that chopper doesn't come and get us. We're banking everything on that. If we can't raise base on the radio, or the heli can't get in, we're going to be screwed. Judging from what's happened so far, our comms are screwed anyway, so we're not going to get through.'

Dinger said, 'Yeah – you're probably right. We'll cancel that one.'

'And besides,' I told him, 'it isn't our mission to go and take out an AA position. Our mission's here, in the OP. If we can't stay here, we'd better go back.'

The others continued to fart around, and it wasn't until 1400 that they decided to drop the idea of attacking the AA site and go for a relocation. Having spent hours encoding a long message about the plan, they began to make up a new signal. But we still couldn't get through on the radio; by then the ionosphere had dropped, and contact was impossible. We also tried using our Satcom telephone. We didn't want to speak for long on it, because we'd been told that it threw off an enormous electronic splash, and that any call which lasted more than twenty seconds was liable to be picked up by direction-finding apparatus. So we switched the set to listening-wait, hoping to hear a call from base. Then occasionally we would come up on the call-sign with a quick request for a comms check: 'Hello Zero Alpha, this is Bravo Two Zero, radio check, over' – but nothing happened.

It looked as though we were going to have to rely on our Lost Comms procedure. That would mean pulling back down the wadi to the drop-off point, and being there when the chopper came in at midnight. Naturally we hoped that it would lift us out to somewhere more favourable, but, more likely, it would bring us a new radio: the CO would be advised that our set had gone U/S, and he would naturally want us to continue our mission.

Either way, after dark the whole patrol was going to move back, and we sat there thinking what a pain in the arse it would be to walk that distance humping our kit, and then hump it all the way back, just to pick up a new radio. We weren't looking forward to making the effort.

Then, about four in the afternoon, everything went to ratshit. Once again we heard the herder boy calling his bloody goats. This time he sounded closer, and coming directly for us. I'd been talking to Andy and Dinger about the radio, and I was under the overhang when the boy started shouting, from a point directly above my head, but some way out behind me. The three of us lay rigidly still – but when I looked across at Vince, on the other side of the rock, he was craning his head to see if he could spot the boy. Mouthing at him furiously, and giving tiny, frantic movements of our fingers, we tried to make him keep his head down.

If we'd all stayed still, we might have been OK. Nine times out of ten, if hidden people don't move, they get away with it. What betrays them is shape, shadow, shine, and above all movement. It's the same with birds and animals in a wood: as long as they keep still, you don't see them, but the instant one moves, that's it.

It was Vince who moved. At the time he didn't admit it, but later he came clean. Overcome by the temptation to see what was happening, he eased his head up until the boy caught sight of him.

At the time we weren't sure what had happened. All we knew was that the shouting stopped. There was no particular cry of alarm, but the sudden silence itself was ominous. It was pretty obvious that the boy had run off. I crawled round to Vince and hissed, 'Did he see you?'

'No, no, no,' he answered. 'We're OK.'

I left it at that, but I didn't believe him. Things were getting scary: there wasn't exactly a panic, but we knew we were about to be rumbled. I felt fear starting up in my stomach. Legs was still at the radio, trying to get through. 'What's happening?' I demanded.

'I'm trying,' he said. 'I'm trying.'

'Have you been on the guard net?' I asked him.

'No.'

49

'Well, get on the guard net and start tapping Morse.'

The guard net sends out new frequencies, and I knew that if we came up on it, we would compromise its entire operation for the current twenty-four-hour period. But in this emergency such a procedure was justified. Legs started working on the text for a burst transmission. 'High possibility compromise. Request relocation or expel,' his message read; but just as he was tapping it in, we heard the roar of a heavy engine and the squealing and grinding of what we thought were tank-tracks, approaching up the wadi.

That was when the adrenalin started to flow. There wasn't any more creeping about. We were all buzzing round. Wild thoughts raced through my mind: the damage a tank could do with one round into the end of the wadi – it would destroy us all. There's a form of anti-personnel round like a huge shotgun; if they whipped one of them up there, that was us finished.

'Get the 66s open,' somebody shouted, and we cocked our rocket-launchers. The guys had spread out round the end of the wadi, lying behind whatever cover they could find. Dinger chose that moment to light up one of his filthy, home-rolled fags, amid strong protests.

There we were, waiting for this tank to come into view round the corner. Every second the squealing and grinding got louder. We were stuck, pinned like rats in the dead-end of the ravine. We couldn't tell what else might be coming at us over the flat ground above. The chances were that the Iraqis were deploying behind us, too; even at the moment, they were probably advancing on our position. A couple of hand grenades tossed over the edge would make a nice mess of us. Even so, if the tank came into view and levelled its gun on us, we'd have no option but to run up on to the plain, and chance it with the AA positions on the high ground.

By then it was 1700 hours, but still full daylight. Someone said, 'Let's get some water down our necks, fellers,' and everyone started drinking, because we knew that if we had to run for it, we'd need the liquid inside us. Other guys began frantically repacking their kit, pulling off the warm jackets they'd been wearing and stuffing them into their bergens. A couple of the lads struggled out of their NBC suits and stowed them.

No one gave any orders about what to do. We just decided

that if a tank or armoured personnel carrier came round the corner, we'd try to take it out, and then go past it down the wadi, using the dry watercourse as our escape-route. The rockets wouldn't have been much use against a tank, but they might have disabled it by blowing off a track.

So there we were, getting water down our necks and having something to eat. Then I looked round at the tail ends of the rocket-launchers in front of me and said, 'Hey, fellers – watch the fucking back-blast on these things. I don't want my face burned.' When a 66 is fired, the danger area behind the tube extends for twenty metres. There was silence for a minute. Then, suddenly, out of fear and tension, everyone started laughing. They couldn't stop. I thought, 'This is bloody ridiculous. There's a tank coming round the corner, and here we all are, giggling like schoolgirls.'

Dinger pointed at my German Army cap and shouted, 'Hey, Chris, you look like Rommel.'

'Fuck off, Dinger,' I yelled back. He was dragging desperately on his fag. 'Put that fucking thing out!'

'Ah – fuck the SOPs,' he said, and everyone laughed some more.

I checked my 203 magazines again, tapping them on the bottom to make sure the lip was properly engaged in the breech. I had the mags taped together in pairs, head to toe, so that I could load the second instantly by turning the empty one upside down. Each could hold thirty rounds, but I'd only loaded them with twenty-eight, to leave the springs a bit looser and cut down the chance of a stoppage. The spares were in my left-hand lower pouch.

Then suddenly round the corner came . . . not a tank, but a yellow bulldozer. The driver had the blade high up in front of him, obviously using it as a shield; he looked like an Arab, wearing a green parka with the hood up. We all kept still, lying or crouching in firing positions, but we knew the man had seen us. He was only 150 metres away when he stopped, stared, and reversed out of sight before trying to turn round. Obviously a local, he must have known that the wadi came to a dead-end, and his only purpose in coming up it had been to find out who or what was in there. We held our breath as the squealing and grinding gradually died away.

For a minute or two we felt more relief than anything else. Then it was, 'Get the radio away, Legs,' and everyone was saying, 'We've got to go. We've got to go.' Dinger lit another fag and sucked on it like a dying man. Now we felt certain that the local militia must be deploying behind us, and one or two of the lads were being a bit slow, so it was 'Get a fucking move on' all round. We'd already decided to ditch the surplus kit we couldn't carry, but we pulled our bergens on and were ready for the off. As we were about to leave, I called, 'Get your shamags round your heads.' So we all wrapped our heads in shawls, in case we could bluff our way and pass as Arab soldiers, even for a few minutes.

As soon as Legs was ready, we started walking southwards, down the wadi, towards our emergency rendezvous point. Finding myself at the front, I led the patrol out. Call it arrogance, if you like, but I didn't trust anyone else to go first.

Dusk was already coming on, and I was hoping we could reach the drop-off point, less than two kilometres to the south, and put down enough fire to defend ourselves until dark fell – and then we'd have to wait until the chopper came in.

Moving out, I kept close in to the left-hand wall of the wadi, because that was the steepest, and in the lee of it we were out of sight of the AA guns. When I turned round, I found that the guys had opened up to a tactical spacing of maybe twenty metres between each; but I was thinking, 'If we have a nonsense here, we want to be tight together.' So I yelled back, 'Close up!'

The bulldozer had gone out of sight, but we were moving towards where we'd last seen it. All too soon the wadi began to flatten out, and on our left a long slope ran up to the plain above. As we came clear of the steep part of the wadi wall, I suddenly saw two Arabs on the high ground above us, guns down by their sides. They were barely 200 metres away, and were standing motionless. There was something oddly inert about their appearance; they showed no surprise and did not move as we walked into their view. Both were wearing dark overcoats on top of their dishdashes (native cotton robes), which reached down to their ankles. Also they had red-and-white shamags done up on top of their heads like turbans. I reckoned they were civilians or possibly militia.

'It's that sodding boy,' I said to myself. 'He's run like hell and tipped them off.'

'Close up!' I yelled again, because it was obvious the shit was going to go down. Next behind me was Bob Consiglio, and I shouted back to him, 'Fucking hurry! Catch up!'

We kept going. But the two Iraqis began to parallel us, moving forward. In case anybody hadn't seen them, I called back, 'We've got two on the high ground to the left, and they're walking down. Keep going.'

Behind me everyone started cursing. The tension in the patrol was electric. I felt fear rising in my chest. Afterwards, I realised that the two Iraqis were waiting for reinforcements to come up; also, they were probably a bit confused, not knowing who the hell we were. But at the time I was wondering if we could outrun them, or lose them somehow, without starting a firefight.

Then I blew it in a big way. I thought, 'I'm going to try the double bluff here,' and I waved at them. Unfortunately I did it with my left hand, which to an Arab is the ultimate insult – your left hand being the one you wipe your arse with. The reaction was instantaneous: one of them brought up his weapon and opened fire. Suddenly he was putting rounds down on us. We swung round and put a couple of short bursts back at them. Both dropped on to one knee to continue firing. As I stood there, I saw Vince take off down the wadi. In spite of the danger, there was something ridiculous about his gait: a pair of legs, going like the clappers under a bergen, and not making much progress either.

'Stay together!' I yelled. 'Slow down!' We began to run, turning to fire aimed bursts. The secret is to keep them short – no more than two or three rounds at a time. Otherwise the recoil makes the weapon drift up, and the rounds go high. We ran and fired, ran and fired.

Within seconds a tipper truck with metal sides screeched to a halt beside the two Arabs, and eight or ten guys spilled out of it. Stan also saw an armoured car carrying a .50 machine gun pull up. Somehow I never saw that; it may have been behind a mound from where I was standing. Some of the Iraqis began firing from the back of the truck, others from positions behind it.

It looked as though there were about a dozen altogether. They had automatic rifles – almost certainly Russian AK 47s – and at least one heavy machine gun. But their fire was inaccurate, and we could cope with them. In my mind they weren't the real threat. What worried me much more was the thought that a bigger force was probably driving round ahead of us, out of sight, to cut off our retreat.

Looking back, I found that our guys were running across the open ground, struggling under the weight of their bergens. Even though the packs weren't as heavy as before, trying to run with them was a nightmare. At one moment the patrol seemed to converge into a tight group, then we spread out again, some running, others taking turns to stop, turn and put down rounds, then run again.

If anyone says he's not frightened in a firefight, I don't believe him. I was shit scared, and so was everyone else. I know the SAS has a high reputation, but the guys are not superhuman: they may have enormous courage, but they are subject to the same fear as anyone else. The regiment's strength lies in the fact that its members are highly trained to control their fear and respond positively to whatever threat they are facing.

In this contact, panic threatened. The flow of adrenalin was fearsome: you can do a lot when someone's shooting at you. But then you get desperate for breath, and your chest and stomach start to burn. On we went, legging it up the slope now, swivelling, shooting at the enemy as they ran back and forth between vehicles. Three times I saw men go down when I fired. One went down behind a mound and never came up. Two others rolled over as they were running. At one point there was a hell of an explosion from one of the vehicles.

Green tracer started coming across, whizzing past our heads. I could hear the odd *doof!*, then *crack!*, then *prooh!*. We were right in the open, like ducks in the water, with all this shit coming in. Whenever one of us stopped to turn and fire, the enemy seemed to concentrate on him, and we could see the tracer close in on the stationary target.

Luckily the Iraqis seemed to have the intention of coming after us. Rather than dropping down into the wadi, and putting themselves at a disadvantage, they preferred to stick to the high ground. As the tracer flew, I got out my TACBE, pressed the tit, and began screaming into it, 'TURBO! TURBO! This is Bravo Two Zero. CONTACT! CONTACT!' Andy was doing the same. He, I and one of the other guys had TACBEs set to American frequencies, so that we could speak to American pilots. The other sets were on British frequencies. Every one of them should have produced an answer within seconds. Every one of us expected to hear a voice come back out of the air – but nothing happened.

'My TACBE's fucked!' I yelled to Andy.

'Can't get through on mine, either.'

'Keep trying.'

Then somebody shouted, 'I'm ditching my fucking bergen!' Someone else yelled, 'You're fucking right! I am too!' Next second, I was doing it myself, fighting to get the straps off my shoulders. Then I was kneeling by the pack, struggling with the clips on the top flap to free my 66. My lungs and heart were bursting, my whole body heaving and shaking. I said to myself, 'Slow down, slow down – or you're done for.'

I got one clip undone. Just as I reached my hand towards the other, the thing exploded in pieces, hit by a .50 bullet. I never felt anything – no wind or burn – but if my hand had been four or five inches farther forward I would have lost it. The heavy round put the bergen down flat beside me. I leapt on it, grabbed the 66, whipped it over my shoulder, and started off again. Ahead of me to the right I saw big splashes of soil or rock coming up. I thought, 'Fucking mortars! Now they're firing mortars, and some dickhead has failed to take the pins out of the shells.' That's what it looked like: as if the Iraqis were forgetting to pull out the safety pins from their mortar rounds, so that the bombs were merely kicking up dirt and rock, rather than exploding. What had happened, in fact, was that the AA position had opened up on us, and rounds from those things were coming across as well.

By now we were walking. We couldn't run uphill any more. I remember Legs being just ahead of me, in the middle. But as I moved away from my bergen, I was thinking, 'What is there in there that I should have?' Then I remembered: it was the medic pack. 'Fuck the medic pack!' I shouted to no one in particular. When I'd gone about twenty metres from the bergen I said to Legs, 'Have you got the radio?'

'No,' he gasped. 'I had to leave it.'

'Fuck it,' I said. 'Keep going.' But then, suddenly, I thought, 'Jesus! My hip flask! The hip flask that Jan gave me for Christmas. Bloody hell – I'm not leaving *that*. The rest of the stuff is military kit, but that's mine.'

I don't know what happened. The sensible thing would have been to leave it behind. But something clicked, and without hesitation I ran back down the slope. As I reached the bergen, I thought, 'You idiot – you're going to get shot now.' I bent down, my back to the Iraqis, and I was thinking, 'You're not going to be walking far at all, because there's going to be a round come through you any second.' I imagined parts of my chest hurtling out in front of me, and wondered what they would look like. Would my clothes tear apart, as in a movie, and bits of flesh and bone fly out? But I stuck my hand into the top of the pack, found the flask, brought it out, stuffed it into a trouser pocket and started forward again.

By then I was finding it hard to walk. My breath was roaring in my throat. I had the sensation of suffocation. Never in training had I pushed myself so hard. I seemed to be going through the movements of breathing but getting no oxygen in. Yet fear was driving me on.

Then we were probably out of range, too far to have any real chance of dropping more of the Iraqis; but the occasional guy would still turn, put rounds down, and look to see where his mates were. The whole scene was becoming surreal. People didn't seem to be heading in any particular direction; they were weaving back and forth in front of each other, like eddies in a stream. I remember seeing Bob, who was behind me and lower down, throwing a couple of white phosphorous grenades to get some smoke up, and thinking, 'You brave bastard!'

I looked at Legs, and saw tracer going across the top of his head. Knowing that tracer flies higher than normal rounds, I couldn't understand how the other stuff wasn't hitting him. I thought, 'He's going to get it here.' Then I wondered if the Iraqis were firing all tracer, instead of one round in five, as we would. Then the stuff was coming past *us*. Andy and I were walking up together, and tracer was flying between us, rounds right between the pair of us.

At last we got over the top, into dead ground, and collapsed on to the deck. Andy gasped, 'Fucking hell! I don't know how we managed that.'

'Nor do I,' I said. 'But look at this – at least I got my flask back.'

'Where was it?'

'In my bergen. I had to go back for it.'

'Christ!'

I unscrewed the top, took a swig of whisky, which was sixteen-year-old Lagavulin, and handed it to him.

'Jesus!' he gasped, as he felt the impact of the spirit.

For a few seconds we lay there, trying to get our breath, and when we stood up again to see where the guys were, we were amazed to find everyone in one piece. I'd thought we must have lost two or three – but they all appeared and came round, just like that, nobody so much as touched. At the very least I'd been expecting to have to dress wounds – although, with the medical pack gone, there was very little I could have done except stuff holes with bandages.

Everybody was talking, but I can't remember what they said. It took us only a few seconds to reach a group decision. If our Lost Comms procedure worked, the Chinook would come in to the drop-off point at midnight; but now that we'd stirred up such a hornets' nest, and the Iraqis knew we were in the area, the chances were that they'd ambush the helicopter and shoot it down. We decided it was safer to make for the Syrian border. First, though, we'd head south and put in a dog's leg, as a feint, to throw the Iraqis off our track.

'Right,' I called, 'let's go.' Without consciously trying to take command, but wanting out of this bloody place, I led off, with Andy behind me and the rest in line. By then, we thought, we were out of range of the Arabs' original position, but some of them had worked their way round on to a closer ridge, and as we came up out of the depression they opened up again. Also, we were back in view of the anti-aircraft gunners, who resumed firing. Some rounds were going *boosh* past us, others landing ten or fifteen metres away – but we weren't interested; we just kept walking like mad. Then the vehicle with the .50 came up on to a crest and started cracking rounds over us again from a range of 400 or 500 metres, but luckily for us the light was dying, and the rounds were going far too high.

So we set off, and walked for our lives into the gathering night.

Chapter Three

Down To Two

Until we cleared the second long valley, the occasional AA round was still falling in. Some burst in the air with a puff of black smoke and a crack, and others hit the ground. Then we were in the clear, out on the barren gravel plains, and we headed due south, marching as fast as we could in single file. Every now and then we'd shout to Mark to get a fix, and he'd switch on his Magellan and hold it up until it locked on to a satellite. After a couple of minutes, he'd call, 'I've got one,' and the guys would go to ground while Andy and I closed up to look at the map and check our position. Mark would read off the coordinates from his little illuminated screen, look down at the map and say, 'OK, we're just there' – and we'd know our position, within ten feet or so. Encouraged by such precision navigating, we'd carry on.

It was a great shock to us that we seemed to have been abandoned by our own people. It's an unwritten rule of the Regiment that if guys need help, their mates come and get them. Wherever you are, even in the shittiest area in the world, if you get into a firefight and give a shout on the radio, they'll come and find you. Now we'd yelled ourselves hoarse on radios and TACBEs, and there had been no result. The disappointment was horrendous. When I'd got out my TACBE, I'd thought, 'This is my last resort,' and I'd fully expected to hear an AWACS pilot answer my call; I had no doubt that he'd have half the regiment coming out in search of us. What we could not have known at the time was that the nearest AWACS aircraft was 500 kilometres to the east – about four times the maximum range of the TACBEs – and that we had been given the wrong radio frequencies, so that none of our calls on the 319 had gone through unscrambled.

Now, deprived of our food, water, warm clothes and other essential kit, we set our faces to the south. After half an hour someone shouted, 'We're getting followed up!' Looking back, we saw the lights of a vehicle. At first we couldn't tell whether or not it was moving, but then through Vince's night-sight we made out that it was definitely coming after us. In some places the desert was completely flat, with no features of any kind, and obviously the vehicle could make good speed across those pancake areas; but luckily for us there were also a lot of wadis, in which the going was rough and the driver had to crawl. There was no way he could still see us – the night was too dark for that – but he knew the line we'd taken down the first wadi, and he was driving on the bearing he had seen us follow, 180 degrees.

The ground varied from hard-baked clay to gravel and loose rock, on which our boots inevitably made a crunching sound. There was also the rustle of clothes and pouches rubbing on each other. We could have been quieter if we'd gone slowly, but the paramount need was for speed, and I pressed on as fast as I could in spite of the noise, with the other guys close behind, at intervals of no more than two metres between each man. All the time I was thinking that, because the AA positions we'd seen were obviously guarding something, the military there would radio ahead, organising searchers to come round in front and cut us off. We already knew that although the desert seemed so empty there were outposts dotted all over it, and we could have walked on to a position at any moment. There was also the risk of stumbling into a bedouin encampment.

After an hour, and maybe eight or nine kilometres, we stopped and came together in a group. Dinger took off his duvet jacket and started covering it with rocks.

'What the hell are you doing?' I asked.

'I'm ditching this fucker. It's far too hot.'

'Keep the damn thing,' I told him. 'Tie it round your waist. You're going to need it.'

Later he thanked me, and said I'd saved his life. But for the moment he cursed as we got going again. I kept thinking of all the stuff I'd left behind. I hated the idea of the Iraqis pillaging our kit. No doubt they'd already whipped the patrol camera away – but unfortunately for them none of the film had been exposed. And what would they make of Tom Sharpe's *Riotous*

Assembly? They'd also have got my dark-blue Patagonia thermal top, my bivvy bag, ten days' rations, the medical pack, a pair of land-line telephones, a couple of anti-personnel mines and some demolition equipment. At least they hadn't got my precious hip-flask. With a flicker of satisfaction I remembered that we'd left the claymores and anti-personnel mines buried in the floor of the wadi, and wondered whether they'd taken any of the enemy out. I wished I'd kept more food in my pouches, and less ammunition. As it was, I had nothing to eat but two packets of hard, cracker-type Compo biscuits, five in each packet. At the very least we were in for forty-eight hours of hard going, on little food and water.

When you're moving in a straight line, and have a contact, it's usually the Number One who gets hit and, even if he isn't shot, it's Numbers Two and Three who have to get him out of trouble, a.s.a.p. On that march our SOP – which everyone knew by heart – was that if we hit trouble the lead scout would put a 203 round towards the enemy and empty a magazine in their direction. By that time Two and Three should already have gone to ground, and be putting rounds down. Number One would then spring back, zig-zagging, and go to ground himself, to cover the other two, while the rest of the guys fanned out. Equally, though, it was important not to panic and start firing at phantoms, as shots would immediately give our position away.

Contact SOPs were second nature. But Vince, who was Number Two, kept dropping back, as if he didn't want to be near me. More than once he stopped and said, 'If we get a contact in front, whatever you do, don't fire back. You're better off sticking your hands up.'

I said, 'Hey – if we get a contact, I'm shooting. Because if we get captured, we'll get done.'

'Don't,' he said. 'If you shoot one of them, they'll kill the lot of us.'

'Bollocks!' I said.

'You've got to think about it,' he insisted. 'I'm not doing it.'

By that time the patrol had closed up again, and there was a bit of an argument. 'Get your finger out,' somebody told Vince. Nobody supported him. I just said, 'Stick behind me,' and led off again. A few minutes later a message came up the line, to slow down and stop. Somebody shouted, 'Stan's gone down!'

Stan! I thought, 'Jesus! He's one of the strongest guys in the patrol. What the hell's the matter with him?' I ran back and asked what was wrong, but he was on the deck and seemed to be nearly unconscious. All he could do was grunt. It was as if he was drunk, only half there. I'd seen students like that on selection courses, so knackered that you couldn't get any sense out of them.

'What's happened to him?' I asked the next guy.

'Dunno. He just went over.'

'Did he hit his head on a rock or something?'

'I don't think so.'

'Stan!' I said. 'What's wrong?'

He just went '*Urrrhhh!*'

One of the guys said, 'I reckon it's heat exhaustion. He's sweating like hell.'

'Never!' I said. 'It can't be. The night's bloody freezing.'

I'd been sweating a bit myself – but not that much. What we didn't know was that Stan was still wearing his thermal underclothes under his DPMs. He'd been caught out with them on when the contact started, and hadn't had a chance to take them off. The result was that he'd become seriously overheated and had sweated himself dry.

Anyway, we got out our water bottles. I tipped sachets of white rehydrate powder into four of them, and started pouring the water down his neck. He drank three bottles straight off – one of mine, one of Andy's, and one from one of the other guys: six pints at least. That should have pulled him round, but it didn't seem to have much effect. He was still dizzy and exhausted, not making much sense.

Somebody said, 'We've got to look for a safe spot and leave him. Find a hole in the ground.'

There was no way I'd do that. We couldn't leave one guy by himself – not when there were seven more of us, all strong and still fresh. I bent over Stan and said in a menacing voice, 'Listen: if you don't start walking, we're going to fucking leave you. Understand?'

He nodded and gave a grunt.

'Get up, then,' I told him. 'Get on my arse, and don't leave it. Just fix your eyes on my webbing, and keep that in sight.'

Someone said, 'OK, Stan – give us your kit.' Andy took his

61

Minimi, then said to me, 'Chris, take this,' and gave me his night-sight (generally known as a kite-sight), which Stan had been carrying slung round his neck.

'I don't want that fucking thing,' I protested. The sight weighed four or five pounds, and I thought it would be a pain to have it dangling on my chest. But I took it – and thank God I did, because without doubt it saved my life. I also took a box of 200 rounds for the Minimi and slung it over my shoulder.

We couldn't hang around any longer, because the vehicle lights were still bobbing about in the darkness behind us. I got hold of Stan again and repeated, 'Just walk behind me – and whatever you do, keep going.'

He went, '*Urrrhh*, yeah, yeah,' then he got up and we kicked off again. Once more I led, with Stan at my back, Vince behind him, and the rest of the patrol following. Lead scout is a tiring job, because you have to be looking ahead all the time; but, being quite observant, I reckoned that if there was something in front of us, I would see it as quickly as anyone else. Andy was in the middle, the normal slot for a patrol commander.

Every time we stopped for Mark to do a Magellan check, I'd say, 'Stan – lie down. Get your head down for a minute,' and he'd lie down without a word, as if he were semi-conscious, obedient as a dog. When we were ready to start again I'd give him a kick and say, 'OK, Stan, let's go,' and he'd get up again and start walking right behind me – only to fall back, farther and farther.

When this had happened two or three times, I tried to provoke some reaction by saying, 'Stan – if you don't keep behind me, and keep up with me, I'm going to leave you.' He did react in a way, by promising to fix his eyes on the back of my webbing, and not let that out of his sight. That kept him going for a while, but still, whenever we stopped, he would lie down like he was dead.

Once again the sky was partly overcast, but a cold north-west wind was keeping the clouds on the move, and whenever the moon came out, it lit up the desert brilliantly. Often I saw some dark object standing out from the background. Usually it was a mound or rock, but it could have been a building or a vehicle, and it needed checking. The moment I had a doubt, I'd stop, lie down and watch for a while, to see if anything moved – and whenever I did so, the other guys automatically went down too, flat on their stomachs, forming an arc.

The little binoculars we'd bought in Abu Dhabi were a distinct asset, as they drew in what light there was and often enabled me to work out what it was that I'd seen. But the kite-sight, or image-intensifier, proved a godsend. Basically a black tube, it was designed to fit on top of a 203, but it made the weapon heavy and unbalanced and I found it easier to put the sight up on its own, holding it like a telescope. To use it, I had to switch it on and wait ten seconds for it to warm up. It gave out a faint, high-pitched squeal, and produced a clear, fluorescent green, white-flecked picture of the ground ahead, with much more detail than the naked eye could pick out.

The more I came to depend on the sight, the more anxious I was that I might switch it on accidentally while walking and run the battery down, so as I was moving I kept a finger on the button, to make certain that it was turned off. The penalty of using the sight was that it reduced my natural night-vision. Whenever I'd taken a check round, and lowered the sight, I could see very little for a minute or two.

In spite of the danger, I enjoyed being out at night. We had done a lot of training in the dark, and I always felt safe, protected by the fact that nobody could see me. I thought of the time when I was a boy, out shooting pigeons with my father, and we were coming home in the dusk one evening. As we passed along the edge of a wood, I felt really frightened by the intense blackness under the trees. It was the sort of place where, in a children's book or a movie, witches would lurk. I said to my dad, 'I'd be scared stiff to go in there.'

'Why?' he said.

'Well, you can't see.'

'Come on, then.' He took my arm and walked in fifteen or twenty metres. I was terrified, and stuck close by him, holding his jacket so that he couldn't do a runner on me. Inside the wood, we sat down.

'Just keep quiet, and listen,' he whispered. After a while he said softly, 'There you are. If anyone was trying to creep up on us, we'd hear him. You can't walk through a wood at night without making a sound. What you've got to realise is that if there are people in here, and we can't see them, they can't see us either. This is the safest place to be.'

The lesson stuck, and I was never scared of the dark again.

At every halt Mark took a fix with his Magellan until we were confident about our route. But the vehicle lights were still coming up behind us, so we decided to put in the dog-leg. Until then we'd been heading back towards the Saudi border. Now we resolved to turn right – westwards – for a spell, then right again, and head northwards across the MSR which we'd been watching. The loss of our jerricans had forced us to modify our original plan of going north-west, straight for the Syrian border. Obviously we would need water, so we decided to aim due north, for the Euphrates, and follow the river out to the frontier.

So, after sixteen quick kilometres southwards, we turned due west and did ten kilometres in that direction, hoping that the Iraqis were wasting their time and resources by throwing out a cordon ahead of where they'd last seen us. The pace was very, very fast – speed marching, with everyone in line-ahead, going as fast as they could without running, probably at nine kilometres or six miles an hour. Now and then we crossed a dry wadi like the one in which we'd lain up, but for most of the way the desert was completely open, without landmarks, and we kept going on a bearing. Whenever we heard the sound of jet engines overhead, we'd switch on our TACBEs and shout into them – but answer came there none.

By the end of the ten kilometres westwards, the strain was starting to tell. We'd been moving at high speed, with fifty-pound belt kits and our weapons, and we were sweating quite a bit in spite of the cold. That meant we were all thirsty, and soon we'd drunk nearly all our water. Whenever we stopped, we made sure to get more liquid down Stan's neck. He had kept going by sheer will-power; admittedly he had been relieved of the burden of his weapon, but even so, after such a collapse it was a major feat to maintain the pace we were setting.

As soon as we'd fully lost sight of the vehicle behind us, we made our second right turn and headed north, stopping frequently to check our position with the Magellan. This went on until we thought we were back within about seven kilometres of the MSR. Then, as we went to ground for yet another map-check, I said to Andy, 'Right: from now on, we're coming to the most dangerous bit. What I'll do is push as hard as I can until we've crossed the MSR. There could be people looking for us along it. If we get caught on those tracks, out in the open, we're going to be knackered. If there are any enemy on the ridge beyond the road, we want to be up on the high ground as soon as we can.'

'Yeah,' Andy agreed, 'push it out.' And he told everyone else, 'We're going to walk real fast until we cross the MSR. OK?'

So we started again, travelling at an even faster pace. By then I was using the kite-sight most of the time, with my weapon tucked under my left arm. It was awkward and tiring to walk in that attitude. After a while my eyes started to hurt as well, because looking through the sight continuously was like staring at a light. But there was no alternative. Soon I could make out the ridge on which the AA guns were mounted, and I kept scanning for lights or artificial shapes, focusing my attention on what lay ahead.

Disaster hit us without warning. We'd been walking for an hour since I last spoke to Andy, when at last we came to the MSR and started to cross the tracks. It turned out that there were about a dozen of them, running side by side, marked in hard mud, and they seemed to be spread over 200 or 300 metres. Out on that open expanse, obviously well used, I felt horribly exposed, so I turned up the pace even faster. Then, just short of the high ground, I looked through the night-sight yet again and saw what I thought was a building or vehicle. I couldn't be sure what it was, but the object certainly looked artificial, so at the foot of the slope I stopped to confer with Andy.

Looking round, I saw Stan behind me, with his head hanging down, then Vince . . . but no one else.

'Where the fuck's the rest of the patrol?' I demanded. Vince just said, 'I don't know. We've lost them.'

'What d'you mean, lost them?'

'They split off somewhere.'

Vince didn't seem too concerned. But I thought, 'Oh my God!' I was on the verge of panic, but all I said was, 'Right – let's get up on the high ground, fast.' I took one more look at the black object, decided it was a rock, and hustled forward as fast as I could. Just short of the top of the ridge I stopped again. Stan lay down like he was dead. Vince was completely zonked as well – he just sat there and couldn't speak.

By my calculation, it was at least an hour since the patrol had split. Looking back across the open gravel plains with the kite-sight, I had a clear view for miles. It seemed impossible that the others could have gone far enough to vanish. I kept scanning and thinking that at any second I would see five black figures trudging in single file – yet I couldn't get any movement anywhere. Men walking in that bare landscape would have showed up large as life – but somehow the desert had swallowed them.

For a few moments I was dumbfounded. Then I thought: 'My TACBE and Andy's are compatible; if both are switched on at the same time, we should be able to talk to each other.' The SOP for this situation was that anyone in difficulties would listen out on every hour and half-hour; so I waited five minutes till midnight, pressed the button and called: 'Andy! Andy!' No answer. I kept on for five minutes, fully expecting him to shout back, but no call came.

Things were going from bad to worse. We were down to three men; one of them was out of the game, and the other didn't want to be in it. We had only two main weapons: I had my 203, and Vince a 203 and a pistol. Stan had nothing but a bayonet. I felt a kind of jealousy and resentment start to burn inside me. The other group was larger, a stronger fighting force, most of them armed with Minimis. If anybody was going to get out, they were. I felt I'd much rather have been in their party than in ours.

Already thirst was a problem. We'd done a fearsome tab, and Stan had drunk all my water. We had also lost the Magellan, which was with Mark. From now on we'd have to navigate by map, compass and dead reckoning – and this depended on knowing how fast we were covering the ground. Experience told me that the error was likely to grow ever-larger as we became more tired and tended increasingly to over-estimate the distance we'd gone. I regretted never having done a course in astral navigation: I could recognise the Plough, Orion's Belt and a few other constellations, but that was all.

I looked round. Stan was asleep on the ground beside me, but Vince had moved off about fifteen metres and was squatting down. I thought he was having a shit, and that if he was, I'd better go across to make sure he buried it. But when I walked towards him, I found that what he was doing was burying his ammunition – a box of 200 rounds and a sleeve of 203 grenades.

'What the hell are you doing?' I hissed.

'I'm not carrying that stuff,' he said. 'It's too heavy. If we get into a big contact, we'll all be wasted anyway.'

'You've got to fucking carry it,' I told him.

'I can't.'

'Give us those rounds here, then.'

I was fuming. We only had the two weapons, and might really need the ammunition. But I couldn't turn round and order Vince to carry it. So I slung the 203 bandolier over my shoulder and let him bury the box. But I knew that from that moment I couldn't rely on him.

I went back, sat down, and waited until 00.30. Then on the half-hour I tried the TACBE again – but still the night yielded no reply.

I felt angry as well as scared. I simply couldn't make out how the patrol had split. But whatever had happened behind us, I could see no future in sitting where we were; we had to get away from the MSR and put more distance behind us, in case the Iraqis tried to follow up. So we cracked on, walking again, with Stan on my shoulder and Vince behind him.

For the next four and a half hours, we slogged on and on. By then, on the high plateau, the ground was flat as a billiard table, but it was covered with loose rocks the size of your fist. These made the going rough, and I could feel I was starting to get blisters along the sides of my feet.

Every time I stopped to check our position, I'd say, 'Stan – just lie down,' and he'd lie down and go straight to sleep. If I tried to get Vince to help me plot where we were, he showed no interest in the map, because he was knackered, mentally as well as physically. I had a small torch attached to my compass, and I'd covered the lens with black masking tape, with just a pinhole in it, so that a very fine beam of light shone on the map. Whenever I tried to work out where we were, Vince would agree with anything I suggested. I would have preferred him to argue. I kept wanting him to say, 'No, look: I think we're *there*,' because it would have made me think harder – but he'd gone completely inert.

Anyway, we kept going until 0500, by which time we were all at the end of our tether. That was hardly surprising, as we'd covered the best part of seventy kilometres during the night. I was thinking, 'Dawn can't be far off. We'd better find somewhere to hole up for the day,' when we came across an old tank berm. This took the form of a bank of soil about six feet high, built in the shape of a big U or horseshoe with one end open, so that a tank could drive into it and be hidden from the other three sides. Just short of it, and leading into it, were two tracks about twenty-four inches wide and fifteen deep, where a tank had sunk into the ground on its way in or out.

There was no future in lying up inside the berm itself; the wind was blowing straight into its wide, open end, so that its walls gave no shelter, and anyone passing could look in. Equally, we couldn't lie outside the walls in the lee of the wind, because we'd have been in full view from the other direction. The only shelter from the wind, and at the same time cover from view, was in the tank-ruts outside.

'We're going to have to stay here,' I said, and we lay down in the deepest part of one of the tracks, head to toe, Vince at one end, me in the middle and Stan beyond me. Down flat, we were more or less hidden, but I only had to raise my head an inch or two to see out. It was a precarious refuge to say the least – and if anyone came to visit the berm for any reason, we would obviously be compromised.

While we'd been on the move, the wind hadn't seemed too cold; but now that we'd stopped putting out energy, it cut through our thin clothes viciously. That was bad enough, but when daybreak came I looked out, and the first thing I saw was heavy clouds piling in from the west, black as the ace of spades. I said, 'Oh, Jesus, fellers. The sky's really dark over there. It's going to piss down with rain.' Then I looked in the other direction and saw something square, about 600 metres off. It was either a little building or a box-bodied vehicle, with antennas poking up out of it, and at least two men round it. This showed how right we'd been to remain alert during the night: here was some small military outpost, miles from anywhere – exactly the sort of place we might have walked on to.

Back at Victor we'd shared some jokes about how shy Arabs are about shitting. The SSM had told me that an Arab will walk miles rather than shit in front of his pal, and this berm seemed just the place one might choose. I couldn't see any old turds lying about, it was true, but the bank was just the right distance from the outpost. So I said to the guys, 'There's an enemy position across there. We're going to have to be careful in case one of the fellers there comes across for a crap. We'll have to take turns to stay awake. Vince, you do the first couple of hours' stag.'

Not that I'd worked out what we'd do if anybody did approach; we'd either have to leg it across the open ground or take the person out – and neither seemed a good option. There was no other cover for miles around, and if we killed anybody it would inevitably reveal our approximate position and throw away the advantage we'd gained from putting in the dog's leg. Nor did it seem likely that any of us would get our heads down, it was so bloody cold. The wind came knifing through my DPMs and smock, so I opened my canvas map case and laid it over my legs. Also I wrapped one shamag round my head, and pulled the other round my shoulders. Even then I was still freezing. But somehow I must have dozed off, because I woke up shaking violently, with what felt like pins and needles in my face. When I opened my eyes, I couldn't believe it: it was snowing, and we were covered in white.

Big flakes were teeming down, coating us with slush as we lay there. I thought, 'Oh, for fuck's sake!'

'Look at this!' I exclaimed bitterly. 'You'd think we were at the fucking North Pole.' Nobody answered, so I said, 'Vince, are you all right?'

He grunted something back.

'Stan, how are you feeling?'

'Oh, a lot better.'

That lifted me – just to hear him sounding more like himself. He seemed a hundred per cent livelier than he had been.

'Thank Christ,' I said. 'Well – get something to eat.' All I had was my biscuits, so I ate two of them, chewing slowly to produce saliva and work them down. Stan and Vince both ate something too.

'What was wrong in the night, Stan?'

'I had my thermal underwear on, Chris. Sweated myself dry. I didn't have time to take it off when the contact started.'

'You lucky bastard!' I said. 'Now, I mean.'

'I'm still fucking freezing, though.'

'So am I.'

The worst result of the night – though I didn't realise it immediately – was that I'd badly burnt my feet. At first I couldn't understand what had happened; my boots were well run-in and completely comfortable, and had never given me the slightest trouble. Later I realised that the problem was my socks. They were German Army issue, made of rough grey-brown wool, and because our build-up had been done in such a rush, I'd worn them for four or five days on end before the deployment. By the time we started walking, they were already stiff with sand, dust and sweat – and now, as a result, they'd chewed the sides of my feet into large blisters.

The normal treatment – which we'd used on selection courses – would have been to push a needle into each blister, extract the fluid, and inject tinc benzine, or Friar's Balsam. The process hurt like hell – it felt as if a red-hot poker had been laid against your foot – but it toughened the underlying skin enough for you to be able to walk on it. Even washing my feet and putting on plasters would have helped. But there, trapped in the tank track, I couldn't even take my boots off to inspect the damage, let alone do anything to repair it.

From time to time we talked in whispers. At one point Vince said, 'I knew we'd been compromised in the wadi.'

'How?'

'That fucking goatherd – I saw him.'

'He must have seen you, then.'

'Must have.'

I cursed silently to myself. If Vince had admitted that at the time, we'd have got out of the wadi a lot quicker before the bull-dozer appeared, and before the two guys appeared above us. We might even have made a clean break back to the drop-off area.

Now and then during the day we saw military-looking vehicles driving in the distance. I lay in the tank-track thinking, 'This is shite!' The snow turned to rain, then back to snow. Our ditch filled with water. The water dissolved the earth into mud, and soon we were wallowing in an icy quagmire. There was mud all over us, all over our weapons. We were becoming sodden with the filthy stuff. But all we could do was lie there in it, from six o'clock in the morning right through till dusk.

I'd often been cold before, but never in my life had I been as cold as that. The cold bit into our very bones. Time slowed to a crawl. Now and then we heard a vehicle drive past, but otherwise there was nothing to occupy our minds. I became so frozen that I didn't even want to move my arm so that I could see my watch, and I asked Stan what the time was. 'Twelve o'clock,' was the answer. Jesus! Was this day ever going to end?

Trying to escape from reality, I thought back to other times when I'd been frozen. Once when I was seventeen, on my first escape and evasion exercise with the Territorial SAS, up at Otterburn in the middle of the winter, I was caught by the hunter force of Three Para. They got us, gave us a good kicking, stripped us naked, tied our wrists and anchored us up to the chest in the middle of the river until we were completely numb. Then they took us into an insulated airborne shelter, with five gas heaters blazing, where the temperature was about 120 degrees. As our circulation got going again, the pain became excruciating – and it was then, when we were doubled up in agony on the floor, that they started interrogating us about who we were and what we'd been doing. As soon as we were warm and starting to recover, they put us back in the river and so began the whole process again . . .

In the tank-ruts, it was impossible to concentrate on anything for long, the discomfort was so intense. I tried to think of places where I'd been warm, like Africa, but I couldn't stay long in any of them. The one big plus was that Stan seemed to be back in his normal spirits. He'd brought a proper boil-in-the-bag meal in his belt-kit, and once he'd got that down him, he was ready to go. Vince, on the other hand, was feeling the cold worst of any of us. He wasn't whingeing, but he kept saying, 'Chris, I can't feel my fingers. I'm bloody freezing,' and I was saying, 'So am I. But we can't do anything, Vince. We can't move, so we've just got to stick it out.'

'Can't we cuddle in together?'

'Not yet. It's too dangerous to move.'

The temptation to get up and go, to start moving again, was colossal: anything would be better than enduring this agony. But one of the regiment's most fundamental SOPs is that during escape and evasion you don't move in daylight, and I decided that we must stick by it. If we were spotted walking, Iraqis would come at us from all sides. Grim as it was, I insisted we stayed where we were.

Then, late in the afternoon, Vince put the wind up me by saying, 'Look – I'm going down here.'

We had to do something.

'What's the time, Stan?'

'Four o'clock.'

'Let's cuddle in, then.'

Vince and I wriggled further down to where Stan lay, and the track was a bit wider. At that point we were all coming out into the open, but we took the risk and lay together, cuddling in for warmth, with me in the middle and the other two on the outsides.

After what seemed an age, I asked again, 'What's the time, Stan?'

'Five past four.'

'Fucking hell!'

This was real torture. It seemed like eternity, lying there caked with freezing mud, with icy water soaking through to our shreddies. Whenever the snow stopped, the wind would get up and bring on the rain, and then the snow would start again – as if someone was programming the weather to cause maximum discomfort.

At last, at about five-thirty, darkness began to fall, and we decided to crawl inside the berm so that we could shift around and get some feeling back into our bodies. But until we tried to move, we didn't realise what a state we were in. Then we found we were truly in the shit.

My fingers and toes were numb, but that was to be expected. It was when I went to stand up that I really got it: the pain in my knees and back was outrageous. I felt as if I had acute arthritis in my spine and hips. Suddenly I thought, 'Jesus, we really are going down here.' For a moment I was hit by despair.

Anyway, we dragged ourselves inside the berm and started trying to run back and forth, to start the energy going and get some heat moving inside our bodies. But my feet were still numb, and clay built up on the soles of my boots so that I could hardly make any progress. Our hands were so dead that we couldn't pick up our weapons – but luckily they had slings, and what we did was duck down, put our heads through the slings, and stand up.

As Vince did so, he said, 'Chris – I can't carry my weapon. I just can't.'

I heard a note of desperation in his voice, so I just said quietly,

'Stan, you take it for him.' So Stan took Vince's 203, leaving him with his pistol.

My memories of the next few hours are hazy, because I was being hit by hypothermia. All three of us were. But even though my mind was becoming clouded, I knew we had to keep moving.

'Right, fellers,' I said. 'We're going to have to start off again.' So away we went. I was stumbling with my weapon slung over my shoulder and my hands tucked under my arms, trying to get some feeling back into them. I kept thinking, 'If we have a contact, we're knackered, because we're not going to be able to shoot back.' I couldn't have pulled the trigger or changed magazines to save my life.

Stan and I were doing the navigating, but he was getting his compass out more often than I was.

'Where are we heading?' I'd ask, and he'd say, 'Due north. We're all right.'

Then the clouds thickened up. Another flurry of snow drove into our faces, hurtling in from the north-west, and soon we were tabbing over ground as white as on a Christmas card. One advantage of the blizzard was that it hid us; no one was going to see us while so much snow was falling. But equally, we ourselves were blinded, and could easily walk on to an enemy position without spotting it.

When the moon came out again, the desert was light as day, and I could read my map without the torch. Vince, who kept lagging behind, called, 'Hey, you're going to have to slow down. I need a rest.'

'Vince,' I told him, 'you can't rest. We've got to keep moving, see if we can warm ourselves up.'

The worst thing was that we were walking hard but not getting any less cold. Normally, after you've walked for an hour, your circulation's really going, and you're warm all over. But because our clothes were soaked through, and this bitter wind was blowing, the chill-factor was keeping our body temperature right down. Also, there was no fuel left in me to re-stoke the fires: I'd burnt it all up. I thought, 'If it's still like this tomorrow morning, we're all going to be dead.'

I knew that in our state, without warm clothes or shelter or food, we couldn't survive such conditions much longer. In fact I thought it was likely we would all die that night. I'd never experienced such pain from cold, such agony in spine and legs. In the course of training I'd had plenty of lectures on hypothermia, and now I recognised some of the symptoms in myself: disorientation, dizziness, sudden mood swings, outbursts of anger, confusion, drowziness . . . Normally a man in that state would be put into a sleeping bag or a space blanket and brought round – but here there was no respite.

So we kept walking – until Vince really started going down. 'Wait for me,' he called. 'You've got to wait.'

We waited a few times. But then I decided that shock tactics were necessary. I knew that at home he had two young girls and a little baby, and that he was nuts about his family. So I gripped him by the arm and said, 'Vince, if you don't fucking keep going, you're never going to see your kids. Think about your home. Think how they'll want you back. Now – get your finger out and start moving.'

'Listen,' he said, 'I want to go to sleep. I'm too tired. I've got to sit down.'

'Vince,' I said, 'we can't sit down. If we stop, we're going to fucking DIE. Get that? If we lie down and sleep, we'll freeze to death, and never know anything about it.'

We carried on walking for a bit, and then he shouted at me, 'Chris!'

'What?'

'My hands have gone black.'

I thought, 'Jesus! Frostbite!' My own fingers were still numb, and I wondered what state my hands were in under my gloves. I walked back to Vince and found him staring down at his hands. He was wearing black leather gloves.

'My fucking hands have gone black,' he repeated. 'My fucking hands!'

I realised his mind was wandering, so I just said, 'OK, Vince, put them in your pockets. Get them warm, and the colour'll come back to them. Come on now: keep up with me and Stan, mate. Keep going.'

At that point I can't have been thinking straight. What I should have done was to keep hold of him, or actually tie him to me. But that didn't occur to me, and I just kept walking. Stan and I would tab on for a bit, then wait for Vince to catch up.

Then the same again. I tried to alternate, being sharp with him one moment, kind the next. One minute I'd shout, 'Get a grip!' trying to spark him into action. Then I'd turn comforting, tap him on the shoulder, and say, 'Come on, Vince, keep walking. Everything'll be all right. We're going to get out.'

Vince's own behaviour was swinging wildly. Several times he started yelling out loud – which of course was bad for our nerves, as anybody could have heard him from hundreds of metres off. Stan hissed, *'Vince – be quiet!'* and he shut up for a while.

Because hypothermia was hitting us, our navigation had become erratic. For some time I'd had the feeling that I was drifting away from reality. The map was saying one thing, and what was happening on the ground seemed to be quite different. Somehow we were getting dragged off to the north-east all the time. I don't know why, but something in me kept pulling me that way.

I saw what was happening, and began to wonder – quite illogically – if I had a tendency to head north-east because I'd been born in the north-east of England. Basically we were wanting to head north-west, and we kept having to correct ourselves, constantly checking on the compass. Every few minutes Stan would say, 'Eh – we're coming off. We're coming off.' Then the clouds would open, and we'd get a glimpse of the Plough, and we could bring ourselves on course again. Then more snow flurries would come in, the stars would be blotted out, and we'd veer off once more. Because it was so cold, I had one hand in my pocket or underneath my arm. Whenever we stopped, the shivers came on, making it hard to concentrate on the map. Spells of weakness kept sweeping over us, fogging our minds still more.

Struggling as we were, we cracked on for a while – but then, as we stopped once again, we realised that Vince was no longer with us. When Stan shouted back for him, there was no answer. 'Chris,' he said, 'we've lost him.'

'We can't have,' I answered stupidly. 'He must be just behind us.'

We started back on our tracks. Naturally I was worried, but I felt bad-tempered about having to retreat. Where snow was lying, it was easy to follow our footprints; but then there were long stretches of bare rock from which the snow had been blown clear, and whenever we crossed one, we had to cast about on the far side, working forward and back to pick up our trail again. Now we realised how much we'd been veering about as we advanced, zig-zagging all over the place.

After twenty minutes there was still no sign of Vince. We called as loud as we dared, and we could see a reasonable distance – but I suddenly realised that our quest was hopeless. The truth hit me with a jolt: it was half an hour, at least, since we'd seen him, and we had no idea what he'd done. He might have walked off to the right; he might have walked off to the left; he might be walking straight backwards; he might have lain down in a hollow and gone to sleep. This last seemed the most likely; that was all he'd been wanting to do for hours – stop and get his head down. If he had curled up somewhere out of the wind, we could spend all night walking in circles and never find him, probably killing ourselves in the process.

'Stan,' I said, 'I'm making a decision. We're going to turn round and leave him.' I could feel my companion's hesitation, so I added, 'Fuck it – I'll take the responsibility. We've got to leave him, or we'll kill the pair of us.'

'OK, then,' said Stan. 'Fair enough.'

It was a terrible decision to have to take, but I saw no alternative. I kept thinking of the times I'd been out on the hills in Scotland, and the weather had turned really bad. In the Highlands, there'd always been the comforting thought that we could get into a barn or a bothy, or go to a hotel. The same applied in Norway – we could always take refuge in a hotel or a hut if things became impossible. But here there was no such facility: nowhere to go, nowhere to escape from the wind and snow, nowhere to dry our kit and warm up, nowhere to find food. I felt all the more certain that if conditions were the same in the morning, Stan and I would die as well. There was no way we would resuscitate ourselves with no shelter and absolutely nothing to light a fire with. So with heavy hearts we turned round and cracked on again, and left Vince on his own.

Chapter Four

Down To One

Our only hope was to get down off the high ground into warmer air, and gradually, as we tabbed on, we did seem to be descending. We never went down any steep gradient, but all the same it felt as if we were losing height. I hoped to God that Vince was doing the same – that he would find his way down off this cruel, high plateau, reach low ground somewhere, get his head down in a hollow, and wake up in the morning.

Our map showed a line of pylons running across our front, and another line that terminated in the middle of nowhere. So we thought that if we hit the first set of masts, and then the second, we'd know exactly where we were. But it didn't turn out like that. We only hit the one line of masts, and couldn't find any more. Later we discovered that the second line didn't exist except on the map.

But at least we seemed to be coming down. The snow flurries died out, and the wind became less bitter. Then through the kite-sight I saw a black-looking band running across our front. We sat down to study it, and presently made out that it was another main road. Approaching cautiously, we lay in a hollow which turned out to be full of mud: somehow, in the middle of the arid desert, we'd chosen a place like a miniature peat bog.

In front of us we saw a chain-link fence running parallel with the road, maybe ten metres on the far side of it, and shining faintly in the moonlight. Beyond the fence something pale was looming. It looked like a strip of concrete, and we thought we'd come on some form of installation. As I followed the line of the fence with the sight, I muttered, 'Christ – it must be a massive place. This bloody barrier goes on for ever.' Then at the last minute we realised that what we could see was a railway line, fenced to keep animals off the track.

The chain-link was only about six feet high. Any other time, we'd have scaled it in seconds. But we were that cold and pissy helpless we just couldn't climb it. Our hands and arms were almost useless, and wouldn't pull us up and over. Stan brought out his set of folding Leatherman pliers and, with an all-out effort to make his hands work, cut a vertical slit in the mesh. We knew it was wrong, and a departure from the SOP, because anyone who came along and saw the gap would realise that somebody had been through there – but it was the only way we were going to cross the track.

Anyway, we squeezed through the gap and found ourselves on the railway line. 'Jesus!' we thought. Shall we walk along it?' It would have been easy going, tabbing on the concrete sleepers. A check on the map showed that it ran straight to a town on the Syrian border. But then we reckoned that probably the line would be patrolled, or that someone on a train would be bound to see us. There was nowhere to hide near the track, and if a train came along, we'd be caught in the open.

We decided to continue northwards. At the fence on the far side of the line Stan gave me the pliers and said, 'Your turn.' My fingers were so numb that I could hardly grip the handles, and putting pressure on them hurt like hell. But wire by wire I cut a slit, and we wormed through, pulling the chain-link back into place behind us so that the gap wasn't too obvious. With any luck it would be days before anyone noticed the damage.

Leaving the railway, we found a big, rounded hill ahead of us and started up it. A few yards short of the summit we stopped, both in the same stride. In that split second we'd spotted that AA gun barrels were pointing into the sky no more than four or five metres in front of us. Standing still and staring at them, we realised we could see the top of a wall of sandbags, almost under our noses. Obviously there were Iraqis inside the sangar but, thank God, they seemed to be asleep.

Without a word, without turning, we back-tracked down the slope, inches at a time, watching for any movement to our front. Nothing stirred. Once we were clear, we pulled away eastwards in a big loop, leaving the mound on our left, and then came back on to our northerly heading. But the incident gave us a fright, because we'd been walking carelessly, not worrying about the scrunching noise our boots were making on the loose rock and gravel.

By the early hours of the morning we were back into a system of shallow wadis and dry channels maybe thirty feet wide, but only two or three deep. These river-beds were full of little bushes which threw thick, black shadows in the moonlight, so that every hollow seemed to be full of quite dense vegetation. I thought, 'Great – we'll be able to get our heads down in here. It should be warmer, too.'

About 05.30 we started looking for a place to lie up, and settled in a hollow. As I lay down next to Stan, I pulled out my hip-flask and offered it to him. I thought the dickhead would realise what was in it, but no: he expected it to be water. I watched as he put it to his lips, and then – his face! His eyes bulged. He went *pwhhhoohhh! mphhhh!* and then 'Fucking hell! What the hell's that?'

'Whisky, you clot!'

'Bloody hell! I thought it was water.'

'You dick, no.' I took a sip myself and told him, 'That's the last time you're getting offered any of this stuff.' So I whacked the flask back into my pocket. Stan took off his webbing and laid it down in the middle of some bushes, and we cuddled down together on top of it. It was really embarrassing, because we were front to front, with our arms round each other, and we had to take turns on whose head was at the bottom.

So we lay there, shuddering, drifting off into sleep, waking with a start, shaking all over, until dawn broke. By then I was bitterly regretting some of the mistakes I'd made in choosing and packing my kit. Apart from the brew-kit, which would have been a great morale-booster, I should have had a goretex bivvy bag or at least a space-blanket in one of my pouches.

When daylight came, we found that some of the mud had dried on us, aided by our body heat, and our clothes were all stiff and covered with ice-crystals, as if they'd been left out on a frosty night. Looking up, I saw that the sky was clear and blue, and thought, 'Thank God, it's going to be a fine day.' Light revealed that the bushes which had looked promising at night were nothing but thorny skeletons, eaten down by goats; there wasn't a leaf on them, and they weren't going to hide us from anyone. So we crawled across and tucked ourselves into the wall of a wadi that ran north and south.

At ten o'clock the sun came up and shone on us as we lay

against the western wall. I'm sure that saved our lives. One more wet, windy day, and we would just have drifted off into unconsciousness and never come round. The sun never felt very warm, but it definitely made the air less cold, and we began to sort ourselves out a bit. We took off our webbing, and I spread out my map case to dry. We also cleaned the mud off our weapons and reloaded magazines. I found I'd fired about 70 rounds during the contact. Stan produced a sachet of American corned-beef hash from his belt-kit, and as I watched him eat it, I was thinking, 'Why the hell didn't I bring my own rations with me?' All I had was two biscuits, my last.

At one point I said, 'Stan – can you tell me, what the fuck are you doing sitting in the middle of Iraq? You're supposed to be a dentist, with a Porsche 911, living in the middle of Sydney – and now you're in fucking Iraq, with nothing!'

'You know, Chris,' he replied, 'I'm asking myself that, right this very minute' – and he burst out laughing. 'I bet we look a bloody state now.'

'Too right we do.'

'What about *you*, then? What are *you* doing here?'

It was a good question – and when I thought about it, I saw that my involvement in the SAS could be traced back to my love of being in open country. It was that, more than anything else, which had determined the course of my career.

I grew up in Rowlands Gill, a small village in the country just outside Newcastle, and went to the junior school there. From our house, I could walk straight out across the fields and into the forest, and the result was that as a kid I was constantly playing in the woods, making camps and sleeping out. My father worked on constructing sites, driving plant machinery, but he generally got laid off during the winter, when work on the sites shut down, and that suited him fine, because all his life he'd been keen on shooting. He'd been brought up in the hamlet of Blanchland nearby, where his uncle had been a gamekeeper, and he'd spent his own boyhood roaming the woods and fields. He'd take me with him out into the country round Rowlands Gill, where he had permission from the farmers, and also near Blanchland, where he was friendly with a farmer called Clive. We used to build hides, in which we'd wait for pigeons, or ferret rabbits out of burrows in the hedges. On winter evenings we'd stand in the woods and flight pigeons as they came into roost.

My dad had a five-shot Browning automatic 12-bore. Once, as we came round a corner, we saw five rabbits on the edge of a field. He got them all, one after another. With feats like that he soon became my hero, and I loved every minute of our expeditions.

Whatever we shot, we ate. My dad would skin the rabbits or pluck the pigeons – as well as the odd pheasant, partridge and grouse – and my mum would cook them. I used to listen fascinated to the stories he told about himself and my cousin Billy, and the times they used to go shooting together as young men. In time I came to resent the fact that Billy seemed closer to him than I ever was, and had got a lot more out of him.

But then came a great change. Some time in his thirties, my dad decided it was wrong to shoot birds and animals, and stopped altogether. By then I was mad keen, and kept suggesting we should go out, but he said, 'No – you're better off just watching them or taking pictures, capturing them on film. If you want to go, shoot with a camera.' It may have been something to do with the fact that myxomatosis was at its height. The sight of sick rabbits blundering about, bouncing off each other, with their eyes closed by purulent swellings, disgusted him, and he was upset by the thought of so many animals dying in pain. As we drove into Blanchland, he'd say, 'God – that bank used to be *covered* with rabbits, and now there's nothing.' He may have thought that if he laid off, it would help the rabbits recover.

At an early age I started asking if I could have an air-rifle, and my parents kept saying no. At one point my dad bought me a .410, but I was only allowed to take it out with him, under close supervision. Later, when I was thirteen or fourteen, I saved up my pocket money and asked again if I could buy an air-rifle. Still the answer was no, so my brother Keith and I went out with some older boys and bought one, a BSA .22. I kept the precious weapon in the loft, along with a few dirty magazines and bottles of cider that we'd managed to tuck away.

Again I asked my mum, 'Can I buy an air-rifle?' and when she answered, 'No,' I said, 'What if I just get one?'

'You wouldn't be able to keep one in *this* house, without your dad and me knowing.'

Keith and I were looking at each other, thinking, 'Yeah – right!' What we used to do was smuggle the air-gun out over an outbuilding at the back. Keith would wait on the ground, while I climbed out of my bedroom window and handed the gun down to him. Then we'd run off into the woods and go shooting.

One day, as I came home from school, I found that Keith had got there before me; he grabbed me, his face all fearful, and said, 'Dad's just bought a new TV, and the man's in the loft, putting up the aerial. You'd better get up there quick.'

The hatchway going up into the loft was in my bedroom. I stood there with Keith, waiting anxiously, when my dad called cheerily up to the fitter from downstairs, 'I don't suppose there are any bottles of beer hidden up there?'

'No,' the man answered, 'just a couple of dirty books and . . . some cider.'

Keith and I stared at each other in horror. Luckily my Dad took the answer as a joke and started laughing. The aerial guy said, 'No, no – there's nothing up here.'

The rifle was never discovered – but when I was sixteen or so I declared it, and by then it was too late for anyone to worry.

My Mum came from Lynemouth, a mining village on the coast of Northumberland. A quiet, very modest woman, she had the patience of a saint, and a tremendously strong sense of right and wrong. Nothing on earth would make her break the law – and sometimes she drove the rest of us crazy by her insistence on absolute honesty, even in the smallest things. But I grew up with enormous respect for her integrity. In bringing up three boys, without any modern appliances, she worked all hours of the day – and I'm ashamed to think how little help we gave her.

At school I was quite soft, and used to get bullied. If a girl started making up to me, I'd have the shit kicked out of me by someone else who fancied her. If there was going to be a fight, it took place when school finished. There'd always be a big crowd gathering at the gate, waiting for the action, and I'd be nearly crapping myself as I approached. Sometimes if my brother Keith got the worst of an argument, he would say, 'Right – my big brother'll see to you.' Then he'd find me at playtime and say, 'By the way, you're to have a fight tonight.' Sometimes I'd go over the back fence and do a runner across the fields to avoid facing the music.

But then came a transition. When I was sixteen I decided that this sort of thing had to stop, and I began fighting back. It wasn't a personality change; just that I went on to the offensive. I realised that if you have a fight, you probably get hurt, but it doesn't last for ever. Listening to my dad, and taking a grip of myself, I put a stop to the bullying.

I also started judo lessons, and couldn't get enough of them. At first, for a couple of months, I was taught by a Japanese who practised a pure form of the ancient martial art, but then I progressed to an instructor in Newcastle, an ex-Olympic champion who taught me to fight dirty – how to disable an opponent by kicking him in the balls, and how to knock somebody's head off. I became so keen that I'd go into town almost every night, and I started winning competitions; in my first fight I floored my opponent within seconds, and hurt him quite badly. But I gave up judo when, in a fight with a bigger boy, my clavicle became detached from the rib cage. Although I finished the fight, I lost on points – and afterwards the injury caused me so many problems that I thought I'd better stop.

I found judo a wonderful means of channelling aggression to a useful end. Not that I see myself as aggressive – determined, yes, perhaps a bit short-tempered, but not aggressive. If things start going wrong, and I tell someone not to do something, and he does it again, I might have an emotional outburst – but on the whole I'm easygoing.

With a jolt I remembered the sick fear I once felt when I was a kid of about thirteen. We were playing Knocking Nine Doors, and a big guy rushed out and chased us down the street. He was known as a really hard man, and when we belted on his door, he was waiting behind it. He flew out, and we went hurtling down the road. He chased us for a couple of hours, and the terror I'd felt then was exactly the same as what I experienced during the contact in the wadi.

That wasn't by any means the only time I'd been on the run. Once my younger brother Keith and I had been playing football with some boys in Blanchland. I must have hurt one of the locals in a tackle, and he went off in a rage. Later, Keith and I set out with our cousin to get conkers. I'd just climbed the tree and started hitting the conkers down, with Keith gave a horse cry: 'Chris – look!' Peering down through the leaves, I saw a gang of ten or twelve kids from the village, all armed with sticks, heading for us at a run.

'There they are!' the raiders shouted as they spotted us. 'There they are!'

I jumped down from the tree. 'You run back up home that way,' I told Keith, and I took off in the other direction. The pack came after me – and it was like hare and hounds for the rest of the day, four hours at least. I ran until I thought I was going to die. I ran through the forest, waded the river, ran up on to the moors – and still the little bastards were after me, determined to get me. In the end I spotted a neighbour of my aunt's, a man who worked as a gamekeeper. I came tearing down the road with the hunters close behind and threw myself into his arms, unable to speak.

I hated school work. I was all right at maths and technical drawing, but never much good at basics like reading and writing, and I took little interest in most of my lessons. Part of my trouble, I suspect, was that the school was in a period of transition, changing from grammar school to comprehensive, and the teachers were not interested in the less able children, so that it was easy to sit at the back of the class and do whatever one wanted.

Afterwards, I bitterly regretted my lack of motivation, especially when I found that, as an adult, I had a perfectly good brain. When I joined the army, I realised I had to pass the exams in order to survive, and so I really got down to work. I found the German course, which I took before going on the Alpine guides' course, a severe effort, as I had no real grounding in English grammar and vocabulary, let alone German. So I had to learn English properly first – and there I was, sitting alongside brigadiers and colonels in Beaconsfield, struggling to keep up. But in the end I surprised myself by passing, and in Mittenwald I went on to receive lessons in Bavarian-accented German on the weather, rock-formations and so on.

As a boy, though, I was more interested in making a camp in the woods or racing about with the other kids on the estate at home than in going to school; every now and then I'd play truant, or try it on at home by pretending to feel ill.

My father never took much interest in my education, and it was my mother who always read my school reports first. She was forever disappointed – and I'd beg her not to show them to my dad. After reading one report, she made an extraordinarily prophetic remark. 'Chris,' she said, 'I hope you've got a sturdy pair of boots.'

'Why?' I said.

'Because you're going to have to do an awful lot of walking one day.' She meant that I'd have to walk round looking for jobs, and she started singing that song, 'These Boots are Made for Walking'. I remember pulling faces behind her back, mouthing, 'Shut up! Shut up!' – but she went on singing and laughing.

By the time I was sixteen, all I wanted was to join the army. I didn't get much encouragement from my dad, because when he'd been caught for National Service in the Royal Horse Artillery, he hadn't liked the army one bit. Probably it was because he was the youngest child, and a bit spoilt. The sudden strict discipline kicked him into shape, but also it gave him an unpleasant shock, and once he came out he had nothing more to do with the military.

At least he didn't oppose me when I wanted to join up. At the local recruiting office I did the first tests to become a boy soldier, and passed them fine. For the final tests I was due to travel to Sutton Coldfield, but because I went down with jaundice, I missed the interviews. I felt destroyed at having lost the chance of joining. I remember lying in bed, feeling lousy, and seeing two men in uniform, an officer and an NCO, come to the house, to tell my parents that the army suggested I should join up for man's service when I was seventeen or eighteen.

Luckily at that point my cousin Billy was in 23rd SAS, the territorial unit, and one day he said, 'Well, why not come up, and we'll get you out on a couple of weekends? Then you'll see what it's like to be in the army.'

Until then I'd only been in the Air Cadets, and knew practically nothing. When Billy came down to pick me up, I was still at school. I said, 'What do I need?'

'Oh, just get a set of spare socks.'

My mum was clucking round me, getting out tins of soup and making sandwiches, but Billy said, 'Don't worry – he'll be fine.' So we went up to Prudhoe, in Northumberland, where 'C' Squadron of 23 SAS had its base. At that time – the late 1970s, before the siege of the Iranian Embassy in Princes Gate – the

SAS was nothing like as well known as it later became; but the Regiment was flourishing, and there was much territorial activity. I was just a naive lad of sixteen, and as I walked through the doors of the drill hall, I saw all these guys who looked tremendously old. Probably their ages ranged from thirty to forty-five, and a lot of them had seen service in Suez and other campaigns, having served in the regular army. No doubt I looked a bit of a twerp to them. But nothing could damp down my excitement; when the SQMS took me into the stores and gave me a camouflage suit, a set of webbing pouches, a poncho and a bergen, I was over the moon.

A bunch of recruits had assembled for a weekend's training – some were civilians, others from regular army units. Their average age must have been about twenty-five. As I arrived, they were about to have a map-reading lesson, so I sat down with them and did that. Next, we all scrambled on to trucks and drove up to Otterburn, where we walked out on to the moors. 'Right,' somebody said, 'tonight we're going to sleep against this wall, under ponchos.' I thought it was terrific – to spend the night outdoors. I was so excited that I couldn't go to sleep, and I lay for ages gazing up at the stars.

Next morning, after no more than a couple of hours' sleep, I was up early, and we spent the day walking. We'd walk for a while, have something to eat, get another lesson in map-reading, then go on again. The exercise ended with a long hike, which left me knackered. Back at Prudhoe, I thought, 'Well – that was great. But that's it.' I imagined that after my introduction to the army, I wouldn't be asked again. But luckily for me the OC happened to be there. He was a scary-looking guy, with ginger hair and little milky-bar glasses, and looked a right hard nut. He came over to speak to me and said, 'You're Billy's cousin, aren't you? Would you like to come back up?'

'Fine,' I said. 'Great.'

'Good,' he replied. 'But you must understand that you won't be on the books. You shouldn't be here, really, because we're breaking the law. If anything happens, you won't be able to lay claim on the army.'

That didn't worry me one bit, and from then on I went up to Prudhoe every weekend. The selection course went on over a period of three months, with the recruits assembling only at weekends. At first the group had consisted of sixty people, but every week a few of them decided they'd had enough and threw their hand in. Whenever I got out of the wagon at the start of a new exercise, the number had gone down. But for me things became more and more exciting, because we went from being in a big group to working in pairs, and in the end I was on my own. It was a big thrill when someone told me to walk alone from Point A to Point B; I had become confident with my map-reading, and between Friday night and Sunday morning we'd cover up to 60 kilometres, carrying a bergen. On the last weekend of the course there were only four of us left, and I was the only one who finished the march.

Completion of that march was the prerequisite for going on to a Test Week in Wales. Normally, anyone who passed would be tested for two weeks down the Brecon Beacons. But I was too young to go, and they told me that I wouldn't be ready to take selection for 23rd SAS until two more territorial selection courses had gone through. In other words, I was going to have to wait a whole year.

That was disappointing, but I was so keen that I volunteered to keep going out on the territorial weekends when the next course started. By that time I knew all the routes, and I could run from one check-point to another without having to consult a map. I'd also learnt how to cut corners and cheat a bit. At the end of that course only one man passed: he and I were the sole survivors.

By then I'd become a bit of a joke in the Squadron. None the less, on the third course I had a still greater advantage. I was so fit, and knew the ground so well, that I finished each leg before the other guys were half-way.

Now at last I was old enough to go down to Wales for the Test Week. After two weeks on the hills, based at Sennybridge, I passed out and at last became a member of 'C' Squadron. My aim, of course, was to join 22, the regular SAS; normally, to do that, you have to enrol in another regiment first, and then obtain secondment. My best course seemed to be to join the Parachute Regiment – but all the guys said, 'Don't bother with that. Once you've served here in 23 for a bit, you can go straight on to selection for 22.' Apart from that, 22 were holding a lot of courses and exercises down at Hereford, and there were often spare places – so I was going south a good deal.

Between all my outdoor activities at weekends, I had various jobs. I worked in a fibre-glass factory, then in a garage, where I got an apprenticeship as a mechanic. But I really had very little interest in the work. Instead of concentrating on the job, I'd be thinking about morse code or demolitions, and in the evenings I'd listen to tapes or study manuals on such subjects. The result was that I could never hold down a job for long; I was always wanting to go off with the TA, and my employers wouldn't give me the time. Someone would ring up from Hereford and say, 'Right, we've got three slots here on a jungle trip. Send two guys down.' But if I went into work and said, 'Listen – can I have four weeks off, from tomorrow?' of course the answer would be no. One day I went in knowing there was a possibility of an exercise in Belgium. After that I was planning a summer holiday in Greece, and immediately after that, there was an exercise in America which would last six weeks. When I asked my manager if I could have the time off, he said, 'Not a chance,' so I said, 'OK – stick your job,' and packed it in.

During the exercise in Belgium our patrol commander began breaking SOPs by walking during daylight. We were moving up the edge of a field on a hot, sunny summer's day when suddenly we got a contact. As I was coming over the brow, a line of red berets popped up out of the golden corn, and we were captured by Belgian paras. I spent my eighteenth birthday being interrogated, put through TQ (tactical questioning) in stress positions, and I thought, 'There's no way I'm ever going to get captured again.'

Back from exercises, I started labouring on building sites for a friend of my father who had his own business. He allowed me to work for him more or less when I wanted, and the money was all under the table. If a TA exercise came up, and I wanted three weeks off, there was no problem.

By this time I was extremely fit. Every day I'd do a ten-mile run, followed by a 16-mile bike ride, and then swim for a mile, and run the three miles home. I seemed to go through this routine with the greatest ease, and maintained it for months on end. Out running, I had the lovely feeling that it was no effort, but that I was coasting comfortably through the country lanes. One day, for some reason, I didn't go out – and in the house I simply couldn't sit down. My mum was cooking dinner, and I was driving her crazy by jumping up and down. 'For God's sake, go for a run, will you?' she said, and I ended up doing just that – and after ten miles I felt fine.

When I asked at Hereford to go on selection for 22 SAS, there was no problem. But first I was taken on an LTM (laser target marker) exercise by Jack, one of the permanent staff instructors. It was here I met a few of the regiment's characters, not all of them admirable. We went out to the Black Forest in southern Germany, where our patrol's task was to put a marker on a farm building, so that a jet could fly across and bounce a signal off the target. I was mustard keen, but there was a guy from 22 who just sat out in the middle of a field smoking, not bothering even to unpack his equipment from its plastic bag. I didn't think that was very professional, and when he said, 'You're a dickhead to get your LTM out – you'll just have to clean it,' I felt quite annoyed. I couldn't see the point of going to Germany and being deployed into the field, and then not doing the exercise properly. Later someone explained that I was doing what I was doing as a hobby, and that once I'd joined up it would become a job and I'd think differently. But Jack turned round and said, 'Don't take any notice of what happened here. That isn't the regiment.'

At last the time came for me to go down to Hereford and take the 22 Selection course, which was spread over six months. We did four weeks on the hills, two weeks' tactics training, five weeks in the jungle in Brunei, then combat survival followed by continuation training. In the hills there were some days when I felt we were being crucified, but on the whole it wasn't too bad. In tactics training, I found I was confident with a weapon, but I was shocked by the state of some of the troops who came up: their weapon-handling drills were poor, to say the least.

In the jungle we were put into six-man patrols, and sent to live in a base-camp from which we moved out every day to do range work, navigation or RV drills. I found it tough going. Navigation posed no problem, and I discovered that I could mix with other guys easily enough; but I didn't like the physical difficulties of living in the jungle, where you're wet, filthy and stinking for weeks on end. Also, I had difficulty assimilating spoken orders. Many of the other guys had led patrols in Northern Ireland, and some had been in the jungle before, so that they were all more experienced than me.

Back at Hereford, at the end of the course, we were all taken into the camp cinema. Nothing had been said about who had passed or failed. Then the sergeant major, whose sense of humour was all his own, announced that he would read out a list of names. The people on it were to go back to the accommodation block, wait there, and return in fifteen minutes' time. He read out twenty names, including mine – more or less half the people on the course. Had we passed or failed? Nobody knew. We walked across to the accommodation block silent and numbed. Then someone said, 'Well – hell! So-and-so's a wanker, and he's still over there. *He* can't have passed.' Somebody else said, 'But Smith's over there too, and he's a good bloke.'

Returning to the cinema a quarter of an hour later, we found that the other half of the course had disappeared, and we sat down again. The sergeant major stood up and said, 'Right, you lot. You haven't passed . . .' There was an intake of breath, and a pause long enough for everyone's heart to hit the floor before he added, 'yet.' Faces lit up. Everyone burst out laughing. There was continuation training to come – but so what?

We did combat survival – in which six more of the guys failed – and after that, build-up for Northern Ireland and the counter-terrorist team. Then at last the survivors passed, and we were given our berets.

Normally, before joining the regular SAS, a soldier would have to put in three or four years of TA courses and exercises; but I had already done seven years as a territorial, and so was able to skip that requirement. It was a tremendous thrill for me. I'd achieved the goal on which I'd set my heart. But I soon found that the regulars were not particularly pleased about TA guys coming into the regiment by the route I'd taken – as they saw it, by the back door. Some people thought of the TA in terms of *Dad's Army*, and didn't realise that I'd already done more work than many members of 22. So one or two of the guys gave us newcomers a hard time, forcing us to prove ourselves even more. For instance, when I did Junior Brecon – a six-week tactics course aimed at anyone who had not been in an infantry unit – someone told me, 'Go down there, and make sure you get a distinction.'

Luckily I managed to do just that – and from then on, everything was fine. I soon developed fierce loyalty to the regiment, and saw that anyone who worked really hard to achieve his best earned a lot of respect and credibility within the unit. I realised that in any small group the key thing was to keep tight, and for everybody to work as one; by that means, sticking together, you can get through quite a lot.

Next stop for me was the Parachute Regiment, which I joined as my parent unit. After Christmas at home I reported to Aldershot with Barry Hilton, who'd come from the Navy, and also needed a parent unit. I'd had a real skinhead haircut, because I knew the other recruits would be the same. Barry turned up with long hair. We went in to see the Company Sergeant Major, who acted the part for all it was worth. He had the pair of us standing in front of him and said, 'OK, I want you to come back to me in uniform.' Glaring at me he added, 'And make sure that tart's had a haircut.' Then we were marched out.

Round at the hairdresser's, Barry only had a trim. 'Jesus!' I said. 'Get a shorter cut.'

'Not a chance,' he answered. 'I'm in the Regiment now. I'm not getting my hair cut for anyone.'

'Oh, for God's sake! Please, just get one, or we're in for some flak.'

When the CSM saw us again, he said, 'Right, I told you to get him a haircut,' and he started bollocking me.

After that short, sharp introduction, we started working with the recruits, lads straight from civvy street who looked up to us because of our experience. Unlike the SAS, where you're left largely to make your own decisions and make sure that you turn up in the right place at the right time, here people were yelling at us the whole time. The activities were all done in groups: team running, a steeplechase, a log race, the assault course and so on. There was always someone on top of us, kicking us to get from A to B, and some of the young guys of seventeen and eighteen began getting hammered. The instructors just beasted them, hitting and kicking them so that they were frightened and didn't learn anything.

Being five or six years older, I found I could cope pretty well. I was living in a room with eight or nine recruits, and in the evening I used to teach them map-reading. One instructor was having trouble with his wife; now and then she'd kick him out of the house, and he'd come down to live in the accommodation block. To relieve his feelings, he'd knock a couple of the young lads around. One night he came in screaming and shouting. I walked up to him and said, 'Hey, cut it out now, or I'll go and see somebody.' He didn't know what to say, because to all intents and purposes I was an ordinary recruit – but he knew I'd passed SAS selection, which he would probably never get through. He just muttered something, slammed the door and got his head down.

I realised how bad the atmosphere was one Saturday, when most people had knocked off for the weekend. I had collected the lads who were left behind and taken them map-reading in a training area called Long Valley. I told one of them, 'Right – you're leading the way now. Can you use a compass?'

'Yes, yes!' he said quickly. But it was quite clear that he couldn't, and when I asked him why he'd lied, he said, 'I thought you were going to hit me.' That was the mentality they'd got into.

Another day one of the instructors came up to us and said that his mother was ill and he ought to go home, but he had to give a lecture that Friday evening on the gympi, the general-purpose machine gun. I volunteered to take the period in his place. While I was in the middle of my talk, in walked the OC of the camp. He sat there and listened, and at the end, thinking I was one of the regular instructors, came up to tell me off for being improperly dressed (I didn't have my belt on or my wings up). I apologised and said, 'I'm Private Ryan from Hereford.'

'What are you doing here?' he asked.

'Just working with the guys.'

'You're wasting your time down here.'

I believe he telephoned Hereford and said he was going to send us back – but outside events accelerated our return anyway. At that time, law and order were breaking down in Aden, and the order was given to evacuate all British personnel; the QE2 was going in to pull them off the beaches, and 'B' Squadron was detailed to parachute into the sea to secure the beach-heads. Everyone was loading up, and my sergeant major rang the Parachute Regiment, asking to have us back immediately, as he needed everyone he could get.

The original intention had been that Barry and I should spend three months with the Paras – but now we were leaving after only eight weeks. In the morning we had to say goodbye to the CSM. I knew Barry hadn't enjoyed himself at all, so as we were about to go in I told him, 'Whatever they say, just tell them you've had a good time. Say you thought it was great, and you've learned a lot – because that's what they want to hear. Then we'll leave.'

'Yeah, OK,' he went.

So we marched in and stood to attention in front of the OC, with the CSM behind us.

'And did you learn a lot?' the OC asked.

'Yes,' I said, 'a great deal.'

'And how about you?' he asked Barry. 'What do you think?'

'I think it's a load of crap.'

Fucking hell! The CSM was right behind us.

The hair on my neck stood up, and I started shaking.

'RYAN!' roared the sergeant major. 'Atten-SHUN! About TURN! Quick MARCH!'

Out I went in double time, with the others yelling at Barry behind me.

Back in Hereford, we found that the trouble had run ahead of us. The OC saw us, also with the sergeant major in attendance.

'One of you two didn't enjoy himself down there,' said the colonel. 'Who was it?'

We stood there looking at each other. Inside I was screaming, 'Come on, Barry, say something!' I thought, 'You wanker!'

Then the OC said to me, 'Chris – thin out. You've got to go to "B" Squadron.' So off I went, and Barry got a terrible bollocking, because obviously they knew already what he'd been saying. Looking back on my stay with the Paras, I realise that all the ferocity and bullying had the desired effect, in that they produced a breed of fearsome fighting men – as testified by the actions at Goose Green in the Falklands, and many other campaigns.

As soon as I joined 'B' Squadron I did a couple of exercises with Government agents in the United Kingdom and Europe. In one, which was highly realistic, we flew into Jersey in the middle of the night, our helicopter landing in a public park, to kidnap an industrialist who – according to the scenario – had been in touch with the Russians and was liable to defect. Wearing civilian clothes, we booked into hotels and made contact with agents who already had the target under surveillance. Then, having hired a van, we snatched him as he came out of a restaurant late at night. After a quick transfer to a car, we drove to a pre-designated pick-up point on the coast and the helicopter, which had been cruising out of sight off-shore, slipped in at wave-top height to land on the beach and collect us.

That was the first time I'd been exposed to anything of the kind, and I thought, 'This is for me!'

Next I went on to the SP or anti-terrorist team, and found it really exciting. Part of the team was on stand-by the whole time, for immediate response to a threat like the hijacking of an aircraft, and we all trained to a very high level, each guy putting down at least a thousand rounds a week.

Within the squadron I found a wide mixture of people. Some guys were really quiet and tended to withdraw into themselves; but the chief requirement was that everyone should mix and get on with each other, so that they could work together under extreme pressure. Everyone was highly motivated by pride in the job and the determination to be best – and with a lot of healthy young guys thrown together, the competition was intense. At times when nothing much was happening, this could lead to back-stabbing and unpleasantness; but when things were moving, and the guys were working together, nobody could compete against them.

One thing I couldn't help noticing was the speed at which people seemed to age. Guys of twenty-three or twenty-four were still relatively fresh-faced; but by the time they reached thirty, a lot of them were wrinkled, with their hair turning grey. By that age nearly everyone had some injury – broken legs, broken wrists, back strains, hearing problems brought on by firing weapons and detonating explosives . . .

As I lay against the bank of the wadi, Hereford seemed a long way off. I took off my boots – one at a time, in case we were surprised – to have a look at my feet. As I thought, they were badly blistered along the sides, especially round the ball, and on the heels. But I had nothing to treat them with, and could only put my boots back on again.

We'd become so confused during the night that it took us

some time to work out which day this was. We decided it was
the morning of Saturday 26 January. Time passed slowly, but we
weren't too uncomfortable. The sun was reviving us, we were
chatting in low voices, and our spirits were kept up by our belief
that the Euphrates was only just over the next hill to the north.
Because we'd walked all night, I knew we'd covered a long distance, and thought we must be within a couple of kilometres of
the river. We said to ourselves, 'We'll hit the river, get some
water, and walk out into Syria – no problem.' We managed to
convince ourselves that we were safe for the time being. We'd
put so much ground between us and the scene of the contact
that we didn't think anyone would come looking for us.

Of course, we were wondering about Vince. I hoped against
hope that, like us, he'd come down off the plateau and found a
warmer place; but in my heart of hearts I felt that he was dead. I
imagined him lying down in a hole among the snow, falling
asleep, and drifting away, without any pain or knowledge of
what was happening. At the back of my mind I kept hoping that
we would see the rest of the patrol appear – that we'd hear one
of them say something and they'd pop up out of the ground.

Together we did a map appreciation, trying to work out how
far we'd come in the night. There was no feature on the ground
that we could identify, but we knew that we'd been on the move
for eleven hours. Some of that time had been spent back-
tracking in search of Vince, but we calculated we must have
advanced about forty kilometres. We thought that one more
good night's push would bring us to the Syrian border.

We spent a profitable hour cleaning our weapons, which were
covered in mud and grit, doing them one at a time in case we
got bounced. In my right-hand pouch I had a small but comprehensive kit – pull-through, four-by-two cleaning patches, oil,
rag, and a tool like a pocket knife fitted with screwdriver,
scraper and gouge. With this I gave my 203 a thorough going-
over. I pulled a piece of four-by-two through the barrel, cleaned
and oiled the working parts, and checked the loaded magazines
to make sure no grit had got in among the rounds. By working
carefully, I stripped the weapon and reassembled it making
hardly a sound.

Then, at about midday, we heard the noise we'd already
learned to dread: the jingle of bells. Fucking goats! Again! We

went down flat with our weapons and looked along the little valley. There they were, a scatter of brown, black, grey and dirty white animals, coming slowly into the wadi from the north-east. Then their minder appeared and sat down on a rock in full view, only fifty metres away. He was a young man with thick, curly black hair, and stubbled cheeks, dressed in a big old overcoat of what looked like dark grey tweed. There he sat, day-dreaming, kicking his feet, chewing on stalks of dead grass.

The goats began feeding our way. Stan and I lay still with our 203s ready. 'Right,' I whispered, 'if he comes up on us, we're going to have to take him out.'

'Wait a minute,' said Stan. 'He might have a land cruiser, or even a tractor – some vehicle he'd lend us.'

It went against the grain to kill a civilian. But I felt certain that if the man saw us at all, he'd go back to the nearest habitation and give us away. It flashed through my mind that we could tie him up – but if we did that, he might die of exposure. I thought, 'He's either going to escape or die – so we might as well do him now.'

The goats kept feeding and moving towards us. I began to fancy eating one of them, a young one – goat steak. Goat curry – even better. Also, I liked the look of the coat the guy was wearing – it was obviously a hell of a lot warmer than anything I had on.

The lead goats reached our position, walking on, stopping, nibbling. When they saw us, they jerked their heads up, but that was all – a jerk, and on they'd go, meandering past within a few feet of our faces. All this while the herder was sitting there, looking up at the sky now and then, but basically doing nothing except minding his herd and his own business. Certainly he hadn't locked on to anything.

'He's bound to come after them,' I breathed, 'and if he does, we'll do him.'

We didn't want to fire a shot, for obvious reasons, but both of us had knives. Mine was a folding knife – a good one, but with relatively small blades. Stan had a k-bar bayonet on his webbing with a six- or seven-inch blade. 'I'll grab him,' I muttered, 'and you run up and stick him.'

But Stan, being a gentleman and a good soldier, wasn't happy. He didn't want to kill an innocent civilian. 'Shouldn't we take the chance of seeing if he's got some vehicle? We could nick it and drive off.'

'No, we'll do him.'

Then the man stood up. On his feet, he looked quite a big guy – about the size of Stan, and hefty with it. Immediately I changed my plan. 'Fuck it,' I whispered. 'Stan, give us that knife. You grab him and I'll do him.'

'No,' Stan muttered. 'I don't think . . . You're not having it.'

'Then *you'd* better do him . . .'

Suddenly it was too late. With the guy nearly on top of us, Stan jumped up and grabbed him.

'Siddown, mate!' he said loudly. '*Hurrh!* How're you doing? Good? Right! Siddown!'

The guy jumped and let out a stream of Arabic, but Stan forced him down on the bank-side. I sat down too, staring at him. He was only a young fellow, in his twenties, but of low intelligence, I guessed. He was dressed like the village idiot, dishevelled, with several ragged jumpers under his overcoat, and dirty bare feet in slip-on leather shoes. He kept looking at me, but I didn't say anything.

Stan did all the talking. 'Car?' he said. 'Tractor?' He made driving motions with his hands. 'House?'

He drew in the air, but our visitor didn't understand a word of English. All he said was, '*Aiwa, aiwa*' – 'Yes. Yes.' It was *aiwa* to everything. In between, he jabbered Arabic and pointed down the wadi.

'Where's there a vehicle?'

'*Aiwa.*'

'How far to walk?' – with walking motions.

'*Aiwa.*'

I exclaimed, 'Ah, bollocks, man, he's just saying yes to everything.'

After a bit Stan said, 'Listen – I'll go with him and see if we can get a tractor.'

'Don't do it!' I said fiercely. It seemed incredible to me that Stan should want to go off with a total stranger. I reminded him that we were aliens in a foreign country, where we had no business to be. I knew we'd get no friendly help from the Iraqis. The natives weren't going to do us any favours. Quite apart from being enemies in war, we were infidels. This man would sell us down the wadi – but Stan couldn't seem to see that.

'Listen,' I said. 'Suppose this was World War Two, and we were a couple of German paratroopers, lost in the Welsh mountains. We meet this farm lad and try to chat him up. Of course he says he's going to help us. But what does he want really? To get us in the nick. Nothing else.'

Even that didn't change Stan's mind. 'It's OK,' he said. 'I'll take the risk and go with him.'

'Stan! You're fucking not. You're staying here.'

'Chris – I want to go.'

This was a big shock to me. I thought he was crazy. But I couldn't force him to stay, because that sort of thing doesn't hold water when you're on the run. So I said, 'Well, OK. I can't order you, because we're on our own. But listen, mate: I don't *want* you to go. It'll mean us splitting up. You'll be on your own. You're making a big mistake here.'

'No, no,' he said. 'What I'll do is leave my weapon and webbing with you. Then I won't cut such an aggressive figure. I'll just walk next to him. Why don't you come too?'

'Not bloody likely! I disagree with what you're doing. It's dangerous, and stupid too.'

But I could see that he was determined, so I said, 'Well – I'll wait here for you till six-thirty, last light. If you're not back by then, I'm off on this bearing.' And I gave him the northerly course we'd already decided on.

'Fair enough,' he said.

'Go on, then. When you're out of sight, I'll take your weapon and webbing fifty metres up that dry stream bed, and hide them there.'

'Yeah – OK.'

So Stan stood up with the Arab and said, 'Come on, cobber. Let's go,' and the two of them started walking off, with the Arab whistling for his goats to follow. I crawled down to the bottom of the wadi and sat and watched them. When they'd made a couple of hundred metres, I suddenly thought, 'NO! This is wrong!' and I yelled out, 'STAN! Stan, come back here!'

Back he came, almost running.

'For Christ's sake, think about what you're doing,' I told him. 'Leave your webbing if you like, but at least take your weapon.'

'I don't want to look too aggressive.'

'Sling it over your shoulder, then, and carry it down the side of your body – but have it with you. And if you change your mind when you get back down there towards him, just drill him, like I said. Put one into him, and we'll sit the day out together.'

But Stan was overboard about his new friend. 'No, no, Chris,' he said. 'He's quite all right. He's offered me food.'

'What food?'

'It's only a few berries.'

'Bollocks to the berries,' I said. 'Just drill him.'

'No – I trust the guy. He seems like, you know, friendly. If we get to a vehicle, I'll give him a sovereign.'

'Drill him,' I repeated. 'Go back and shoot the bugger.'

But Stan wouldn't have it. Away he went with the Iraqi, meandering down the dry stream bed. For nearly a kilometre he remained in sight. He'd wrapped his shamag round his head, and from a distance he looked quite like another Arab. I could see the two of them trying to chat together, matey as anything. In the end they went round a bend to the left and disappeared.

'Jesus!' I thought. 'Now I'm on my own.' I wished I hadn't let Stan go – but for the moment I didn't feel too worried. I found it difficult to keep still. For a few minutes I'd sit against the bank in the side of the wadi; then I'd come up on to a mound in the middle of it and scan with my little binoculars. Looking straight down the line of the watercourse I could see for miles, up on to a big hill in the distance. Again and again I looked for the two men walking up there. Then I'd go back into cover.

Time crawled by. After a couple of hours I took Stan's webbing and tucked it into the side of the stream-bed, where I'd told him it would be. On top of it I left four of the extra 203 rounds which I'd taken from Vince during the night. Then I had nothing to do but wait for dark.

As the hours dragged past, I grew more and more jumpy. Several times I imagined I heard something. Whenever that happened, I'd creep round to one side of the mound and look out, hoping like hell that I'd see Stan returning.

Dusk came on. By 1730 I was in a state of high anxiety. Very soon I was going to have to make a decision. I was hungry and thirsty and cold, and on my own. Six o'clock came, and I thought, 'Jesus, this is it.' I took one last look back down the wadi. Night had come down, and there was still no sign. I still kept hoping I'd see the lights of a vehicle heading out – but no.

It was a tough decision. My last friend had disappeared. He could still be on his way back. But when 1830 came I thought, 'This is it. You can't sit around here any longer.' So I checked my compass and started walking north.

For fifteen minutes I tabbed it steadily over level, open ground, with darkness settling in on the desert all round me. Then I happened to look over my shoulder, and I saw a set of headlights coming up the wadi I'd just left. 'Bloody hell!' I thought. 'Stan's got a vehicle after all. Brilliant!'

I started running back as fast as I could. I must have been halfway back to my start-point when suddenly I saw that it wasn't one set of lights coming towards me, but two. Immediately I thought, 'Shit – he can't have two vehicles. He must have been captured, and this is the enemy. If he'd been on his own, he'd never have brought two vehicles.' So I turned and ran north again.

Already I was out of breath. Glancing back over my shoulder to check the vehicles' progress, I searched desperately for cover on the flat plain. A burning sensation seared the top of my throat and forced me to slow down. Behind me, the vehicles had driven up the side of the wadi and were heading straight across the open desert for me. Then the clouds parted and the moon shone through, lighting the place up like day. It may have been my imagination, but my smock seemed to have become luminous, shining like an electric beacon. The old adrenalin had started up, and my heart was going like a sledgehammer. Then I saw a little bush with a shadow behind it, and threw myself down into that tiny patch of black.

As I lay there panting, I frantically sorted out my kit. I checked the magazine on the 203, and piled spare mags in a heap beside me. I opened out the 66 so that it was ready to fire. I even bent together the ends of the safety pins on my white phos grenades, so that I could whip them out quickly if need be.

For a moment I got a respite. The lights swung round, whipping wildly up and down as the vehicles went over bumps, and headed back into the wadi. There was a lot of banging of doors. Obviously some guys had got out to have a look round the place where the goatherd had found us in the morning. I squinted through the kite-sight, trying to make out what they were doing, but the glare from the lights shone everything else out. Then the vehicles moved off again and started driving about the floor of the wadi.

The moment the lights were away from me, I picked up my kit, stuffed things into the webbing pouches down my front, and legged it. Now I was really running, looking right and left for cover – and suddenly the lights swung round and they were coming for me again. I dropped down and got my kit out once more. I set up the 203 with the battle sight, and as I piled the spare magazines, it went through my mind that this was just like range practice. I cocked the 66 again, lifted the bomb sights on the 203, and waited.

Whether they'd seen me or not, I couldn't tell. But they were driving towards me at a steady roll. I got the 66 lined up on the leading pair of lights – and then I became aware of this amazing noise: *ke-kik, ke-kik, ke-kik, ke-kik.* It sounded like a steam train, and I thought, 'Jesus! Here's another vehicle, and the engine sounds really rough. Where is it? Where's it coming from?' When I closed my mouth, I couldn't hear the noise any more. I strained with my ears and wondered, 'Have they switched off, or what?' Then I opened my mouth to breathe, and it was *ke-kik, ke-kik, ke-kik* again. Suddenly I realised that what I could hear was the accelerated pounding of my own heart.

The lights were still coming. Obviously the vehicles weren't going to stop. Someone on board must have realised that I would be heading due north, for the river, and they were driving on that bearing. The wagons were rolling at maybe 15 m.p.h., and the lights were quite steady. They would pass so close that there was no chance of them not seeing me. It was going to be them or me. I hugged the ground and tried to stop myself shaking. An age seemed to pass as the vehicles ground on.

Now I thought, 'This is it. You're going to get killed here.' The worst thing was that I suddenly saw an image of my daughter. 'I'm going down here,' I thought, 'and Sarah will never know how her dad died.' I felt sudden fear that if I did get killed, she wouldn't remember me. She would never really know who her father was or what he'd been like. She was never going to understand how or where my life had ended – and I found that desperately sad.

Fifty metres, and they kept coming. Two Land-Rover-type

vehicles, advancing at a purposeful crawl, obviously in search of me. I couldn't tell how many men they might contain. I held the sight of the 66 aligned between the front pair of lights. When they were twenty metres off, I pulled the trigger.

Whhoooosh! went the launcher, right in my ear. Out front there was a big *BANG* as the rocket took the vehicle head-on. Oddly enough, I remember no flash, just this heavy explosion, and a cloud of white smoke billowing out in the moonlight. The vehicle rolled to a stop. I dropped the 66, grabbed the 203 and lined up the grenade sight on the second pair of lights, a few yards to the left of the first. From maybe forty metres I smacked that one right in the bonnet. Then I was up and running toward the enemy.

In a moment I had reached the first vehicle and put a burst into it. Coming to the second, I sprayed it all down the side, through the canvas back. Then I looked into the back and put another burst in. There were men in the back wearing dish-dashes. I let off another burst over the backs of the front seats into the driver's compartment. Then I had to change magazines. At the front again, I put more rounds into the first vehicle. Suddenly I thought, 'Fucking hell! I've left all the other magazines.' I sprinted back to them, snatched them up, stuffed them down the front of my smock and ran.

I ran till I thought my heart was going to burst. I imagined that everybody was on to me and chasing me. The moon was so bright that I felt as if a spotlight was beaming down on me. I was swept up in panic, just as I had been when chased as a kid. It was as if I'd been found out, and was on my own. I ran till I had to slow down, because I was feeling like I had during the initial contact: my throat was heaving, my chest exploding, my mouth dry as the desert. I'd had no water all through that day, and soon I was so knackered that it was painful even to walk.

All the time I was turning to look behind, to see if any more lights were coming up – but nothing showed. At last I thought it was safe to stop, sit down and sort out my equipment.

After a contact like that, it takes time to recover. Gradually I chilled out and got myself together. One minor improvement was that I had less to carry: once I'd fired the 66 I threw away the tube, which was useless to the Iraqis.

Walking again, I kept on for a couple of hours towards the

north. All the time I was wondering what had happened to Stan, and hoping to hell he hadn't come back in one of the vehicles. Or had he sent them up to me? No, I decided: he couldn't have. It must have been the goatherd who brought the Iraqis back to the wadi; no one else could have directed them on to my position with such accuracy. Thinking over our confrontation with him in the morning, I realised I should have done him there and then. Of course I should. My intuition about him had been right. I should have done him with my own knife, but he was a big guy, and somehow, with Stan not keen, it hadn't been on. Then I should never have let Stan go off with him: I should have put a round through the bugger myself. But then, if he had come back in one of the vehicles, maybe in the end I'd done him after all – because I don't think anybody in either of them could have survived.

The question was, what had happened back on the site of the contact during the last couple of hours? If anyone had got away from one of the vehicles I'd hit, or if someone else had found the wrecks, word might have gone out that another enemy soldier was on the run. People would surely guess that I was heading for the Euphrates. From the firepower I'd put down, they may have thought that there were several guys at large.

I tabbed on and on through the moonlight. Now the desert was rolling in gentle undulations, and I believed that the river was going to appear over every rise. Then, away to my right, I heard dogs barking, kids shouting, grown-ups calling. As I went down on one knee to listen, I saw the red tracer of anti-aircraft fire going up in the distance. Obviously there were habitations somewhere close to me, and the people I could hear were watching that nice firework display on the horizon. Then I heard the far-off roar of jets; I couldn't see them, but the sound of their engines was unmistakable. They must have been miles off, attacking some target, and the red tracer was curving silently up towards the stars.

Half an hour later I spotted a glimmer of light ahead. The kite-sight picked out three stationary vehicles, with light coming out of the side. I went down and watched for signs of people on foot, in case a mobile patrol was being deployed to cut me off. Men on foot could be strung out in an extended line, sweeping the desert ahead of them. After a careful search with the kite-sight, back and forth, I saw nothing more, so I boxed the vehicles and carried on.

Again, as I came to the top of a rise, I was convinced that I must find the Euphrates in front of me – but no. The next thing I saw was a set of pylons. I'd been expecting them for some time, because they were marked on my map. Beyond them was an MSR, and some fifteen kilometres beyond that, the river. When I sat down under the power-lines and scanned ahead, I found I could see the road, and a wide-open flat area beyond it – but no water. By then it was two in the morning, and nothing was moving on the highway. Coming down to the MSR, I found this was metalled. By then I was almost on my knees, and when I found a culvert under the road, I crawled into it and stretched out. All I could think was, 'I've got to get my head down,' so I took off my webbing and lay on that. I was also desperate with thirst, and I kept tipping up my two water bottles to see if I could get a drop out of them – but not one. I felt relatively safe in the culvert and closed my eyes – but anxiety was gnawing at me, and so was the cold.

Within ten minutes I was shaking all over, too frozen to stay still any longer. On again, then. From the map, I thought that if I crossed the MSR and kept heading north, I must hit the Euphrates, flowing from north-west to south-east. From talking about the river to Jan, I knew that in Biblical times it had been a mighty waterway, and I assumed that it must still be pretty big. But what I hit next was a huge system of dry wadis, with steep walls up to twenty metres high, all made of dead rock. Obviously they'd once been a river bed. Maybe in wet weather flash floods would turn the channels into a rushing river again. I was gagging for want of water, and getting so confused in my mind that suddenly I thought, 'Jesus – I hope this isn't the Euphrates. Surely it can't have dried out since the Bible? If it has, I'm fucked.'

Panic was making me walk faster and scrabble down through the tumbled, loose rock. I kept thinking, 'There's got to be water at the bottom of this.' At its lowest point the river-bed seemed to open out, and as I looked down through the kite-sight, I made out a line of palm trees running across my front from left to right. Also, away to my right, I could see the houses of a village – pale, flat-roofed blocks glowing in the moonlight, with a breeze-block wall running down one side, and the shapes of cultivated fields outside it. I still couldn't see any water, but I thought, 'This has got to be the river – the Euphrates at last. Great!' I started walking down towards the trees, which I presumed were growing on the bank.

The closer I came, the warmer the air seemed to be – or at least, the atmosphere seemed stiller and calmer. I kept about 300 metres from the breeze-block wall, but dogs came out and started barking. As there was no wind, they could hardly have smelt me. More likely, they had picked up the noise of my feet, first on the rock and then in the dry grass of the fields. The houses were dark; they may have been blacked out, but probably the people in them were asleep.

Moving parallel to the boundary wall, I made my way carefully down to the river through oblong fields. No crops were sprouting as yet, but the ground had been well tilled, and the fields were divided up by irrigation ditches, with grass growing on bunds. I tried to keep out of the fields, for fear I would leave footprints in the soft soil. Rather than cross the cultivated areas, I kept to the ditches, which as yet had no water in them.

At last, between the trunks of the palm trees, I saw water. Irrigation pumps were working all along the bank: the night was full of their quick, steady beat – *boop, boop, boop, boop*. I could hear many different pumps working up and down the valley. For several minutes I kept still, watching for any movement. The cultivation seemed to end about ten metres from the edge of the water, and my kite-sight revealed piles of cut bushes, each about two metres square, sticking out from the bank into the stream, one about every fifty metres. At first I couldn't make out what they were for, then it occurred to me that they were probably makeshift jetties, for men to fish off or to bring boats alongside. In any case, using one for cover, I crept right down to the water's edge.

Crouching next to the pile, I got out my waterbottles, but found that at the bank the water was only a few millimetres deep – a thin skin over mud. I tried to wade out, but I hadn't taken three steps before my feet plunged deep into silt. In a second I was up to my knees, then up to my bollocks. I thought, 'Jesus, I'm sinking!' I threw my rifle back on to the pile of bushes and dragged myself out, soaked up to the waist and coated in slimy, silty mud.

For my next attempt, I crawled out over one of the platforms of bushes. As my weight came on to it, the whole structure sank into the stream. I could feel water coming through my clothes at the front – legs, crutch, chest – but I filled both bottles, crawled back out, and drank one down.

I swallowed and gasped and choked, trying to stifle the noise. The relief of getting water down my neck was incredible. I shone my torch beam down the neck of the full bottle, and saw that the water was black and foul-looking, but it tasted quite good. I crawled out to fill the empty bottle again.

At that point the river was a couple of hundred metres wide, and I could see no buildings or cultivations on the far bank. In the moonlight the land beyond glowed white, as if it were encrusted in salt. Because there seemed to be no habitations over there, it occurred to me that I might swim across and make better progress along the far side. I'm a strong swimmer, but I thought that to go in with my weapon and webbing would be asking for trouble. The water was icy cold, and although the surface was smooth, I could see that a strong current was flowing out in the middle of the stream. If I'd got into difficulties halfway across, that would have been it.

By then it was nearly five o'clock, and I needed somewhere to basha up for the day. I moved cautiously out between scattered houses, up to a dirt road. Again a dog started barking, so I waited a couple of minutes before going on up into the dry wadi systems. Once into the rocks I turned on my TACBE and tried speaking into it. Getting no response, I left the beacon on for a while. As I climbed, the rocky channels grew steeper and steeper, and a couple of hundred metres above the road, they came to a dead end. There I found a rock a couple of feet high which was casting a black shadow in the moonlight. I curled up beside it, with my map case beneath my legs, one shamag round them and the other round my head, and lay there feeling relatively secure in that patch of deep darkness.

Before settling down, I gave myself the only treat at my disposal: I got out my flask, and took a nip of whisky. The old Lagavulin burnt as it went down into my empty stomach, but it gave me a momentary lift. I was so exhausted that in spite of the cold I kept falling asleep, only to come round with a start a few minutes later, racked by shudders. It was a real pain to be wet again; having spent hours with Stan getting dry, I was now soaked all up the front, with my sodden clothes clinging to me, and the damp intensifying the cold.

When first light came, with dawn breaking early under clear skies, I realised that I wasn't really in any sort of cover. At night the shadow of the rock had looked comforting; if someone had walked past in the dark, he wouldn't have seen me. Now I found I was lying out in the open.

Looking up on to the north bank of the wadi, I saw a hollow among some loose rocks. I walked up to it, lay inside it, and piled up a few more rocks at either side to break my outline. That was the best place I could find in which to spend the day – and that was when it really hit me how much I was on my own.

Chapter Five

Boxing Clever

In the days and nights that followed, there were several moments when morale plunged to rock-bottom – and this was one of them. A wave of loneliness swept over me, as I realised that I was utterly alone. I thought, 'This can't get any worse.' I was hungry, wet, tired, cut off from all communication with friends, and still far inside a hostile country.

'If things get on top of you,' my mum always used to say, 'have a good cry.' So I lay there in the rocks and tried to cry – but I couldn't. Instead my face crumpled up and I started laughing. 'Dickhead!' I thought. 'Here you are, deep in the shite, and all you can do is laugh!' But somehow it did the trick; it let go the tension and sorted me out. I daydreamed wistfully about the glorious puddings my mum used to make – particularly her rice pudding, with its thick, sweet, creamy inside, and its crust baked to a crisp golden brown. I could have done with a helping of that, there and then. But from that point I wasn't bothered about being alone. I seemed to have made a transition into feeling that I'd been on my own for the whole trip. I was used to it now – all I had to do was get on with heading for the border.

It was the morning of Sunday 27 January, my third day on the run. I would have liked to let my feet breathe, but that would have involved too great a risk. I had to be ready to leg it at any minute: so it was one boot off, one sock off, check that foot, and get sock and boot back on. Then the other foot. The blisters looked bad; they had long since burst, and the underlying skin was raw and bleeding. My toenails had started lifting, and there were blisters under my toes. I had no means of treating them, and could only hope that my feet would hold out until I reached the border.

With my boots back on, I devoted the best part of an hour to cleaning my weapon. Again, I took care not to make any noise that would carry. If you release the working parts of a 203 normally, they snap forward with a sharp crack, but if you handle them gently, you need make scarcely a sound. Once I had everything squared away, I lay back with my belt undone but my webbing still in place, straps over my shoulders, so that I could make a rapid getaway if need be. Even down there, almost on the level of the Euphrates, the air was still icy cold, and I shivered continuously. I lay on one side, with my hands between my legs, tucked in under one big rock, with smaller rocks pulled into position shielding my head and feet, and bare rock beneath me.

From time to time I dozed off, but always I woke with a start a few minutes later, shaking all over. It was my body's defence to bring me round like that: if I hadn't kept waking, I would have drifted off and been gone for ever. Aching from contact with the rock, I would shift about, trying to find a more comfortable position. There was always a pebble or bump of rock digging into some part of me, and the pressure-points on the outside of my knees, hips and spine had already begun to rub sore.

The drink had made me feel better in one way; the trouble was, the intake of all that cold water had given me the shivers, and all I wanted to do was press on again, so that I could warm up. The hardest thing was to keep still in daylight. The urge to start walking, to make progress towards the border, was almost overwhelming.

Below me, the wadi dropped towards the river in a V-shape, snaking left and right. Its flanks consisted of tumbled grey-brown rock, devoid of vegetation, but the bottom of the channel, where water would run after rain, had smoother sides. There was nothing whatever alive to keep me interested: no bird or animal, nothing moving. Boredom soon became another powerful enemy: it took all my will-power to resist the urge to move on, or even just to have a look round.

The day was quiet: I never heard voices or traffic movement, but now and then the wind would stir among the rocks and I would come fully alert, looking round, wondering if a person or an animal had shifted. From where I lay I could see what looked like the remains of an ancient viaduct, jutting out from the bank of the river into the water. There were three tiers of pale yellow arches on top of each other, and they looked as though they were made of stone. I'd spotted the structure when I was getting water, and now, if I lifted my head, it was still in sight. I wondered how old the remains of the bridge were, and whether they could date back as far as the Romans. Round the base of the arches the water was obviously deep, for through my binoculars I could see the current swirling fast. The river was brown with silt, a strong contrast with the salty-looking land on the far bank.

What kept my spirits up was the thought that I must be close to the Syrian border – within no more than thirty or forty kilometres. Looking at the map again and again, I worked out that I was much farther west than I had thought I was. I reckoned I was within one night's march, possibly two, of safety.

Until then, the longest I'd ever gone without food was four days, on combat survival training in Wales. Even then, an agent had brought me one slice of bread or a little piece of cheese every twenty-four hours – but I remembered feeling pretty weak at the end. The furthest I'd ever walked in one march was 65 kilometres – the final march on Selection. Now, I reckoned, I'd covered about 150 kilometres in three nights, and already it was five days since I had had a proper meal – the big blow-out at Al Jouf. With my biscuits finished, I inevitably began to worry about how long my strength would hold out. How long could I go on walking? Would I slow right down, or even be unable to keep going at all?

I knew from weight-training, and books about the subject, that when the body is under stress it starts to burn its own muscle, trying to preserve fat for emergencies. I was carrying very little fat anyway – so the only realistic prospect was that my muscles would deteriorate quite quickly, especially as I was burning yet more energy by shivering all the time. In lectures on combat survival we'd been told that a man lost in the desert can only survive for a day without water – but this wasn't by any means a typical desert, and the temperature, far from dangerously high, was threateningly low.

Of course I kept wondering about the rest of the patrol. I greatly feared that Vince was dead, and in a way I felt responsible. Lying all day by the tank berm had undoubtedly contributed to his collapse, and it was I who had decreed that we should follow SOPs and stay there. If we'd been a bigger, more heavily-armed party, we might have risked moving to somewhere warmer in daylight – and that might have saved him, at any rate for the time being. Then, in the night, I should have tied him to me. As a qualified mountain guide, I could have handled the situation better. But at the time I'd had a lot on my mind. I myself was going down with exposure, and not thinking as clearly as I might have.

Vince had been fit, but he had carried no surplus weight. Taller than me – maybe 5' 11" – he was skinny, with the build of a runner. In fact, as we'd sat discussing what might happen if things went wrong, he'd told me he reckoned that if he stripped down, he could run and walk thirty miles in the night, so that he should make Syria in two nights at most. The trouble was that, like the rest of us, he hadn't reckoned with the cold. Exposure can catch people in different ways. Even when I started to go down, and was slipping back and forth between feelings of drunkenness and being clear-headed, I still knew what was happening to me. I don't think Vince did; he was deteriorating so fast.

What about Stan? It seemed certain that he'd been captured, and I could only hope he wasn't having too bad a time. As for the other five – I reckoned that the chopper must have come back and lifted them out. I felt sure that the aircraft had been inbound towards our original position, following normal Lost Comms procedure, and that it would have flown around until the guys made contact with the pilot. 'By now,' I thought, 'those lucky sods are sat back in base, pissing themselves with laughter.'

Trying to concentrate on pleasant subjects, I thought about my family – about Sarah and Jan, and, before Jan, Susan. During my time with 23 SAS, I was engaged to a pretty, tall, blonde woman called Susan who lived in the same village. I met her while I was still at school, and for seven years we went everywhere together, even on holidays. She had a job as receptionist for a firm of lawyers in Newcastle. We'd meet for lunch, and often she'd come back from work to stay the night at my home. In the evenings I wasn't interested in doing anything except listening to Morse code or reading through my technical manuals, but she'd sit around patiently enough.

My mum kept saying that I was too young to get married – and I was certainly too inexperienced. What she was trying to tell me, but couldn't in so many words, was that I ought to go out and sleep with other women, and live life a little rather than tie myself down with the only girl I'd ever known. 'You're a man now,' she'd say, 'and you've got to get around a bit.' I couldn't understand what she was on about – but now I see how right she was. I was extremely naive, having been strictly brought up never to drink or smoke, and my horizons were very limited.

When my selection course for 22 SAS was in the offing, Susan and I planned to get married and move south – provided I passed. Once in the regular SAS, I'd be on a good wage, and everything would be all right.

Or so I thought. In fact, with my own move south all that went by the board. Suddenly I was thrown into the company of guys of thirty, who were constantly going out humping and drinking, and it was a real eye-opener for me. Hereford was alive with young, single girls, all determined to latch on to the guys in the regiment. With a new intake, especially, their behaviour became outrageous. Rapidly I saw the other side of the coin. My long-standing engagement seemed like a big mistake, and I started to play the field like everyone else.

The difficulty was to break the news to Susan. After returning from the Parachute Company to the Squadron, I did a couple of short exercises, and then went on a three-month trip to Botswana. Immediately after that I joined the SP team, which meant that for nine months I was on thirty minutes' notice to move, and couldn't leave Hereford. The result was that I didn't visit home for more than a year. Susan and I did talk on the telephone, but in the end she wrote saying, 'This is no good, and I think it's best if we finish.' So I took the easy way out, rang her, and said I agreed.

At least the break meant that I was unattached when I met Jan. That was in 1986, when she was serving in Queen Alexandra's Royal Army Nursing Corps, and working as matron in charge of the hospital at Airport Camp in Belize. I was out there on a three-month deployment with a troop called F Company, which organised jungle training courses for the resident British battalion, and also gave guys new to the SAS their own first jungle experience.

Boxing Clever

One of my jobs was to run a range, and when I saw this gorgeous blonde walk past our accommodation on her way from the hospital to the officers' mess, I immediately decided to invite her up for some pistol shooting. The only slight difficulty was that I didn't know her name – so I decided to cast my net wide.

The sergeant in charge of the hospital was a bit of an SAS groupie, always snivelling round the guys, so I asked him if he'd like to bring his staff up to the range. He made enquiries and reported that his people were keen. When I asked who was coming, he gave me a list of names – but this still didn't tell me what I wanted to know, as it just said 'Major This' and 'Captain That'.

'Have you got a woman in there?' I asked – knowing full well there was one.

'Oh yes – that's Captain James, the matron.'

'Well – invite her too.'

He went round and asked her, and the answer was that she'd be along as well.

We set the ranges up, and I had all the guys detailed off so that I'd be free to grab the matron and give her some personal instruction. Alas, she failed to appear, and I stumped off in dudgeon. But just as I set off across the football field, I saw her coming in the opposite direction. 'Damn!' I thought, 'I've screwed this up.' As we passed each other, I said 'Hello,' and when I saw her reach the range, I ran back, pretending I'd been to fetch something. Then I grabbed her and took her to one side, inviting her for a drink.

Back in England we met up again, and we saw a good deal of each other when I did my training to become a medic. For a month I was attached to the John Radcliffe Hospital in Oxford, where she also had trained, and as she was stationed at Wroughton, only an hour's drive to the west, she would come up in the car to collect me whenever I had time off. We got engaged in September 1987, and married the following summer.

My medical training was thorough and lengthy. It began with an intensive six-week course in Hereford, where we learnt about anatomy and physiology, and the role of drugs. Then I picked a hospital – the John Radcliffe – to which I was posted for four weeks. My introduction to the place was breathtaking. The day I arrived, the sister – who came from Hereford and knew who I was – introduced herself and immediately said, 'Would you like to see something interesting?'

'OK,' I agreed cautiously.

'Get your white coat on, then, and go through those double doors.'

Inside was the resuscitation room of the emergency theatre. I thought I was going in to watch a video or listen to a lecture. Not at all. As I walked through the doors, there was a lump of meat screaming on the table, with two doctors and three or four nurses working on it. The man, a road casualty, had compound fractures of the legs and arms, as well as big gashes in his face and on his chest.

After that brisk introduction, I was partnered off with a house doctor and put into the Accident and Emergency room. I'd go into the little cubicle with my mentor, and be introduced to the patient as another doctor or a consultant. I'd watch and listen as the proper doctor made his diagnosis; then, after we'd come out, he'd ask me what I thought ought to be done. If I produced the right answer, he'd say, 'OK – go in and do that,' but if I was wrong, he'd make alternative suggestions. It was excellent hands-on training, and we had at least one serious road casualty every week, so that I got plenty of practice.

Another useful ally was the matron in charge of the maternity ward. Often she would make sure that the mother-to-be didn't mind a colleague being present, and then bleep me so that I could go in to watch the birth, whether it was natural or Caesarean section.

I was put to live in the nurses' accommodation block, where three bedrooms, a bathroom and kitchen were arranged as a kind of flat. When we arrived, someone said, 'Oh, good, here's our bouncers for the next four weeks.' When I asked what she meant, it turned out that at least once a week a nurse would be attacked, probably by a patient.

Sure enough, one night a drunk came in with his wrist and hand badly cut after punching his fist through a kebab shop window. A nurse began cleaning his wounds, taking splinters of glass out of his hands. Suddenly he went for her, yelling out that she had hurt him. He got her by the neck and slammed her up against a wall, trying to strangle her. Another of the girls came screaming into my room. I pulled on my white coat and ran. It was a horrendous sight. The nurse was up against the wall, with blood all over her face and neck and down the front of her uniform. I thought the guy was murdering her, so I dragged him off and hit him. He looked amazed and said, 'You can't do that. You're a doctor.'

'Just watch this, then.'

Wham! I smacked him again, and put him down with a kind of anaesthetic quite new to him. All the time another of the nurses was crying out, 'Don't hurt him! It's all right.'

'Come on!' I said. 'He *was* trying to throttle her.'

Another phase of our medical training was to watch post-mortems being carried out in the mortuary at St Mary's Hospital, Paddington, and to practise for live operations by doing things like putting in chest-drains or carrying out tracheotomies on the corpses. Again, my first exposure to this peculiar world was a bit of a shock. One day our instructor said, 'OK – there's some bodies you can work on.' There were four old people, one middle-aged man who had hanged himself, another man in his thirties, and a boy of nine or ten, who'd fallen downstairs through a window, so that a piece of glass had pierced the top of his skull. Otherwise there wasn't a mark on him, but strangely enough, there was a rush for the older bodies – nobody wanted to touch the kid. Another day the pathologist brought out the body of a man who'd been in the Thames for three weeks. His skin and clothes were all the same colour – a slimy green – and all round the corpse was a solid wall of stench.

Back at Hereford, I sat various written and practical tests, and so became a qualified medic – though I had to re-qualify by doing a short refresher course every year . . .

Jan and I were married in Hereford during the summer of 1988, and our first child was due early in 1989. But during December, because Jan's blood-pressure kept falling, she was taken into hospital. Being a theatre-sister herself, she knew the score pretty well, and about three weeks before the baby was due she asked for it to be induced, because she knew I'd be leaving the country early in the New Year and she wanted to have it while I was still around. The doctor declined absolutely; but her blood pressure continued to rise and fall, and while she was in for a check during the morning of 21 December, the surgeon told her she must go for surgery immediately, because the baby's umbilical cord was being twisted and compressed, and cutting off the blood supply.

At 9a.m. she rang me at home and said she had to go for a Caesarian section straight away. In the background I could hear the surgeon saying, 'If he wants to be in at the birth, he'd better get down NOW, because you're going straight in.'

I was still in bed, recovering from a late night. I leapt up, threw on the first clothes I could find, jumped into the car and raced through Hereford with headlights and flashers blazing. As I ran into the hospital I saw Jan being wheeled past on a trolley.

The surgeon asked if I'd done the medical course, and when I said I had, he said, 'Come with me, then.' He took me into a room and got me dressed up in green theatre clothes. Then we went through and found Jan already on the operating table. They'd given her a spinal anaesthetic, which left her numb from the waist down but fully conscious, and she was keeping up a running discussion with the surgeons.

'What layer are you going through now?' she asked. I kept looking at her and saying, 'Please shut up!' But she was determined to talk the surgeon through his task. Then suddenly she said to me, 'Just watch your feet. Stand back a bit, or your wellies are going to fill.'

I stepped back, and a few seconds later the surgeon cut through the amniotic sac, so that the fluid flowed out. All I remember after that is this thing like a little alien being pulled out of Janet's belly, screaming.

The baby, a girl, was all but full-term, and perfect – but if it hadn't been for the hospital's prompt action, we might have lost her. We had decided that if we got a boy, he would be Stephen, and a girl would be called Sarah. So Sarah she became. Although Jan was in real pain the next day, she came home a couple of days later, and recovered quickly.

After little more than a week at home with her, I had to leave to go on the German guides' course – which meant that I was away for three months at a time, and could only come back for a week or 10 days before leaving again. The result was that there wasn't much bonding between myself and Sarah until I finished the course. It was sad, because although I had a daughter, she meant little to me. But then, in May 1990, I came home for six months, and after a couple of weeks Sarah suddenly latched on to me. Belatedly I realised what I had, and we became tremendously close.

To me, she seemed the perfect child. Of course my opinion may have been prejudiced by the fact that she looked very much like me, with clear blue eyes, and hair that gradually turned darker as she grew older. But from an early age she was exceptionally well behaved. We only had to tell her once not to do something, and she never did it again. She was never afraid of the dark, but slept right through the night without any light on. Best of all, she was always glad to play on her own. She seemed to have inherited my gift of wanting to get on with life, and to try her hand at everything. Although so good, she had an independent mind, and would happily spend hours on her own, drawing, painting and singing away to herself. She was also a bit of a tomboy, and was often covered in cuts and bruises from falling out of trees or off climbing frames. I smiled to myself as I thought how she would sit in the dog-basket, cuddled up with Jessie, our other Staffordshire bull terrier, reading her picture-books . . .

Up in the rocks, something near me stirred, jerking me back to the Euphrates. I sat up and looked round, holding my breath, listening. Goats? A dog? A human? In a moment or two I was reassured; there seemed to be nothing close to me, and the movement had been only that of the wind. But thank God – at last the light was starting to fail. It wouldn't be long before night came and I could continue on my way.

What I had no means of knowing was that, during that day, the other guys in the patrol had been captured close to the river at a point about 100 kilometres nearer to the Syrian border. As a result of contacts with them, some 1,600 Iraqi troops had been deployed to look for other coalition soldiers on the run, and the civilian population along the river had been alerted: not only the men, but the women and children too had been ordered to turn out.

I came out of my hiding place not long after dark, and began heading north-west, keeping as close as I could to the edge of the cultivated land, where the going was easiest. I was walking more carefully now, because I was in a populated area. I was probably down to three or four kilometres an hour. Occasionally, for a change, I rested the 203 over my shoulder, but for most of the time I held it in both hands, with the weight taken by the sling of paracord round my neck. That way, the weapon was less tiring on my arms, but it was also at the ready: I could have aimed and fired a shot within a second.

Soon I found that there were amazing numbers of Arabs out and about. Every half hour or so I'd come across a group standing or sitting around, chatting in quiet voices. Several times I picked up the glow of a cigarette and had to box round it. Often I just smelt smoke, either from cigarettes or from a fire or stove, and pulled off without seeing anything. (The smell of Arab cigarettes is harsh and distinctive.) I didn't know what the norm was, but it seemed odd that so many citizens should be out of doors on a freezing winter night.

Again and again I saw or sensed people ahead of me, brought up the kite-sight for a better look, and had to make a detour. In the end my lack of progress became quite frustrating, and I started to think that if things were going to be like this all the way to the border, I would never get out. I would become too weak from lack of food, and would end up getting captured.

During that night I was on the move for eight hours, and must have covered thirty or forty kilometres, but I made only about ten kilometres towards the frontier. I would walk gently forward for a while, see someone, back off and box them. Immediately I'd come on someone else, box them, and carry on. It was zig-zag, zig-zag all the time, five or ten steps sideways for every one forward.

I found it incredibly difficult to maintain concentration for any length of time. Wild animals like antelopes and deer, which are preyed on by carnivores, have the ability to remain on the alert for hours on end – and in fact their lives depend on it. But humans have lost the knack, and it takes conscious effort to stay at a high pitch of watchfulness.

Often I found I was having silent conversations with myself.

'I'll walk as far as the top of that hill,' I'd say. 'Then I can have a rest.'

Soon I'd ask, 'How the hell did you get yourself into this mess? And where have the others got to now?' Casting ahead in my mind, I wondered what the border with Syria would look

The Bravo Two Zero patrol before departure on the tailgate of the Chinook—from left to right: Myself; Bob Consiglio; Stan; Legs; Mark; Andy; Vince; Digger.

Magellan GPS (global positioning system)

Satellite communication equipment

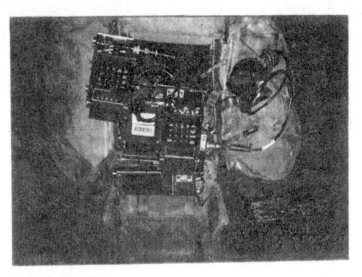

Patrol radio PRC 319

Minimi light machine-gun

The M16 on top, M16 203 and the Colt Commando with the 203 grenade launcher underneath

Nowhere to hide—the flat bedrock plains of Iraq

A Milan post engaging a target, as used by A and D Squadron

BELOW: Deep wadis

The night it snowed, when we lost vince.

The area around the lying up position

SAS 110 Land Rover

Members of B squadron put under secondment with D squadron

The anti-aircraft positions at Al Qaim

A Scud in transit

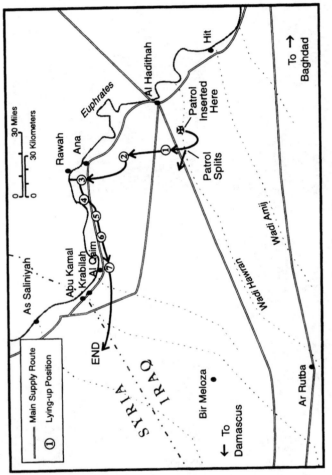

A map of my route

like, and how I'd cross it. People and personalities from my past kept drifting into my head: my mum and dad, my brothers, my schoolteachers. I'd wonder what they'd be doing at that moment – and I longed to tell them where I was. I imagined how surprised they'd be if they knew what I was doing. Often I heard their voices, and these became so real that I'd forget about my own security and pay no attention to my surroundings. Suddenly I'd come to and realise that I'd covered a kilometre or more in a dream.

Whenever I passed a house, the dogs would start barking, and the noise would ricochet down the valley: one lot of dogs would alert the next, and they'd start up before I even reached them. Those tell-tale alarm calls progressed along the river ahead of me, and to my ears they sounded as loud as the wail of a siren.

The dogs were an infernal nuisance. As I was skirting one village, above me on a mound, I looked up at the houses – square, dark silhouettes with flat roofs and no lights showing – and saw a whole pack of them coming down, barking their heads off. Through the night-sight I watched them make straight for me. One ran up to within 10 feet, with three or four more close behind it. If I stopped, they would stop, and also they'd stop barking. But the moment I threatened them or moved, they'd bark like hell again and creep on some more, stalking me.

I kept looking anxiously up at the houses, expecting lights to come on at any second. I felt like the Pied Piper, with all the dogs following me. I kept thinking furiously, 'Oh, for God's sake, SHUT UP!' I stopped, picked up a rock and hurled it. The pack ran away for a few metres, only to close in again. As I cleared the houses, they followed for a couple of hundred metres, then stopped, and stood or sat, watching and barking until I was out of their sight. Then, when my nerves were well in tatters, they'd turn back and troop home. The one saving grace was that their owners seemed to pay no attention whatever. So far as I could see, nobody ever came out of a house to investigate the cause of the commotion.

For a while I stayed as close to the river as I could, partly for navigation, partly so that I could get more water in due course; but then, deciding I was too close to the inhabited stretch, I drew away to the south again and returned to the edge of the desert, where sharp, bare rock seemed to predominate. There I started cross-graining through the wadis, which were running down towards the Euphrates at right-angles to my line of advance. All the time I was trying to find a safe compromise, far enough from the river and its habitations, but at the same time out of the wadis, so that I wasn't forever scrambling up and down.

By five in the morning I was starting to worry about finding somewhere to lie up for the day. At 5.30 it was still fully dark, but when I came to the top of a cliff looking out over the river, something made me decide to scramble four or five metres down the face. There I found a ledge, and at the back of it a nice flat area, with a crack going back underneath the cliff. That seemed as good a refuge as any, and I lay in it until day broke.

When the light came up, I found I could look straight down into the river on my side, and that on the opposite bank there was a small village. The houses were simple, single-storey structures, mostly built of breeze blocks, with flat roofs. They stood in areas of dirt, with not a sign of a garden. Soon, as I watched through binoculars, people started to come out and walk up and down, going about their daily tasks. There seemed to be very few men, but plenty of women, all dressed in black robes from head to foot and heavily veiled: groups of them came down to the water's edge to fill their buckets. Surprise, surprise, the place was alive with dogs. I watched the comings and goings out of sheer interest, but also I was looking for any abnormal activity which might suggest that the area was on the alert – military vehicles driving about, or troops on the move. I was annoyed not to have the camera which I'd left in my bergen: with it, I could have taken pictures of the village and the river.

Two men spent the whole day fishing, paddling up and down in a boat, dropping off gill nets, going round, and pulling in fish. On each pass they let themselves drift maybe a hundred metres downstream. The speed at which the boat picked up confirmed that the current was strong, and I felt all the more glad that I hadn't tried to swim across. In daylight the water looked a dark-brown colour, and a good deal of rubbish was floating about inside my bottle; but the sight of the shining fish reassured me: if they could live in the river, I thought, the water couldn't be too bad.

All that day – Monday 28 January – I lay on the ledge, with

my webbing under my head as a pillow. Up there in my vantage point, under the overhang of rock, I felt secure, almost peaceful. It was the sort of place, I thought, in which an eagle or a peregrine falcon would nest. My main enemy was boredom. I spent hours studying my map, trying to work out exactly where I was. Again I managed to convince myself that I was well to the west of my true position, and a great deal nearer the border.

Throughout all the hours of daylight there was never a movement close to me, either above or at the sides – just the activity in the village across the water, with the odd car coming in and out, and the people going steadily about their business. From among the ploughed fields below came the constant sound of an irrigation pump – a distinctive *dyoot, dyoot, dyoot, dyoot*, the only noise in the valley. It was great to have a live cabaret to watch.

I tried not to think about food, but inevitably, with all that time on my hands, it had become a major preoccupation. Every one of those houses opposite had food in it, even if it was only flour or bread. But for the dogs, I could nip into one under cover of darkness and steal a loaf. In my mind I kept seeing the sachets of fruit that I'd left in my bergen. What wouldn't I give for some pineapple in syrup? 'When I get out of here,' I thought, 'I'm going to eat a gallon of ice-cream.'

All the dogs made me think of Turbo, my Staffordshire bull-terrier. What a character! What chaos there would have been if he'd been with me! He'd have fought every dog along the Euphrates, and sent the whole lot packing.

A friend in the squadron had got him for me. He was supposed to have been eighteen months old when he came; but he already had grey hairs on his muzzle, and healed-over scars on his face – which made me think that he was a good bit older than he was supposed to be, and also that he'd been entered in fights. His official documents turned out to be extremely elusive, and we never did establish his age properly.

When we first had him, he couldn't pass another dog without looking for a fight. If I took him walking on a lead, and we met another dog, Turbo would apparently pay no attention. But the moment I let him off, he'd turn back, go like hell and get stuck in. In this way he managed to start dozens of battles – although after a while he seemed to settle down.

Alas, he came to a sad end. When we moved house, the

change of routine seemed to upset him. Until then he had always been the cleanest dog you could imagine, but now he began to wet indoors – and when Jan came home with the infant Sarah, he growled at the baby.

That put us in a fix. We couldn't give him away, because we couldn't be sure how he would behave with someone who didn't know him; even though he meant no harm, he was strong enough to knock small children over, and generally be a nuisance. So we decided with great sorrow that we would have to put him down. Remembering how my father had always shot dogs when they became too old or infirm to carry on, and hating the idea of taking Turbo to the vet, I resolved to do the deed myself. So I got a pistol and drove out to the range – but then I looked at him and thought, 'Jesus, I can't do this.' So I reprieved him and brought him home.

All too soon he growled at the baby again, and I decided his time had come. I drove him out into the country with a .357 pistol in my trouser pocket. But when I jumped out of the car and said, 'Come on, Turbo!' he just sat bolt upright, gazing ahead. Normally he'd rush out at the first opportunity, but he knew something was up. In the end I shouted *'Cats!'* and out he hurtled, between my legs. I put one round straight down into the top of his skull but he stayed on his feet, his tail wagging against my knees. A split second later I gave him another, and then, as he was still standing, I put one between his eyes. Poor Turbo! I brought his body home and buried it in the garden.

From my perch on the cliff face, I watched the shadows lengthen in the village opposite. Gradually the grey-brown fields beyond the houses faded into the dusk. As evening came on, I began itching to get going again, and had to hold myself in check. When darkness fell at last, I moved out, climbed to the top of the cliff and started walking. That night, thank goodness, activity seemed to cease as people disappeared into their houses, and after dark there was nobody about. But to keep out of the way, I pushed up towards the wadis, between a line of pylons and the main road. Up there, I found myself in steep country. I kept coming to what looked like small quarries, so that I'd have to climb down, walk across a flat floor, then scramble up again and along the top. It was really tiring, and my feet had become seriously sore. After my prolonged study of the map, I thought I'd identified the spot I'd reached – a big bend in the river with a village on it. This looked only about a day's walk from the border – a fact which lifted my morale and gave me strength.

Again I walked all night. The occasional car went along the MSR, which was three or four hundred metres down to my right. Some had headlights on, others were driving blind. At some point late in the night the headlights of a car illuminated a motorway-sized sign. I was too far away to read the names, but I got the idea of moving down to the road so that I could check what the sign said.

It was then that I saw the only wild animal in the whole of my trek. As I dropped towards the road I looked through the kite-sight, and there, on top of a mound, stood a big fox, staring down at me. I knew what he was from his sharp-pointed face and sticking-up ears. For a whole minute I watched him, and he never moved; then I went on, and left him in possession of his territory. In that fox I recognised a fellow creature of the night. I bet that, like me, he lay up all day and came out only when darkness fell. He can't have been as short of food as I was, but I found it hard to imagine what he lived on, because never in all my time on the move or lying up did I see any form of rodent.

Closing on the sign, I peered up at it and made out the legend – in English as well as Arabic – AL QAIM 50; NEW ANA 50. New Ana was behind me, and I'd known for some time that I was heading for Al Qaim – but 50 kilometres! That was a massive blow to morale. I'd imagined I was almost at the place. Sitting there in despair, I thought, 'I'm never going to finish this damn walk.' When I got out the map and pinpointed my position, I saw I was still 80 or 90 kilometres from the border – at least two days short of the spot I thought I'd reached.

I couldn't believe it. I felt as if I'd had a kick between the legs, and sat down on the side of the road, staring at the sign. But the evidence was there, and everything fitted together, as I worked out where I was and where I'd been. The reality was intensely depressing.

There was nothing for it but to keep going. Weighed down by exhaustion, thirst and fear, I started moving along the line of the MSR. I was only a hundred metres from it when I heard a drone from somewhere along the road behind me. I went to ground and lay listening. The noise was coming from miles away to the east, but it grew steadily until it seemed to fill the night. Presently a four-ton wagon went past – but still the heavy drone was increasing. I moved down to the edge of the road and hid in some rocks, looking along the highway through the kite-sight. For minutes I couldn't see anything. Still the noise built up. Then, as I scanned for the twentieth time, I saw a black dot, which grew bigger and bigger until it resolved itself into a massive vehicle, filling the sight. With a tremendous roar it came level, and suddenly I realised I had a Scud going by me. The TEL vehicle was a huge articulated truck, with the missile canopied-up under tarpaulins on its trailer, and a convoy of smaller trucks behind it, all heading out towards the Syrian border. In one of them, with an open back, I could see a whole gang of squaddies.

'Jesus!' I thought. 'That's what I'm here for – to find Scuds!' I never imagined I'd get as close to one as this. Should I have opened fire on it? I couldn't have destroyed the missile, but a grenade from the 203 into the front of the truck might have put the launcher off the road. Yet I would have marked my position, and the guys in the convoy would have been on top of me.

If only I could report back what I'd seen: this was exactly the information the Coalition needed. I whipped out my TACBE, switched on and spoke into it, but as usual got no response. I was left with the mortification of hearing the drone of the engine and big tyres gradually fade into the distance. I imagined the drama of a couple of A-10s coming in to take the launcher and missile out – but it was not to be.

Then again I felt crushed by the disappointment of finding myself so far from safety. How could I have miscalculated so badly? I cursed the wretched, useless map.

On the move once more, I crossed the MSR, so that I was between the road and the river, which at that point were maybe fifteen kilometres apart. Now the ground was really flat, and again I started crossing ploughed fields. It was time to look for a lying-up position, but here in the farmland I couldn't see any rough, broken areas. So I planned to move back across the road and regain the higher ground beyond. Then I came to a culvert, about six feet high and eight wide, underneath the highway, obviously built for pedestrians and animals to walk through.

Boxing Clever

I was feeling so knackered and let-down that I decided to lie up in the tunnel. It was a bad decision, but I can see why I took it. I was thinking, 'You're going down. You're not going to last much longer. Why not take a vehicle and drive to the border?' The culvert would make a good base for such a hijack.

I sat there in the tunnel having this discussion with myself. My lazy side was saying, 'Just do it: grab a vehicle and drive out.' The other side was saying, 'What happens if there's two people in it? How are you going to make them stop? What if there's only one man, and he just drives on? Once you've been seen and reported, that's you finished.'

I went through the scenario again and again. I imagined myself standing on the road, putting one hand up, levelling my weapon – and the car accelerating past. Then I'd have given my position away and lost all the advantages I'd so painfully built up. Suddenly I thought that if Stan had still been with me, the idea would have been even more tempting – but even if we got a vehicle, the chances were that we'd drive into a control point.

I decided not to risk it. But I'd landed myself in a hell of a place. While I'd been dithering, the sky had begun to lighten, and it was already too late to move on. Safe or not, the place was horrendously uncomfortable. The wind was blowing straight through that culvert as if from the North Pole. Soon I was absolutely frozen. I tried moving rocks to make a little shelter, yet still the wind whistled through the gaps. In the gloom I could see that bushes were growing in the floor of the tunnel, and I thought that maybe I could pile some into a barrier; but when I grabbed one, I got a handful of vicious thorns. There seemed to be no way of improving my shelter, so I lay down, determined to stick it out.

Just at full daylight, I heard the sound I wanted least in the world: goat bells. I'd had enough of goats and goatherds already. Looking through the tunnel towards the river, I saw the lead animal come into view, heading confidently into the culvert, obviously on its way through. I just had time to scoot out the other end of the tunnel and up the sloping embankment of the MSR. As I ran towards the top of it, a car was approaching at speed, so I flung myself into a shallow ditch which led down the bank at an angle from the road-edge.

There I lay on my back, trapped, looking straight down over

my boots to the top of the culvert exit. In a few seconds the lead goat emerged below me, not three metres away. More and more goats came into view, pushing and jostling. Their stink rose all round me. Last came the goatherd, an old man wearing a long, woolly coat over several other layers, with a white shamag wrapped round the top of his head. He was leading a donkey, which had a blanket over its back, and five or six dogs jostled at his heels. As he walked out, the top of his head was barely three feet below my boots.

I lay rigid, with the 203 down my front, praying that he would not look back, and that the dogs would not get wind of me. Had they done so, I'd have had to drill him. Little as I wanted to kill an innocent civilian, I was desperate. If I had shot him, I would have been in a dire position: I'd have had to run off into the wadi system with the pack of dogs after me, and even if I'd made a temporary getaway, the old man's death would have put down a great big marker. Obviously he came out that way every morning, and people would be expecting him back.

How the dogs failed to smell me, I still cannot imagine – unless my scent was obliterated by the stink of the goats. I held my breath as the party moved slowly away, up into the wadis. The old man never looked back, and the jingle of bells faded among the rocks.

I couldn't go back into the culvert, because it was clear that at some time during the day the flock and their keeper would return. Equally, I couldn't move down anywhere below the road, because the farmland was too open, and too full of people at work. Besides, I felt sure that there must be a village, or at least a few houses, not far off.

I lay still and watched the goats until they were out of sight. My mind was racing. There was only one way I could go – up into the wadis. But traffic had started to build up on the motorway; every other minute a vehicle came past, and if I began moving up on to the high ground, there was every chance a driver would see me from the vantage-point of the elevated embankment. I kept imagining what would happen if somebody spotted me and raised the alert. The hunt would be on, and, because it was still just after dawn, the searchers would have all day to catch me.

I decided to take my chance and make a go for it between cars.

I rolled over on to my belly, slung the 203 on my shoulder, slithered down the embankment and began crawling up a dry river-bed. Every time I heard a car coming, I went to ground, scared stiff that I would be seen. After a hundred metres I came up into a crouched stance, scuttled upwards and got round into the beginning of the wadi system, maybe 500 metres from the road. Then I walked until I found a hollow in the ground, and lay down in that.

There I was, stuck again for the hours of daylight. As a hideout, my hollow was far from ideal. Although I couldn't see the road, I had a reasonable view downhill maybe 200 metres, but behind me the outlook was blocked by a mound. If anyone had come along, I wouldn't have seen him until he was on top of me. This kept me fully on edge. Any sound made me whip round, even if it was only the wind passing over the rocks. My entire world was one of barren, grey, broken rocks, with nothing but the occasional withered bush to break the monotony, and nowhere to hide in an emergency.

I calculated that this was Tuesday January 29, and a map check showed that I was still at least 70 kilometres from the border. Working backwards, I realised that due to hypothermia Stan and I had miscalculated on our last night together, and we'd gone in a much more northerly direction than we'd supposed.

By this stage even keeping still had become painful. Because of the cold, I had to maintain a foetal position, with my knees tucked up to my chest, lying on one side or the other, and I'd lost so much weight that my pressure points had become very sore. I could see that the day was going to be a long one.

Chapter Six

Echoes Of Africa

There was something spooky about my surroundings. The wind blowing through the rocks of that huge wilderness took my mind back to another desert, another time. Africa . . . the Kalahari. My thoughts floated away to the time when 'B' Squadron was deployed on a three-month training exercise, my troop staff sergeant was killed, and we all became caught up in what felt like voodoo or black magic.

For the various parts of the exercise, the squadron had spread out over a wide area. The Air Troop went free-falling; the Boat Troop splashed around in the swamps which were ideal for their purposes; the Mobility Troop drove around the Kalahari desert; and the rest of us went climbing in the Tsodilo Hills. That was my first trip abroad with the Squadron, and the fact we lost one of our guys within days brought home to me how dangerous and close to the mark our training was.

On our first evening in the country, before the troops split up, we had a brief on snakes from an African called Lazarus who'd been a sergeant in the police force. Later we realised what a bullshitter he was when he told us that his skin had originally been as white as ours, and had gone black from exposure to the sun. But when he first started releasing snakes from a sack to show us the various kinds which we might come across, we didn't know what to make of him.

He brought out a spitting cobra, holding it by the throat, and said that if you gripped it like that, it couldn't spit. 'Watch that bloody thing,' growled the SQMS, 'because if it does spit, and the stuff gets in your eyes, you'll have problems.' Sure enough, as Lazarus came past me the cobra spat, and although I closed my eyes, some spit landed on my arm and the side of my face. I wiped it off immediately, but wherever a drop had touched it took the pigment out of my skin. I was left with pale dots all over my cheek, and a patch the shape of the British Isles on one arm.

As a grand finale Lazarus produced an Egyptian cobra – a massive creature, twelve or thirteen feet long – which he set down on the ground. We were gathered round in a circle, and he said, 'Stand still, and let it go through your legs.' All was well until one guy moved – whereupon the cobra chased him. The man ran up on to a water bowser, and the snake wrapped itself round one of the axles, baring its enormous fangs as Lazarus heaved on its tail, trying to drag it off. In the end he got it back into his sack, but it was amazing that none of us had been bitten.

After that little introduction, our troop moved up to the Tsodilo Hills. Our camp was maybe half an hour's walk from the base of the biggest hill – an outcrop of bare, blue-grey rock which rose abruptly in tiers out of a dead-flat plain. From a distance the hill looked strange but not particularly impressive: only when we got closer did we realise that some of the tiers, which went up in vertical rock faces, were 100 or 200 feet high.

In the evening, as we sat round the fire, one of the guys said, 'I'm going out shooting – does anyone fancy coming?' Nobody could be bothered. So he went out on his own, and presently he came back with a small, furry animal, about the size of a hare. A few Botswanan soldiers had been attached to us for training, and when he offered the animal to them, there was a big commotion. The Botswanans were with some Bushmen, who became very agitated. The little men raised a hubbub, rushed about and began lighting more fires. Via the Botswanans, the message came back to us strongly that we shouldn't kill any more animals as it was dangerous, and would provoke the spirits who lived on the mountain.

Next morning we had a brief on the climb. Ian, our mountain guide, had worked out that rain was probably going to come in during the afternoon, so he told everybody to be off the rock by midday. Then he split us into climbing pairs, and sent us off. I was with Ian himself, and when we reached the first of the rock faces, he began showing me how to use various aids, particularly devices called friends, which expand and lock themselves in position when you hammer them into crevices. The mountain rose in a series of well-defined vertical faces and horizontal ledges, almost as sharp as a huge staircase.

Joe Farragher – a staff sergeant and a big, heavy man of about 17 stone, strong as an ox – went off climbing with a guy called Trev, who soon stepped off a rock, and, although he only fell a couple of feet, put his back out, so that he had to be carried all the way back to camp. As a replacement, Joe got the young Rupert to go climbing with him. By the time he left for his second attempt, it was already 11a.m., and he shouldn't really have returned to the mountain, because it was a good half an hour's walk from the camp, and everyone had been told to be off it by twelve.

Anyway, Ian and I were climbing away when suddenly we heard yells from round the corner. It was the officer, shouting down that there'd been an accident. Ian got both of us down on to a ledge, and we hurried round, to find Joe lying on the rock, having fallen about 75 feet. We ran up to him, and I tried breathing into his mouth to give him CPR – but there was frothy red blood coming out of his mouth, and when I touched the back of his head under his climbing helmet, it felt like a broken eggshell. He was obviously dead, so we shouted down to some others to send for the Alouette helicopter, which was on stand-by.

Soon the chopper came in – but further dramas began immediately. The ledge was too narrow for it to land, and the face of the mountain was so steep that the pilot had difficulty hovering close enough for a doctor to abseil down. The heli began rocking, so that the doctor was swinging in and out – if he'd missed the ledge, he'd have gone down a couple of hundred feet. The pilot began making energetic cutting motions, telling the loadie to sever the rope – but in the end the doctor got down safely.

After he'd pronounced Joe dead, we trussed his body into an old stretcher and prepared to lower it down the face. The drop was so long that we had to tie two ropes together, and Ian asked me to abseil down first, to make sure that we could get our figure-of-eight linking device past the knot. I was feeling quite shocked, but also excited to be involved in a real rescue. As I went over the edge, I wasn't sure where I was going to end up, but luckily it turned out that the knot was level with another flat ledge, so that passing it was easy.

It should have taken no more than half an hour to get Joe down; but everything seemed to go wrong. Ropes kept getting snagged or broken, and several times the body nearly fell out of the stretcher. We had to keep tying him back in, and it was awful to see a person we had known and liked trussed up like a stuffed chicken. Like the rest of us he was wearing shorts and a T-shirt, and by the time we got him down he was in a mess, with his skin all scraped. Altogether we struggled for eight hours, and darkness was falling when we reached the plain.

That evening we were all pretty subdued, and we didn't feel any better next day, when the Alouette which flew the body out broke down. Then we heard that while the guys from the Air Troop had been free-falling, the engines of their C-130 had caught fire, and the aircraft had had to land.

We were starting to wonder whether there was some jinx on the exercise when one of the Air Troop produced a paperback copy of the South African explorer Laurens van der Post's book about the Bushmen, *The Lost World of the Kalahari.* 'Listen to this,' he said, and he read out some passages describing how the author had come to this very area, maybe forty years before, in search of Bushmen. When members of his party killed an antelope and a warthog, everything went belly-up: wild bees attacked the camp at sunrise – not once, but every morning – even though it was highly unusual for them to fly at that time of day; when the expedition's cameraman tried to film some ancient cave paintings, the movie-camera repeatedly broke down; their tape-recorder also ceased to function. In the end van der Post became so scared that he decided to leave the area immediately.

First, though, he got his guide, Samutchoso, to communicate with the spirits. After the man had gone into a trance, the answer came back: 'The spirits of the hills are very angry with you, so angry that if they had not known your intention in coming here was pure, they would long since have killed you. They are angry because you have come here with blood on your hands . . .'

To win forgiveness, van der Post wrote a letter addressed to 'The Spirits, The Tsodilo Hills', in which he humbly begged pardon. As 'an act of contrition' he promised to bury the note at the base of the great cave painting which he had found. He then got all his companions to sign the letter, sealed it in an envelope, and placed it in a lime-juice bottle, which he duly buried in the cave. Thereafter he had no more trouble: his Land-Rovers started without difficulty, and the expedition moved on.

His experience sounded uncannily like our own, and the death of that one animal seemed to have put us under the same spell. We decided to go and look for the cave, and I walked round the mountain with one other guy, Merv. We found the place easily enough – at least, we found *a* cave, in which there were primitive red paintings of animals on the walls. I thought it looked a bit creepy, and didn't fancy walking in; but Merv decided it was all right – so we went in, and at the back we found a green bottle, corked up, with a piece of paper inside.

Back at the camp, we reported on what we'd found. People made a few jokes, but Harry (the Everest climber, who had spent a lot of time in mountains, and felt sympathy for the people who lived in them) suggested that we should write a note of our own, apologising for the death of the animal, put it in another bottle, and leave it in the cave.

When our message was ready, Merv and I went back to the cave with it. The old bottle was still there – but something very strange had happened. Although the cork was still in place, the paper inside had been shredded, as if by a hamster. Of course we were disconcerted. Then we thought that some of our own guys must have been pissing around. Anyway, we left our bottle beside the first one, and went back to the camp – only to find that nobody else had been near the cave.

Whatever had happened, the atmosphere was becoming tense. That night, as we sat round the fire, the sergeant in charge announced that we would abandon the climbing equipment that was still on the mountain: if anyone else wanted it, they could have it. But in the morning we went up to look at it again, and when we studied the place where Joe had fallen, things somehow didn't look right. There seemed to be no reason for the friends to have pulled out, as they had, all three at once; so we sent for Ian, the expert. He came up, and also thought there was something wrong; he agreed that the friends should never have come out.

During the recovery of Joe's body, the sergeant had come down and told me to take pictures of the body and the ropes. I got some photos, took the film out and handed it over. Now, with Ian there, I took more pictures of the ropes.

By then everyone was becoming nervous. The place had an unpleasant atmosphere; we felt as though we were being watched. Even off the mountain, mishaps kept occurring. A herd of goats came through the camp and wrecked the tents, knocking everything over and chewing up our clothes. One of the Mobility Troop fell off his motorbike and broke his collarbone. The Boat Troop was attacked by a hippo, which bit off one of the twin tails of a Gemini inflatable. The bang scared the animal off, but the boat was finished. When the RAF flew a Hercules over the top of the mountain and tried to throw out a wreath for Joe, it blew back into the aircraft. So they flew over again, and twice more it came back in. You could, at a stretch, explain that in terms of air turbulence, but it seemed uncanny, and only when they were three or four miles from the mountain did the wreath finally stay out and float away.

All this could have been coincidence – but there was no doubt that the Bushmen believe in the power of the mountain spirits, and by the end of the exercise I was well on the way to doing the same. Though not religious, I appreciated for the first time the sheer strength of some people's beliefs, and began to feel that there were forces at work which we Europeans simply didn't understand. Through the Botswanan soldiers, the Bushmen kept sending us the message. 'Whatever you do, don't kill anything else.' We didn't tell them about our own bottle.

One of the guys came with me to consult a witch doctor in the nearby village and find out what fate had in store for us. After we'd dropped a few boxes of rations in payment, a skinny, middle-aged man, wearing nothing but a loincloth, came out of his mud hut carrying a small leather bag. Having swept a patch of earth clear with one hand, he tipped six or eight bones on to it, and sat staring at them for fully half a minute, muttering to himself. Through the Botswanan who was with us, the message came back that we had nothing more to worry about, and we started to feel happier.

With our squadron exercise finished, we drove away, and as I looked out of the back of the Land-Rover at the mountain, I still had the feeling that there was something there, watching us, glad to see us go. We were told not to mention the story back in

Hereford, for the sake of Joe's family. But that was the first incident for me in which I'd seen someone killed, and it stuck in
my mind for ever.

Remembering Africa helped pass the day. But cold, hunger,
thirst and the pain of lying on rock continually reminded me I
was in Iraq. Somehow the hours dragged by. At about five in
the afternoon I moved up to the top edge of the mound and lay
there gazing into the distance. Ahead of me, in the direction I
needed to go, ridges of bare rock rose one behind the other,
greyer and greyer as they stretched to the horizon. Close at
hand the ground was rolling, and on my left hills climbed
steeply towards a high plateau. Looking west, I could see an old
stone fort perched on one of the ridges running up from the
river valley; it stood in an elevated position, and obviously commanded phenomenal views. I worried slightly that it might be a
manned border post, but somehow the sight of that man-made
structure gave me a lift. The fort made a sudden contrast to the
barren wastes of the desert.

I realised that, as I grew weaker, I was covering the ground
more slowly, and not making the progress I expected. All the
same, after studying the map on and off during the day, I
reckoned that one good night's march would take me across the
frontier.

Then a simple event gave my morale a tremendous boost.
Never mind wind-noises: I really *did* hear a movement close at
hand. Once again goats came into view below me, and I held my
breath as they grazed along the contour. Then I saw their herder, working round the slope below me. Keeping well down
behind a rock, I watched him. The goats traversed the lower side
of the mound, away from me, but the man whipped round my
side of it, out of sight of the road. As I looked down, from about
a hundred metres away, he whipped up his dishdash, squatted
down and had a big old shit. Them, quick as a flash, he wiped
his arse with his left hand, gave it a brisk scrape on a rock, and
was off, running back to catch up with his flock.

Again I remembered how, back in the Squadron in Saudi, the
SSM had said to me, 'You'll never see an Arab have a shit.

They're that bloody shy about it. It's like seeing a rocking-horse shit. It just doesn't happen.' But here it was, happening right in front of me, and I lay there doubled up with silent laughter. 'Wait till I get out of here!' I thought. 'I'm going straight to the SSM to tell him what I've seen.'

Chapter Seven

Over The Border

The crapping Arab made my day. My morale had been down, but suddenly it was back up again. I couldn't stop laughing. A simple thing like that brought me right back on line. Once again I was full of anticipation, waiting for the time to be off.

Water was an urgent necessity. On the map I'd found a pumping station, and I felt I must have a good chance of getting a drink there. Surely a pumping station would have clean water coming out of it? Also I was buoyed up by the hope that I hadn't far to go. I really felt good. I said to myself, 'Eh – you're near the end here!'

This was my sixth night on the run, and in six nights and six days I'd had nothing to eat but two packets of biscuits. I was seriously dehydrated, and my feet were in ribbons. Even so, I felt pretty good, and had that sense of excitement mixed with apprehension that you get before a race or a big football match.

All I had to do was go down to the pumping station, get water, and carry on. By then I'd be only about ten kilometres from the border, and I would either cross it that same night, or reach it the next day.

The sight of the big hills in the distance made me think of the mountains of Wales, and I felt glad that I wasn't on ground as steep as the Brecon Beacons. Seeing how far I still had to go, I reckoned I'd never make it if the slopes were as tough as on Pen-y-fan or its neighbours. The desert might be harsh and hellishly dry, but at least it was reasonably level.

Things didn't work out as easily as I had hoped. I waited till dark and then started walking, but after only a hundred metres I came round a corner and found a small tented encampment to my right, obviously Bedouin, the nomadic herdsmen of the desert. Several dogs began barking, and through the kite-sight I could see two tents and one vehicle. But nobody came out for a look round, so I moved carefully away to the left, boxed the position and carried on.

As soon as I could, I swung down to the right, heading for the pumping station. I began to follow a line of telegraph-poles, which made navigation easy. But by then my feet had become really sore, and I had to keep stopping. I forced myself to do ten poles between each rest – ten lots of 150 metres, every one of them a major effort. According to my map, I was heading for a point at which the telegraph lines crossed a run of pylons. In due course I saw the pylons, coming in on my right. The wadis to my left were getting deeper, the sides steeper. Then I saw that instead of crossing the telegraph line, the pylons were set out parallel with it. The map wasn't making sense. So I said to myself, 'Bollocks – I'll just cut down to the right and head for the river.'

I peeled off the high ground and started on another bearing, confident that I'd hit the river sooner or later. As I went down I spotted a square, white building with a flat roof – the pump house. Coming close, I saw that the end facing me was open, and that a lot of pipes ran in and out of it. There was one main pipe, which I guessed was bringing water from the river, and several smaller ones.

By then I seemed to have grown careless. Whether or not it was the result of exhaustion, I don't know, but I was getting almost blasé. When you're that tired, it's all too easy to decide you'll do yourself a favour, sling your weapon over your shoulder instead of carrying it at the ready, and just saunter along. It's hardly a conscious decision to lower your standards and sink from very, very cautious to plain un-cautious; it's just something that happens gradually, without you noticing.

In any case, I walked straight into this place, lulled by the fact that it was silent and no machinery was working. I wasn't crash-banging about, but I didn't case the building as carefully as I might have. I even got my torch out and shone it around, because I could hear water dripping from a pipe. There it was – a steady drip, glistening in the torch beam.

Then, as I started getting my waterbottle out, I looked up and noticed a little, glassed-in hatchway on the back wall, with a red glow coming through it. Standing up to peer through, I saw a small electric fire with a bar glowing. Across from it lay an Arab, huddled down in a parka and sleeping bag, dossing on a camp bed. He was separated from me only by the thickness of the partition wall.

'Jesus Christ!' I thought. 'I've walked right into this. What the hell am I doing in a building anyway? I've dropped a bollock here.' I tiptoed out, without any water, and crept away. I tried to give myself a shake-up. 'Well, come on. Screw the nut.' It took a fright like that to wake me up. Things had started to seem too easy. I was making good progress. The border was only a short distance ahead. Nobody had challenged me for a while, and I'd started to switch off my defence mechanisms.

Getting over the fright, I moved on in a state of maximum alert. I held my weapon at the ready, and moved very slowly, scanning constantly. But I was hardly clear of the pump-house when, from high ground to my left, an air-raid siren went off. The noise started low, wound up to a high note, then swung down again. I hit the ground, thinking I had tripped some alarm, and lay there listening. Up and down went the metallic scream, swooping high and low. As I searched through the kite-sight, scanning the high ground, I made out anti-aircraft positions with gun barrels showing against the sky and black figures running round them. Then I saw tall, lattice-work towers, maybe a couple of hundred feet high, with what looked like cables slung between them. They seemed to be part of a communications network, and when I heard a drone start up, I thought the noise was coming from generators. I reckoned I'd walked into some sort of signals base. How the hell had I got in among all this without seeing anything? I certainly hadn't crossed any fence or other barrier, but somehow I had landed in the middle of the complex.

I knew I wasn't far from the river; vegetation started only a couple of hundred metres below me, and I thought that must mark the bank. I lay still until the all-clear went up – a noise like a Second World War siren – and everything quietened down. Whatever had caused the alert, it hadn't been me. When I reckoned it was safe to move, I got up and set off cautiously towards the river – only to see a group of five men walking. Back on the ground, I lay still until they had passed and disappeared.

Desperate though I was for water, I decided I had to get out of this thickly populated area. I had seen from the map that the river bent round, and thought I could hit it at another point not far ahead. But now I seemed to be in the middle of numerous scattered positions, and I had no option but to weave my way through them.

I crept onwards. To my front I saw something sticking up into the sky. Peering through the night-sight, I realised that it was the barrel of an anti-aircraft gun. As I looked down, I saw its circular emplacement right in front of me.

I pulled back, boxed it and moved on with every sense at full alert, threading my way forward between buildings which showed up here and there, pale in the moonlight. The place was extremely confusing, as it didn't seem to be laid out in any regular pattern; perhaps because the ground undulated so much, the dirt roads were neither straight nor at right-angles to each other, but coming in from all directions. On the ground, insulated land-lines were running all over the place. I thought of cutting them, to put local communications out of action, but knew that it would only draw attention to my presence. My map was far too large-scale to show details that would have been useful to me, and it no longer bore any relation to the ground.

At one point I could see a big cliff coming round in front of me, like the wall of a quarry – but of course there was no sign of that on my sheet.

Then – wonder of wonders – I reached a stream, with vegetation growing beside it. The water looked crystal clear, and the moonlight shone through it on to a white bottom. I thought, 'Jesus! I'm in luck here. A spring of clean water, flowing down into the Euphrates.' The whole place was so dangerous that I didn't go down for a drink; I just filled my bottles, popped them into my side-pouches, and moved quickly away.

Just as I left the stream I saw a file of seven men walk across my front, two or three paces apart. They were moving carefully, obviously on patrol. I froze, thinking, 'If they've got a dog, it's going to pick up my scent now.' But no – they disappeared, and I moved out on a bearing, going very slowly.

Again I came across an anti-aircraft position; this time I was so close that I peered over a wall of sandbags and saw three men lying on the ground in sleeping bags. For a moment I felt stunned – so close were they, right under my nose.

I seemed to be glued to the ground, staring. Then I felt a surge of fear, rising like acid from stomach to throat. The thought flashed into my mind that if I'd had a silenced weapon, I could at least have taken out anyone who spotted me. But nobody had: the men were all asleep, and within a few seconds I was creeping slowly away.

The next thing I hit was a vehicle laager point. Mounds of rock or minerals stood about, as if in a quarry. As I came creeping round the side, I walked right up to a Russian-made Gaz 80 jeep, only four or five yards away. Again, I got a bad fright. I couldn't see through the vehicle's windows; for all I knew it could have been full of people. For a few seconds I held my breath, 203 levelled, waiting for it to erupt.

When nothing happened, I turned to go back. I found I'd passed other vehicles and wandered into the middle of this park without seeing it. There were four-ton trucks with the canvas backs off, some with the canvas on, buses like ordinary coaches, double-deck car transporters – none of them had armour or weapons fitted, but this was a big collection of general transport. How I'd penetrated in among all these without noticing them, I couldn't explain. With hindsight, I realise that my concentration was coming and going, functioning at one moment but not the next. At the time I merely felt bewildered.

No matter how I'd got in there, I had to get out. Ahead of me were houses, with light coming from one window. Silhouetted figures were moving across it, and I could hear voices calling. I pushed off to the right, sometimes walking on tiptoe, often crawling on hands and knees.

I boxed that particular group of buildings; then ahead of me lay a single, big, whitewashed house, with a steeply-pitched roof and a pale-coloured wall maybe a hundred metres long running round its garden, and trees and shrubs sticking up over the top of it. To the left were two other buildings with lights shining from them and people outside, talking and shouting. I think there was also music playing on a radio.

The big house was easily the most impressive I'd seen, and by far the best maintained. High on one wall, beneath the apex of the roof, was a mural, an outsize portrait of Saddam Hussein. In the dark the colours were indistinct, but I could see that it was a carefully painted head-and-shoulders representation, which showed the dictator bare-headed, wearing military insignia on his epaulettes. The picture reminded me of the violent murals I'd seen in Northern Ireland, and for several seconds I stood looking at it, thinking, 'You're definitely in the wrong place now, mate!' What made me stand there gawping, I can't explain. Again, as in the pumping house, I seem to have grown blasé; it was almost as if I thought I'd become invisible, and didn't need to hide any longer. After surviving so many close encounters, I felt that nobody could see me, and I needn't be so careful any more.

Anyway, as I stood there, a man came round the corner, only fifty metres away – a dark figure, silhouetted against the light. Instinct, rather than any conscious decision, made me control myself. I felt a surge of fear, but instead of bolting I simply turned away and walked casually round the side of the house. In two steps I was out of sight. Then I ran. As I sprinted, I told myself, 'For God's sake, screw the nut. Take a grip.'

The man had seen me. I knew that. But he didn't seem to have followed up. Round the back of the building I spotted a ditch running along the side of the road. I dived into it, and as I lay there two family-type vehicles, like Espace vans, came rolling down. At their approach, the big house suddenly burst into life: security lights blazed on, and people poured out to meet the vehicles, both from the building and from pill boxes at the gates. A man got out of the vehicle, and four of the other guys body-guarded him into the house. As soon as the party was inside, the lights went off, so that the place was plunged into darkness again. It crossed my mind that this could be Saddam himself. The house was an impressive one, and well maintained. Was this his secret hideaway? Then I realised that he would never draw attention to himself by having his own portrait on the wall; more likely, this was the home of the local governor, or some similar official.

The whole incident took only a few seconds, and it left me thinking, 'What the hell is this?' I seemed to have strayed into a nightmare, with unexplained people and events popping up all over the place. I saw that I must have walked right past the sentries in the pill boxes. Again I realised how dangerously I was switching off. In my head I began having a conversation with myself.

'I don't believe I did that.'

'You bloody did! Switch back on.'

By this time I'd been in this complex – whatever it was – for five hours, trying to find my way out. Time was cracking on. According to my route plan, I should already have been on the border. Something had gone far wrong with my map-reading, and I was faced by the prospect of having to lie up without food for yet another day. Oddly enough, I never felt desperate with hunger, I never got pains in the stomach. My biggest worry was that I was gradually growing weaker – less able to walk, less able to concentrate.

My immediate plan was to creep back up to the road and go somewhere beyond it, clear of the buildings, so that I could sneak another look at the map; but before I could move, I heard footsteps and voices coming down the path towards me. By the sound, there were two men at least. I was crouching in a corner beside a mound, without cover, and they were coming right on top of me.

My survival instinct took over – instinct sharpened by years of training. Whoever these guys were, it was going to be them or me. To fire a shot in that position would have been fatal, so I quietly laid my 203 down and got my knife open in my right hand. As the first man came level with me I grabbed him, stuck him in the neck and ripped his throat out. He went down without a sound. When the second man saw me, his eyes widened in terror and he began to run. But somehow, with a surge of adrenalin, I flew after him, jumped on him and brought him down with my legs locked round his hips. I got one arm round his neck in a judo hold and stretched his chin up. There was a muffled crack, and he died instantaneously.

When I got back to the first, he was still quivering. I could feel hot, sticky blood all down my front. There hadn't been a sound. Now I had two bodies to dispose of. To leave them where they were would advertise my presence to all and sundry, but if they just went missing, the chances were that nobody would raise the alarm for a few hours at least.

Luckily the river was less than a hundred metres off, and a gentle slope covered by small, loose rocks led down to it. Luckier still, the bank was screened by a stand of tall grass. Each body made a scraping, rattling noise as I dragged it over the rocks; but I got both to the edge of the water, one at a time, without interruption. Then I loaded them up with stones inside their shirts, dragged them into the water and let them go.

Knowing my bottles were full, I didn't bother to drink any of the dirty water in the river. The encounter had roused me to a high state of alert, and it had all taken an hour. Now my urgent need was to clear the complex before daylight.

Moving silently, I worked my way up to a road that ran along the contour. Under it I found a culvert, and I thought I'd crawl into it for a look at my map; but as I came to the end of the tunnel, I heard a kind of growling. Thinking there must be some animal under the road, I tiptoed forward and peered into the pitch darkness. I couldn't see a thing. Suddenly I diagnosed the source of the noise: it was some local, snoring. I felt slightly annoyed that an Arab had already picked the retreat I fancied. Probably he was a soldier, and supposed to be on stag. Lucky for me, then, that he'd decided to have a kip. Creeping back out, I climbed up on the side of the road and crossed over.

As I did that, I heard a shout from down by the houses where I'd heard people talking. I didn't think the yell had anything to do with me, but I ran across the road, made about fifty metres into the rocks and dropped down. A man came running up the road, which was raised about six feet above the ground. He stopped right opposite me and stood staring in my direction. Evidently he couldn't see anything, and he ran back. A moment later, a blacked-out land-cruiser roared past, its engine screaming in second gear, straight up the road to the junction with the MSR, and disappeared.

For nearly half an hour I lay still, letting things settle. After getting that fright, and the violent expenditure of energy, reaction set in and I felt drained of strength. But I couldn't stay where I was, so I began to work my way round the rocks. On my left was a run of chain-link fencing, quite high. So that side of the complex was protected, anyway.

Coming to a corner of the barrier, I went up on to the MSR and crossed over. As I did so, I looked to my left and saw three guys manning a vehicle control point on the junction of the road coming up from the complex. Dodging back up a wadi, I peeped over the side and saw a line of anti-aircraft positions facing towards the Syrian border.

I pulled back again, stuck. The ground there was almost flat. I couldn't go forward, and I couldn't go back. Dawn was approaching. My only possible refuge was another of the culverts under the road. I found three tunnels, each about the diameter of a forty-five gallon drum and maybe 10 metres long. The first looked clean, and I thought that in daylight anybody looking in one end would see straight through it. The second seemed to be full of dead bushes and rubbish, so I crawled in and lay down.

In the confined space, I realised how badly I was stinking. But my surroundings were no better: there was a powerful stench of decomposing rubbish and excrement.

I was desperate for a drink, and looking forward to one with incredible anticipation. But when I went to compress the plastic clip that held the buckle on my webbing pouch, I found that my fingers were so sore and clumsy that I could scarcely manage the simple task. Gasping with pain, I used all my strength to force the clips together. Then came a horrendous disappointment. Bringing out one bottle at last, I opened it and raised it to my lips – but the first mouthful made me gasp and choke. Poison! The water tasted vicious and metallic, as if it was full of acid. I spat it straight out, but the inside of my mouth had gone dry, and I was left with a burning sensation all over my tongue and gums. I whipped out my compass-mirror, pointed the torch-beam into my mouth and looked round it. Everything seemed all right, so I took another sip, but it was just the same. I remembered that when Stan had collapsed during the first night on the run I'd put rehydrate into my bottles, to bring him round, and I wondered if the remains of it had somehow gone off. Then I tried the second bottle, and found it exactly the same. I couldn't make out what the hell had gone wrong. Whatever the problem, the water was undrinkable, and I emptied the bottles out.

'Now I *am* fucked.' I thought. I was in a really bad state. It was eight days since I'd had a hot meal, two days and a night since I'd had a drink. My tongue was completely dry; it felt like a piece of old leather stuck in the back of my throat. My teeth had all come loose; if I closed my mouth and sucked hard, I could taste blood coming from my shrunken gums. I knew my feet were in bits, but I didn't dare take my boots off, because I feared I'd never get them on again. As for my hands – I could see and smell them all too well. The thin leather of my gloves had cracked and split, from being repeatedly soaked and dried out again, so that my fingers hadn't had much protection. I'd lost most of the feeling in the tips, and I seemed to have got dirt pushed deep under my nails, so that infection had set in. Whenever I squeezed a nail, pus came out, and this stench was repulsive.

With my extremities suppurating like that, I wondered what internal damage I might be suffering, and could only hope that no permanent harm would be done. With the complete lack of food, I'd had no bowel movement since going on the run, and I couldn't remember when I'd last wanted to pee. I yearned for food, of course, but more for drink – and when I did think about food, it was sweet, slushy things that I craved. If ever I found myself back among rations packs, I would rip into the pears in syrup, ice-cream and chocolate sauce.

I felt very frightened. First and most obvious was the danger of being captured – the fear of torture, and of giving away secrets that might betray other guys from the Regiment. Almost worse, though, was the fact that I could see and feel my body going down so fast. If I didn't reach the border soon, I would be too weak to carry on.

Twisting round in the cramped space of the drain, I got out my map and tried for the hundredth time to work out where I was. It was now the morning of Wednesday 30 January. What options were left to me? Already light was coming up, and whatever happened, I was stuck in the culvert for that day. When dark fell again, I could try to sneak back down to the river, cross over and go along the other side – but it seemed a far-fetched hope. In any case, I'd built up a deep dread of going anywhere near the river. Every time I'd tried it, something had gone wrong; one more attempt, and I might easily be captured. At the very least, I still had thirty kilometres to go. How long could I hold out? I just couldn't tell what my body was still capable of.

First, I somehow had to get through eleven hours of daylight – eleven hours, when every waking minute now was agony. At least I was out of the wind, and less cold, so that I could drop off to sleep. I'd go straight off and be fast asleep, and start dreaming, usually about the squadron. I was with the rest of the guys.

145

They were all round me, talking and laughing, getting ready to go. We didn't seem to be in any particular place – unless it was the actual place I was in – but their presence was completely real. Then suddenly, maybe ten minutes later, I'd wake up, shuddering violently, hoping against hope that my mates were still there, and fully expecting that they would be. The dream had been so strong that I felt certain I'd find people lying near me, moving around, and that we were all together. Then I'd open my eyes and realise that I was alone in the culvert with no one to talk to. It was a horrible let-down.

Sometimes, also, I was at home in England with my family. Every time I fell asleep, the hallucinations grew more vivid. The most worrying feature was that I'd become confused between Jan – my wife – and Susan – the woman I was engaged to for so long. I kept trying to imagine Jan's face, but the awful thing was that I couldn't remember what it looked like. I was aware that I should remember her perfectly well, but I just couldn't see her, and I couldn't have described her to anyone else. I knew that she had blonde hair, but that was all. It was terrible to be aware that my own mind was going.

Instead of Jan, I was seeing Susan all the time. I saw her sitting on a fence, or in our house at Rowlands Gill. When I saw little Sarah, it was on Susan's knee that she was sitting.

I saw our home at Christmas, with all the decorations up – and the confusing thing was that this part of the dream reflected reality, not fantasy. The three of us had been sitting at the round table in the living room, and Jan had said, 'Chris, will you switch the Christmas tree lights on?' But little Sarah had jumped up and toddled across, saying, 'No, Daddy, I'll do it' – and she went over and flicked the switch. Now, in the filthy culvert, I saw the whole scene again and heard her baby voice saying, 'Daddy, I'll do it.'

For hours I lay there, drifting in and out of consciousness. At one point I suddenly found myself thinking of the Killing House – the special building at Hereford which the counter-terrorist team uses for a lot of its training. The walls are hung with sheets of rubber – so that live bullets can be fired without danger of ricochets – increasing the sense of claustrophobia. Visiting VIPs are often taken into the Killing House for demonstrations, which usually begin with pistol shooting. My speciality was always these pistol demos, in which I would fire at a 'Hun's Head' target (like a man wearing a German helmet) while rolling around the floor – and expect not just to hit the target, but to put all the rounds through the same hole.

Next, visitors are usually taken into another room and placed in one corner, behind white tape. Touching the tape, on the outside, would be one figure target. Next to that would be a live man – described as the hostage – sitting at a desk, and on his other side, a second figure target. The soldier in charge of the demo stands behind the hostage, commentating, and explaining that members of the SP team are planning to snatch him to safety.

One day the visiting VIP was none other than the Prime Minister, Margaret Thatcher, who was shepherded into the corner behind the tape, together with two bodyguards. The team commander gave his usual spiel, waffling on about the SAS until, with deceptive lack of emphasis, he said, 'Our success depends on three factors, which happen to have the same initials as the Regiment: Speed, Aggression and Surprise.'

On the word 'surprise' a loud explosion blasted off outside the door, simulating the demolition of the hinges. Two men in black ran in, armed with MP5s. Each put a burst of live rounds through one of the targets, so close to the visitors that they could feel the wind of the bullets. A third man dashed in, seized the hostage and dragged him away so quickly that, in the violent storm of noise, nobody noticed he had gone. In seconds the raid was over – and the only visitor still on her feet was the Prime Minister. Both bodyguards had hit the deck. As the smoke was clearing, she turned to them and said, 'What *are* you doing? For God's sake stand up!'

It must have been my claustrophobic surroundings in the culvert that brought back the scene so clearly. Yet another star visitor was the Princess of Wales, who came down with Prince Charles not long after they had been married. Her hair was longer then, and although she dressed up in black to take part in an assault on what was known as the old embassy building, she declined to put on a respirator or pull her hood into position.

As she came out after the attack, one of the guys asked, 'How did you find that?'

147

'It was great,' she replied, 'but I couldn't understand why someone kept hitting me on the back of the head.'

'You will when you look in the mirror,' he told her. What she didn't realise was that her hair had caught fire, and her neighbour had been beating out the flames. It was this slight setback that accounted for the much shorter hairstyle that she adopted for her next official trip.

Such memories helped a few minutes go by. But all too soon I was back in the reality of the drain. I wasn't worried by the occasional rumble of a car going past above me, but soon I began to hear other movement: scurrying, scuffling noises, as if troops were running around. I thought, 'Here we go. The next thing is going be somebody at either end of this fucking culvert, and I'll be caught like a rat in a drainpipe.'

Every time I moved, dust rose around me and filled the tunnel, half choking me and making my tongue cleave to the back of my throat even more stickily. From the scrabbling, it sounded as though squaddies' boots were moving everywhere. I reckoned that the bodies had been discovered, the alarm had gone up, and that a search-party was closing in on me.

Most of the noise was coming from the end towards which my feet were pointing. I tried to turn my 203 to face the disturbance, but the drain was too narrow and I couldn't bring the weapon to bear. Now was the moment I needed a pistol, or better still a silenced one.

The scrabbling noise came closer. I tensed myself, certain that a man would stick his head into the end of the pipe at any second. If he did, my only option would be to try to scuttle out the other end. But what did the intruder turn out to be? A frigging goat!

A herd was being driven up the side of the road. I watched their legs move steadily past, and the scrabble of their feet on rocks, echoing through the tunnel, sounded like a whole company of squaddies on the move. Again I was terrified that they might have a dog with them; if they did, it would surely get my scent.

Tortured by thirst, by noises close at hand, by phantom scenes from home, I somehow stuck out the day. That was the lowest point of my whole escape. I'd lost so much weight that lying down became ever more agonising. Whatever attitude I adopted, bones seemed to be sticking out, with no padding to cover them, and every five or six minutes I'd be in such discomfort that I'd have to turn over. Spine, hips, ribs, knees, elbows, shoulders – everything hurt, and I was developing sores all over. I kept telling myself, 'You've got to clear that border tonight, whatever happens.' But first I somehow had to escape from the trap in which I'd landed myself – and if the night turned out clear again, I didn't see how I was going to avoid the VCP.

Eventually darkness fell, and when I poked my head out of the end of the culvert, my morale took a lift again. Until then the nights had been clear, but this one was black as pitch, with the sky full of storm clouds that looked so threatening I even thought it might rain. The very idea of moisture was exciting. If rain did come, and I turned up my face, at least my parched mouth would get some refreshment. Maybe I could even collect water by spreading out my map case.

I crept out of the culvert. The night was so dark that when I looked in the direction of the VCP, I couldn't make it out. Moving closer, I found that the guards were still standing there, so I eased away until I could no longer see them, and when I was half-way between them and the anti-aircraft positions, I started walking at full speed.

Thank God for the darkness. Behind me nobody moved, and I got clean away. I'd been going for nearly two hours, parallel with a road, when all of a sudden a blinding flash split the darkness. Convinced I'd walked into ambush lights, I flung myself down; but then from behind me came a heavy explosion, and I realised that an air-raid was going in on the installation I'd just left. The same thing happened twice more: a flash, and a few seconds later a really big, deep *boom*. I kept thinking, 'If this hadn't been a dark night, that's where I'd still be.' What effect the bombs were having I couldn't tell, but the explosions sounded colossal, and I thanked my lucky stars that I'd been able to move on.

Occasionally, far away to my left, I saw anti-aircraft fire going up into the sky, and I guessed it must be coming from the airfields designated H1 and H2. No sound carried over that distance, so the tracer arched up in perfect silence – but at least it meant that the bases were under Coalition attack. I knew that

'A' and 'D' Squadrons were operating in that area, and hoped it was they who were hammering the Iraqis.

I knew from the map that the Iraqi town of Krabilah should be coming up on my right. Krabilah lay on the border, and there was a Syrian town beyond the frontier. The thought of it kept me going, but only just. By now my feet were so bad that whenever I sat down for a rest they went from numb to excruciating. Upright, I couldn't feel them much; sitting, I thought they were going to burst. Several times I sat there thinking, 'Fucking hell! I can't take much more of this.' Then the pain would ease off, and I had a few minutes of bliss, with nothing hurting.

The worst bit came whenever I stood up again, and the pain just exploded. Starting off, I couldn't help gasping with the sheer agony. I had to shuffle my boots along the ground like some old comic, and I kept thinking, 'If anyone sees me, doddering along like this, I'll look a right idiot.' It wasn't till I'd taken about ten paces that my feet seemed to go numb again, and I could walk out. Occasionally I'd hit a sharp stone or rock – and boy, was that sore.

Never in my life had I been so exhausted. Often on selection and afterwards I thought I had pushed myself to my limit – but this was something else. I had sunk to an altogether different plane of tiredness and debilitation. The temptation to stop and rest was almost irresistible, but I knew that if I did I would never reach the border before my body gave out.

Helping me, I'm sure, were the years of training that I'd put in: not just the physical fitness which I'd built up, but the mental toughness, which life in the SAS had given me. Always competing with other guys as good as or better than myself, always determined to come out on top, I had learnt to push myself beyond what seemed to be possible. I was used to being hurt, and knew that I simply had to walk through the pain.

I couldn't fall back on religious belief to sustain me, because I didn't have any. As a child I'd gone to Sunday school, but only because someone would read us a story and we played games. In school proper I'd had religion thrown down my neck until I was sick of it; but as an adult I found I was unable to believe in God, seeing how much misery and disease and poverty there are in the world. At the same time, I think that humans do need to believe in something or someone. When you're in trouble you'll always cry for somebody – whether it's God, your mother or your wife. In those dire straits I believed in my wife and child – and the person who dragged me out of it was Sarah. Without warning, the hallucinations began again. Suddenly, out in the middle of the black Iraqi night, there she was, walking in front of me, dressed in the purply-blue top and yellow bottoms, all covered in dots, that she'd worn at Christmas. The image I had of her, and the angle from which I could see her, were exactly the same as they'd been in Hereford. As I hobbled over the rocks and gravel, she somehow kept ahead of me, toddling on, leading the way through the dark. There seemed to have been a complete reversal of roles. Now she was the one who had confidence; I was the one who was afraid. Time and time again I heard her say, 'Daddy, do it.' Her voice was so clear that I thought I could pick her up in my arms. Time and time again I reached out to touch her. I felt that if I could catch hold of her hand, she would pull me out of trouble. Throughout that endless night I was on the verge of tears when I found I could not reach her. And yet, even when I realised she was not there, I knew that it was only the thought of her, and my need to see her again, that were keeping me going.

Towards the end I was stopping and resting on my feet. Because they were so agonising if I sat down, I took to reading my map standing up – which was not a good idea, as my torch was up in the air instead of close to the ground. I'd walk until I was really knackered, then prop myself against something so that I kept the pressure on my feet.

I was so far gone that when I reached some houses I was on the point of giving in. 'If only I were in England!' I thought. 'There'd be milk bottles standing on the doorstep, and a milk-float coming past in the morning.' How many bottles of milk could I have drunk straight down?

I watched the houses for a while. They were only small places, but I'd find water in them, for sure, and food. Suddenly I decided I'd had enough. 'Bollocks to it,' I thought. 'I'll go in, and if I have to, I'll do the people in there. I'll get something to drink and take their vehicle.'

I slid along one side of the nearest house, and found a window in the wall. It had iron bars down it, with a hessian curtain inside. Music was being played inside the room, and a candle or oil-lamp was flickering. I went past the window and reached the front of the building. Outside the door stood a car. 'Now!' I thought. 'Just let the keys be in it!' As I came round the corner I looked down, and there was a blasted dog, lying outside the door. The moment I saw it, it saw me and went berserk, barking frantically. Back I scuttled, along the side of the house, and away off into the wadis. The dog came out, and more dogs from the other buildings joined it. They followed me for about a hundred metres, barking like lunatics, then stopped. Oh for Turbo, I thought. He'd sort them.

Up in the wadis, I came to a railway line, scrabbled under it through a culvert, and was back in the desert. With a jolt I realised that this must be the same railway that Stan and I had crossed all those nights earlier. If only we'd tabbed straight along it, we'd have been out of Iraq days ago.

Galvanised by my latest fright, I kept walking, walking, walking. According to my calculations, I should have been passing Krabilah on my right, but there was no sign of the town. What I didn't realise was that every house had been blacked out because of the war, and that I had already gone clean by the place in the dark.

I reached a refuse heap, where loads of burnt-out old cans had been dumped in the desert, and sat down among them to do yet another map-study. I couldn't work things out. Where was the town, and where was the communications tower which the map marked? Where, above all, was the bloody border?

I started walking again, on the bearing, and as I came over a rise I saw three small buildings to my front. With the naked eye I could just make them out: three square bulks, blacked out. But when I looked through the kite-sight, I saw chinks of light escaping between the tops of the walls and the roofs. As I sat watching, one person came out, walked round behind, re-appeared and went back indoors. I was so desperate for water that I went straight towards the houses. Again, I was prepared to take out one of the inhabitants if need be. I was only fifty metres away when I checked through the kite-sight again and realised that the buildings were not houses at all, but sand-bagged sangars with wriggly tin roofs. They formed some sort of command post, and were undoubtedly full of squaddies. Pulling slowly back, I went round the side and, sure enough, came on a battery of four anti-aircraft positions.

If I'd walked up and opened one of the doors, I'd almost certainly have been captured. Once more the fright got my adrenalin going and revived me.

On I stumbled for another hour. My dehydration was making me choke and gag. My throat seemed to have gone solid, and when I scraped my tongue, white fur came off it. I felt myself growing weaker by the minute. My 203 might have been made of lead, such a burden had it become, so much of the strength had ebbed from my arms. My legs had lost their spring and grown stiff and clumsy. My ability to think clearly had dwindled away.

At last I came to a point from which I could see the lights of a town, far out on the horizon. Something seemed to be wrong. Surely that couldn't be Krabilah, still such a distance off? My heart sank: surely the border couldn't still be that far? Or was the glow I could see that of Abu Kamal, the first town inside Syria, some twenty kilometres to the west? If so, where the hell was Krabilah? According to the map, Krabilah had a communications tower, but Abu Kamal didn't. The far-off town *did* have a bright red light flashing, as if from a tower – and that made me all the more certain that the place in the distance was Krabilah.

Morale plummeted once more. Like my body, my mind was losing its grip. What I *could* make out was some kind of straight black line, running all the way across my front. Off to my left I could see a mound with a big command post on it, sprouting masts. Closer to me were a few buildings, blacked out, but not looking like a town.

I sat down some 500 metres short of the black line and studied the set-up through the kite-sight. Things didn't add up. With Krabilah so far ahead, this could hardly be the border. Yet it looked like one. I wondered whether it was some inner frontier-line which the Iraqis had built because of the war, to keep people back from the border itself. Suddenly I thought of the Int guy back at Al Jouf, unable to tell what the border looked like. 'What an arsehole!' I thought. 'He should have known. That's his fucking job.'

Whatever this line ahead of me might be, all I wanted to do was get across it. I was gripped by a terrific sense of urgency, but I forced myself to hold back, sit down and observe it. 'This is where you're going to stumble if you don't watch out,' I told myself. 'This is where you'll fall down. Take time over it.'

There I sat, shivering, watching, waiting. A vehicle came out of the command post and drove down along the line – an open-backed land-cruiser. Directly opposite my vantage-point two men emerged from an observation-post, walked up to the car, spoke to the driver, jumped in, and drove off to the right. It looked as if the Iraqis were putting out roving observers to keep an eye on the border. I couldn't tell whether this was routine, or whether they suspected that enemy soldiers were in the area; but after a few minutes I decided that the coast was clear, and I had to move.

At long last I came down to the black line. Creeping cautiously towards it, I found it was a barrier of barbed wire: three coils in the bottom row, two on top of them, and one on top of that. Having no pliers to cut with, I tried to squeeze my way through the coils, but that proved impossible: barbs hooked into my clothes and skin and held me fast. I unhooked myself with difficulty, and decided that the only way to go was over the top. Luckily the builders had made the elementary mistake, every twenty-five metres, of putting in three posts close to each other and linking them together with barbed wire. Obviously the idea was to brace the barrier, but the posts created a kind of bridge across the middle of the coils. I took off my webbing and threw it over, then went up and over myself, sustaining a few lacerations but nothing serious.

Still I could not believe I was clear of Iraq. The barrier seemed so insignificant that I thought it must only be marking some false or inner border, and that I would come to the true frontier some distance further on. The real thing, I thought, would be a big anti-tank berm, constructed so that vehicles could not drive across. Maybe this was why I had no feeling of elation; for days I had been thinking that, if I did manage to cross the frontier, it would be the climax of my journey, but now I felt nothing except utter exhaustion.

With my webbing back in place, I set off yet again on the same bearing. Never in my life, before or since, have I pushed myself so hard. I think I was brain-dead that night, walking in neutral, moving automatically, stumbling grimly onwards. Once or twice Sarah returned to keep me company and lead me, but mostly I dragged myself on without hearing, seeing or thinking.

In the end I could go no further. I simply had to sit down and rest. I took my weapon off my shoulder, and just as I was lifting the night-sight from where it hung round my neck, I seemed to click my head, and felt what I can only describe as a huge electric shock. I heard a noise like a ferocious short-circuit – *krrrrrrrk* – and when I looked down at my hands, there was a big white flash.

The next thing I knew I was sitting in the same place, but I couldn't tell if I had been asleep, or unconscious, or what. I was aware that time had passed, but had no idea how much. Nor did I know what had happened to me. But it was a weird feeling, to have been out of the world for a while.

I got my kit back on and stood up. This time my feet were real torture, and I was barely able to totter forwards until they went numb again.

It was still dark. The night seemed very long. Nothing for it but to keep going. Was I in Syria or Iraq? Couldn't tell. Better steer clear of the odd house, then, because every one had a dog. What would I do when it got light? Didn't know. Couldn't think. Should be in Syria.

I woke up a bit when I found I was crossing vehicle tracks – many wheel marks imprinted in dry mud. Then after a while I thought I heard something behind me. As I turned to look, the same phenomenon hit me again: a big crack of static in the head and a blinding flash. This time I woke up on the ground, face-down, and I said to myself, 'Jesus! You picked a stupid place to fall asleep. Get a grip.'

On my feet again, I checked my weapon to make sure I hadn't pushed the muzzle into the ground as I fell, and went forward once more. Now I was walking towards a red light, which never seemed to get any brighter. I would approach the next crest in the ground thinking, 'When I get there, the light will be close in front of me.' But that never happened. The glow must have been miles away.

All this time, although I did not know it, I was drawing away from Krabilah, which lay down to my right in the darkness. I had walked clean past it without seeing the least sign of it. But that was hardly surprising, because things were becoming blurred now. I was in and out of wadis, staggering on. I was on a flat area with more tracks. Presently I came to the wall of one wadi and had another attack: a big crack in my head, the same *krrrrrk* of static, a flash . . .

The next thing I knew, I came round to find my nose blocked and aching. How long I have been unconscious I could not tell. But dawn had broken, so I presumed that an hour had gone by, at least. In my compass-mirror I saw that blood had run down my cheeks and neck, matting in the stubble. Somehow I'd fallen flat on my face.

I propped myself against the rock wall. If ever I had come close to dying, it was then. I seemed to have nothing left. My strength had gone, and with it the will to move. I lay back with my head resting against the rock, feeling almost drunk. Now that daylight had come, I knew I ought to lie up. But no – I couldn't last another day without water. For minutes I sat there in a heap. Then I got out my precious flask and drank the last little sip of whisky. It tasted horrible, like fire. I was so dehydrated that it burnt all the way down into my stomach, and left me gasping and desperate, so that I wished I'd never drunk it.

Then suddenly, to my indescribable relief, out of the wadi wall came Paul, the guy in Bravo One Zero who'd burnt his hand before we left. He was dressed in green DPM, not desert gear, and stopped about twenty feet away from me.

'Come on, Chris,' he said, 'hurry up. The squadron's waiting for you.'

It seemed perfectly normal that the squadron should be there. Painfully I levered myself to my feet with the 203 and shuffled down the wadi, expecting to see the rest of the guys lined up, sorting themselves out, ready for the off. In my mental picture, everyone was in as bad a state as I was – knackered, but preparing to go. Yet when I came round the corner, there was nobody in sight.

To this day I swear that Paul walked out in front of me. I thought I was *compos mentis*, and seemed to know what was happening. I knew I'd passed out. I knew I had fallen and hit my nose – but now I was fully conscious and alert again. I even heard the sound of Paul's boots as he came towards me over the gravel in the wadi bed, and for a few moments I thought my nightmare was over. I thought help and salvation had come. Far from it. I was still on my own. Disappointment dealt another crippling blow to my morale. What the hell was I to do now?

I sat down, trying to get myself together. It was early morning on Thursday 31 January. I'd been on the run for eight days and seven nights. It was ten days since my last proper meal, six days since I'd finished my biscuits, three since I'd had any water. My body wasn't going to last another day.

In a futile gesture I pulled out my TACBE, switched it on and let it bleep away. Then I looked up and realised that in the middle distance, about a kilometre away, there was a barn or house – a combination of both, standing out on a rise in the middle of scruffy fields in which rocks poked up out of the bare grey earth.

As I stood watching, a man came out of the house and walked away with a herd of goats. The people living in that barn must have water. I decided that I had to get some, whatever the cost. If I was in Syria, the people might be friendly. If I was still in Iraq, I was going to have to threaten to kill them, get a drink, and carry on. I'd made up my mind: I was going in there, and I'd kill everybody if need be.

Chapter Eight

Safe Or Sorry?

I left the TACBE on in my pocket as I started forward. *Beep*, it went, *beep, beep*. I began closing on the barn. The building was made of dirty-white stone, with a low wall running out of its right-hand end; and the doorway was open. Outside it was a young woman with a black scarf tied round her head in a band, bending over a wood fire and holding what looked like an upturned wok. I could see that she was cooking pieces of dough, like nan bread, spread over the shallow cone of hot metal. Two or three children were playing in the open.

The woman saw me coming but did not react much. As I approached, my weapon in my hands, she lifted her head and called into the house. I was only five or six metres off when a young man came out – a fellow of maybe eighteen with dark, curly hair. He touched his chest and then his forehead with his right hand, nodding in typical Arab greeting.

I went up and shook his hand, and pointed at the ground, asking, 'Syria? Is this Syria?

He nodded, repeating, 'Seeria! Seeria!' Then he pointed over my shoulder and said, 'Iraq. Iraq.'

I looked back the way he was gesturing, and in the distance behind me, over the mounds to the east, I saw a town with a mast. Krabilah! Looking westward, I saw another town, also with a mast. Abu Kamal! The one to the east was miles behind me. Both bloody towns had masts! I realised that I must have passed Krabilah early in the night, and that most of the walking I'd done since then had been unnecessary – nothing but self-inflicted torture. That line of barbed wire had been the frontier after all. I'd been in Syria for hours.

The young man could see the state I was in. A worried look came over his face, and he began touching my hands. He took me by the sleeve and drew me into the barn. In the middle was a round oil stove with a glass door and a metal chimney that rose straight through the roof. At the far end of the room lay rolls of bedding and some straw. There was practically no furniture, and it was obvious the people were very poor. A woman with tattoos on her face sat breast-feeding a baby, and did not move as I came in.

I sat on a mat on the ground next to the stove with my weapon laid across my lap. The young man looked at me and asked in gestures if I wanted something to eat.

'Water!' I croaked, tipping up an imaginary glass. 'Water!'

A moment later he handed me a shiny metal bowl full of water, which tasted incredibly fresh and cold. Never in my life had I had a more delicious drink. I tipped it straight down my neck. The boy brought another bowlful, and I drank that as well. Next he gave me a cup of sweet tea, thick with dissolved sugar, and I put that down too. Then the woman came in with some of the bread she'd been making, and gave me a piece. It was still hot, and smelt delicious, but when I bit off a mouthful and tried to swallow it, it locked in my throat and would not go down.

I had to get my boots off. It was four days since I'd seen my feet, and I was dreading what I would find. As I undid the laces and eased the boots off, the stink was repulsive. Like my hands, my feet were rotting. I smelt as if my whole body was putrefying. When the man saw the state of my feet, with pus oozing along the sides, he let out a yell. The woman who'd been cooking came up with a wide bowl like a dustbin full of cold water and began to wash my feet. All my toenails had come off, and my toes were numb – I couldn't feel them. But the water stung the rest of my feet like fire.

In spite of the pain, I forced myself to scrape the pus out of the cuts along the sides and round the heels. I also washed the blood off my face. With that done, it was bliss to lie back with my bare feet raised to the warmth of the stove and let them breathe. Another girl appeared from outside, took my socks and rinsed them through. When she brought them back, of course they were still wet, but I pulled them on, and got my boots back on as well.

In sign language, and by making aircraft sounds, I tried to indicate that I was a pilot and had been in a crash. Then I made some siren sounds – *dee-dah, dee-dah, dee-dah* – to show that I wanted to go to the police. A boy of about six had been drawing pictures of tanks and aircraft on sheets of dirty white paper. With my numb fingers I drew a police car with a blue lamp on the roof. Suddenly the message got through: the young man nodded vigorously and pointed towards the distant town.

'Go to the town?' I suggested, and I made driving motions. 'You have a vehicle?'

Again he nodded and pointed. What he meant – I soon found out – was that we should start walking down the road towards the town and thumb a lift.

With the water and tea inside me, my body seemed to have switched back on. My drowsiness and disorientation had vanished. I felt sharp again, as if there was nothing wrong, as if I could do the whole walk again. Everything seemed so relaxed that for a while I just sat there, recovering.

The old man came back with his goats and stood looking at me. Then, to get some action, I dug a sovereign out of my belt and showed it round. I started saying '*Felous, felous'* – 'money, money' – and pointed to the goats, then back at the coin, trying to put over the idea that this represented many animals, or a lot of cash. 'Bank,' I said, 'bank.'

The appearance of the gold galvanised the young man. All at once he became hell-bent on going into town. Maybe he thought that if he escorted me in I would give him the money. Soon everyone was staring at the sovereign. Another girl came in, and somehow I knew she said, 'He's got more on him somewhere.' The old man appeared with a gun – some ancient hunting rifle. 'More,' he said, 'more' – and by gestures he showed he wanted another coin, to make the girl a pair of earrings. Then he started demanding gold for the other girls as well.

'No, no, no,' I said. 'This is for goats, clothes and stuff. No more.'

The Arabs began muttering to each other. For half an hour things remained tense. I lay with my feet against the oil fire, warming up. It was the first time in a week that I hadn't felt half frozen. I had begun to hope that I could sleep in the farmhouse that night; I wanted to tell them, 'Wait awhile – just let me rest here.' But the young man had become determined to go into town, and indicated that I should come outside.

I decided not to wait any longer. But to present a less aggressive figure, I took off my webbing and smock, so that I was left wearing my dark-green jersey and camouflage trousers. With signs I asked the man for some sort of bag. He produced a white plastic fertiliser sack, and I put my kit into that. I then slung the sack over my shoulder and we set off along the road.

Soon I thought, 'It's hardly the thing, to walk into a civilian town carrying a rifle,' so when we'd gone about two hundred metres, I broke my weapon down in two and put it in the bag. I still had my knife, but in this situation I could have done with a pistol – an inconspicuous weapon, which would have come in handy during the emergency which followed.

The young man led off quite fast along the dirt road and I shuffled behind him, in too much pain to move quickly. Every minute or two my companion stopped and waited for me to catch up. Then, seeing I was in difficulties, he took the bag off me, and without the weight I made better progress. I kept saying, 'Tractor? Where's a tractor?' – and I presume he was saying in Arabic, 'One'll come soon.'

Wagons were rolling out from the town, and presently one stopped: a land-cruiser loaded with bales of hay. The driver could speak a little broken English. He said he was a camel farmer, and asked who I was.

'My aircraft's crashed,' I told him.

'Your aircraft? Where is it?'

'Over the hill, over there. I need to go to the police.'

'OK. I'll take you.'

He swung his vehicle round, and I got into the middle of the front seat, between him and the young man. In a minute or two I was regretting it, because he started making aggressive comments: 'You shouldn't be here. This is our country. This is a bad war.'

I just said, 'Yeah, I know,' and kept as quiet as possible. Soon we hit the edge of the town, which proved a severe disappointment. I'd been imagining a fairly sophisticated place, with banks and shops and other signs of civilisation. This place had nothing but crude houses made of grey breeze-blocks, with heaps of rubbish lying round them. There was no vegetation, and not a sign of a garden. The only form of decoration was the odd burnt-out car. One thing that did surprise me was the extent to which the Syrians resembled Europeans – and I was startled by the sight of two men with flaming, carrot-coloured hair, one of them sporting an equally red beard.

My driver pulled up outside a house on the left-hand side of the road and beeped his horn. Out came an Arab dressed in a black dishdash. There was a bit of an exchange between the two; then the driver said something to the young farm lad, who got out of the truck. I felt helpless, because I saw fear in the boy's face, and didn't know what was happening.

'Everything all right?' I asked, but the driver spoke sharply to the lad, who set off walking, back towards home.

The two of us went on into town, and the driver started niggling again. 'You want to go back to Iraq?' he said, and roared with laughter. 'I should take you back.'

'No, no!' I said. I brought out my idemnity slip, written in Arabic as well as English. The letter promised £5,000 to anyone who handed me safely back to the coalition. The driver snatched it and began to stuff it into his pocket, as if it was actual cash.

'You don't understand,' I said. 'I have to be with this piece of paper. Me and the paper at the same time. You only get the money if the two are together.' I took it back from him and put it away.

'OK,' he said, 'OK.'

At least he stopped talking about taking me back across the border. But then he asked, 'You have gun?'

'No,' I said. 'No gun.'

We came to a petrol station, and he pulled up. On the other side of the pumps was a car with a gang of young lads round it. The driver touched my bag, with all the kit in it, and asked, 'What all this?'

'Nothing, nothing. Just my things.'

He reached over to pat me on my stomach, to feel if I had a weapon concealed about me.

'No,' I protested. 'I've got nothing.'

Suddenly he called out to the lads by the pump, and one of them came over. The boy stood by the window and didn't look at me, but kept his eyes straight down on the bag. The driver went on talking to him – until suddenly he ran off into the building.

I thought, 'There's something going on here. There's going to

162

be a lynching party coming out. They're going to do me for my weapon, or put me back across the border.'

It was time to go. I opened the door, grabbed the bag and began to get out. At that moment the driver seized my left arm, trying to restrain me. I dragged him across the front seat and half out of the cab. When I kicked the door shut, it caught his head in the opening and he had to let go of me. He let out a yell, and I took off.

Fear boiled up in me again, almost worse than before. Away I went, running up the street, with the plastic sack in one hand. At least, I thought I was running – but when I turned round I saw a load of old guys easily keeping pace with me. I was running in slow motion. I couldn't go any faster.

Soon there was a big commotion, and a crowd of over a dozen people coming after me. They were barely thirty metres behind me and closing fast. I thought, 'You're screwed here.'

Instinctively I knew that in those Arab border towns everyone is related to everyone else. Although some of these people called themselves Syrians and some Iraqis, they probably all belonged to the same families, and had cousins or even brothers on the other side. I'd seen it on the border between Saudi and Iraq: guys from both sides were driving across to the frontier posts opposite, just to have tea with their friends. Whenever they got a stand-to, they'd merely disappear back.

Now, somehow, these Syrians knew I had a weapon in that bag. They were out to get it, and then to throw me back into Iraq, or worse. A terrific atmosphere had suddenly built up. The pavements were full of people, and the ones on the other side of the road were all looking, alerted by the noise. Ahead of me, more pedestrians were staring. I kept hobbling and staggering along, hampered by the plastic sack in my right hand. I couldn't even wave my weapon in threat, because it was stripped down.To have reassembled it would have meant stopping for at least a minute, and by then the mob would have been on top of me.

Then, as I turned a corner, a miracle: there stood a man with an AK 47, wearing chest webbing. He was right next door to a pillar box, obviously on duty. It flashed into my mind that this might be the Iraqi border post, but it was too late to worry.

'Police?' I shouted. 'Police?'

I don't know what the guy said. I'm not sure he said anything at all. He just pulled me through a gateway and into a walled garden. I saw bunting of triangular flags over the entrance, vegetation all round, and a big bungalow. He had me by the arm and the scruff of the neck, and ran me into this enclosure, out of reach of the crowd in the street, who by then were yelling for my blood. What his motives were, I'll never know. He may have been trying to save me from the mob, or he may just have thought he'd grabbed a prisoner.

Inside the bungalow a man sat behind a desk, smoking. He was wearing a black leather jacket. So were all the other men in there – black leather bomber jackets and jeans – and they all seemed to be smoking. Nobody spoke a word of English. There was a lot of pointing. I said, 'I'm a helicopter pilot,' and made chopper noises, whirling my hand round to indicate rotors, and then diving it down to show that I had crashed.

Very soon they'd opened my bag and got out the 203, together with my webbing. Then the driver who'd given me the lift rushed in and let fly a volley of Arabic, jabbing his finger in my direction. I felt another surge of fear, and motioned to the bomber-jacketed guys, 'Get him out!' They bundled him into another room, protesting all the way.

The air was full of animosity, but I couldn't tell which way it was pointing. These leather-clad guys obviously had no time for the driver, but they didn't like the look of me either. I couldn't blame them. My hair was matted with dirt; my face was emaciated, eyes staring. I had ten days' growth of beard. I was filthy and stinking. I was also an infidel.

They started stripping my kit, and pulled out the two white phosphorous grenades. One of the guys, who was smoking a cigarette, held a grenade up and asked something in Arabic, obviously 'What's this?'

'Smoke,' I told him. 'For making smoke' – and I waved up clouds of the stuff in mid air.

They started lobbing the grenades round, one to another, catching them like cricket balls. The safety-pins, which I'd loosened before our first contact, were hanging out. I knew that if one of the grenades went off, it would kill us all; so I made to stand up and grab them. The movement did not go down well. The instant I was half-upright, three guys pulled pistols and levelled them at me, yelling at me to sit down. So I sat back, and everything gradually calmed down. The man who'd finished up with the grenades brought them over, and let me push the pins back into place.

By then the others were ripping out all my kit: the kite-sight, my little binoculars, my fireflies (the lights which give a high-intensity flash and have infra-red filters for bringing aircraft on to you). All my stuff was disappearing, and I thought, 'I'm not going to see any of this again.' None of it was particularly valuable, but I'd become quite attached to it, having carried it all that way, and now it was being stolen in front of my eyes.

After about twenty minutes I was taken through a door into another room, and in came a man of fifty or so, wearing a grey suit. He was very calm, as if nothing bothered him, and he looked exactly like a Middle Eastern version of the actor Anthony Hopkins. He sat me down at a table with a piece of paper and said, 'Details? Name? Birthday? Country?'

I wrote down, 'Sergeant Chris Ryan, 22 Turbo Squadron, Para Field Ambulance,' and my date of birth – and left it at that. 22 Para Field Ambulance didn't exist, but I thought that if I finished up in a prison camp, and the number, combined with the word 'Turbo', reached the coalition, somebody would click on to the fact that I was a medic in 22 SAS. I gave my rank as sergeant because I knew it would command a bit more respect than if I said 'corporal'; besides, in the SAS corporals get sergeants' pay.

While I was writing, another man gave me a cup of coffee, and I drank it. It was thick and bitter, Arab-style, and made me feel thirstier than ever. The Hopkins character took the paper, went out, then came back in and beckoned me to follow him. I stood up, and as I reached the door two other guys were waiting. I felt as if I was going to run the gauntlet, but they grabbed me by the arms and pulled me into a different room. There they pointed down at a white dishdash and motioned me to put it on.

By then I was really scared. What the hell were they doing, making me dress up like an Arab? The dishdash came down to my feet. Someone came in with a shamag and wrapped it round my head. At first I could just about see out, but then they pulled it right down over my face. Nobody told me where

I was going or what was happening. I felt panic rising. Inadvertently I had handed myself over to these bastards, who had complete control of me.

I saw my bag of equipment go out the door ahead of me. A land-cruiser pulled up outside. Two men armed with AK 47s came in; there was an exchange, and I was passed over to them and marched out. One man climbed into the driver's seat, I was pushed into the middle, and the second man got in on my right.

As we came out of the police station, I held my breath. I felt certain that if we turned right, we would be on our way back to Iraq. If we turned left, there was a good chance that the Syrians would be keeping me.

We turned left. I breathed again. Then we set off at high speed, along rough streets full of kids playing. The fact that humans were in the way didn't deter the driver; he just kept going, with one hand on the horn, swerving in and out of the vast potholes. After a while the passenger made signs to ask if I was hungry. I said 'Yes' and nodded, so the driver stopped and waited while his mate ran out, returning with a bag of apples.

When I ate the whole of the one he gave me – core, pips and all, everything bar the stalk – both Arabs stared at me. The one on my right hadn't touched his apple, and he gave it to me – so I ate that too, core and all again.

On we went, missing hundreds of dogs by inches. We swerved to avoid any number of dead ones, too. Next we cleared the town, came on to a metalled road and down into a big valley. Then we were out in the desert, on a road that ran straight for miles.

I knew my bag was in the back, but I couldn't tell how much of my kit was still in it. I tried talking, and asked where we were going. 'Damascus?' I suggested. 'Damascus?' But my question produced no answers, so I shut up. At one point, to my right, I saw ancient ruins, but, in the state I was, they didn't interest me much.

Ahead of us I saw two dark-blue Mercedes parked on the side of the road, with a group of six men standing round the cars. As we came towards them, my escorts started jabbering to each other. Obviously this was some pre-arranged rendezvous. We began to slow down. Fifty metres short of the cars, I could see that one of the waiting men had a pistol in his hand. Suddenly the guy on my right pulled up my shamag, quite roughly, so as to blindfold me, and grabbed hold of my arm. I thought, 'Fucking hell, this is an execution squad!'

We came to a halt. I was dragged out, run up to the back of one of the Mercedes, thrown down on my knees. Somebody pushed my head forward, and one of these twats came and stood behind me.

Silence followed. Nobody moved or spoke. I thought I was going to die. Until then I'd always reckoned that if anything like this happened to me, I'd make a last-ditch run for it. Watching films of the Holocaust, and imagining I'd been caught by the Nazis, I'd seen myself putting up a last-second fight. But now it wasn't like that. Physically incapable of running, I just knelt there waiting for the bastard to shoot me in the back of the head. It was a terrible feeling, to be on my knees, waiting for someone to do that to me. But I didn't get scenes from my life flashing through my head, like you're supposed to. I just felt annoyed that I'd given myself up to these rotten people.

The silence seemed to last for ever. In fact it probably went on for less than a minute. Then there was a movement. Hands either side grabbed my arms, stood me up, moved me forward and threw me into the back of a car. The doors slammed and we drove off.

Now I had three escorts, all in western civilian clothes. On my left sat the youngest, a skinny fellow with a thin, weasly face and a straggling moustache – the sort of looks that annoy me. He struck me as a weak character. The driver was quite a big fellow, dark, good-looking, maybe my own age, and wearing a black leather jacket. His front-seat passenger was about forty: chubby, and going thin on top, he wore a green safari-type jacket with patch pockets. Al three had ties, but they had pulled the knots loose, and in general their appearance was scruffy.

Who *were* these guys? Police, I hoped. But they gave me no clue as to their identity – and why were they messing about so much? In my state of exhaustion and confusion, I didn't know what to think. Of course I considered trying to take them out. I still had my knife on me – but the car was travelling fast, probably at 70 or 80 m.p.h. for most of the time. Also, there was another car escorting us, and police outriders. The desert we were going through was very open, with nowhere to hide.

My shamag was still on, but the guy in the passenger seat pulled it down far enough for me to see. Then, leaning over into the back, he began to strip-search me: he took off my ID discs by pulling the cord over my head, unclipped my belt, undid my boot laces, removed my watch, emptied my pockets, took my notebook and map. One thing which escaped him was my belt, which had 19 gold sovereigns taped to the inside.

That was another frightening moment, when I felt his hands on me. The guy on my left was holding my arm, and I was thinking. 'Jesus, if I'm going to safety, they shouldn't be doing this to me.' *Could* these fellows be the Syrian police? Or who were they? Why were they behaving like this? It was all very strange and alarming.

Presently they blindfolded me again. They talked a bit among themselves, and played loud Arab music on the stereo. Also, they chain-smoked. Soon I was in agony. In the warmth of the car – the highest temperature I'd been in for days – my feet and knees began to swell. Probably being static contributed to the trouble, and the pain became excruciating. I kept trying to ease the agony by shifting around, but all the time I was finding it harder and harder to breathe. I wasn't exactly hyperventilating, but I'm sure fear was contributing to my problems, and I was being choked by the filthy smoke.

I started feeling claustrophobic, and said, 'Can't you take the blindfold off?' Until then, whenever I'd tried to pull the shamag off my face, the guy in front had twitched it back, but now he seemed to realise that I was in trouble, and let it drop out of the way. I saw that the second Mercedes was ahead of us, and that whenever we came to a village, our outriders went ahead on their motorbikes to seal off any side-roads, so that we could go speeding straight through. Then they'd come howling past us and take the lead again.

The scrawny fellow next to me kept poking me in the ribs and going on about the war, making banal, needling remarks in broken English. 'What were you doing in Iraq? You shouldn't be here. Do you like Americans?'

At any other time I'd have thumped his block off – and I don't think he'd feel very well if I saw him today. As it was, I grunted monosyllabic answers, anxious to give nothing away. I still didn't know who these people were, or what they were doing. I felt fairly confident they weren't taking me to Baghdad, but I thought they might be going to hand me over to some extremist group as a hostage. I knew that both John McCarthy and Terry Waite were being held by guerillas. In my confused state, I couldn't remember who it was holding them – was it Hizbollah? – but I began to think I was going to end up with them.

Sometimes our driver would overtake the other car and lead for a while. Every time we came to a village, one of my escorts would pull the shamag over my eyes so that I couldn't see any names.

After four or five hours we drove down a broad valley, with steep sides set back maybe a kilometre on either side, and high ground rising beyond them. Then, looking ahead, I saw a motorway sign coming up – and all it said, in enormous letters, was BAGHDAD, with a big arrow pointing from right to left.

When I saw that I felt that I'd gone through the floor and my arse was getting dragged along the ground. Just as I spotted it, the driver said something to the fellow beside me, who started poking me in the ribs, cackling, 'Yes, you right. You going Baghdad! You going where Baghdad is.'

I was growing angry – partly with the idiot beside me, partly with myself. How the hell had I ended up in such a situation? All my effort in walking so far seemed to have gone for nothing. Why had I given myself up to these dickheads? Why hadn't I tried to pinch a vehicle and drive myself to Damascus?

The front-seat passenger turned to me and said, 'Yes – we're Baghdadis.'

Then the driver pointed at his own backside and went, '*Ee, ee, ee, ee,*' watching me in the mirror as he did so, obviously meaning that my bum was twitching.

He never realised what a good turn he did me by making that stupid gesture. All at once he infuriated me and steeled my resolve. I thought, 'Fuck you! I can take anything you cunts can give me. I'll keep my mouth shut and take whatever's coming.'

I began struggling to reorientate my ideas. I had to accept that I was going to a prison camp. I was going to be interrogated. I was going to get a bad kicking, a beating. 'Think your thoughts,' I told myself. 'Get organised.'

The One That Got Away

I still considered doing a runner, but it was impossible. I was physically knackered, and wouldn't have gone a hundred yards. 'It's no good,' I told myself. 'They'll have you.' Instead, I sat still, trying not to annoy my escorts by fidgeting; but every part of me was aching: back, shoulders, knees – but worst of all, my feet.

With the view cut out by the blindfold again, I kept trying to visualise where we were. On the highway to Baghdad, I felt certain. But which way did it go? Had there always been a highway to Baghdad, right from Biblical times? And did it run through Jordan, or what?

Exhaustion began sweeping over me again. Although I'd drunk the water and coffee in the barn that morning, I was desperately in need of food, and more liquid. I had been weakened more than I realised. My mind was so confused that I couldn't remember the simplest details of everyday life.

Through my blindfold I could see and feel that we were heading towards the sun, and that hour by hour the sun was going down. But what did that mean? Did the sun set in the east or in the west? Unable to remember, I tried to think back to what used to happen when I was a kid. Gradually I got it: from my bedroom at home I could see the sun coming up over Gibside, the big country estate on the far flank of the Derwent valley where we lived. I tried to project myself out into the sky above our home, so that I was looking down on the house. 'Yes,' I thought, 'the sun's coming up over there. That's the direction of Newcastle, and, further off, China.' That meant the sun rose in the east, and set in the west. Now we were heading into the setting sun: therefore we must be driving west. In that case, I told myself, we couldn't be going to Baghdad. Desperately I tried to visualise the map and remember which part of Syria Damascus was in.

For the final half hour or so they kept my head wrapped up. Then darkness fell, and still we went on driving, until in the end we hit the outskirts of some town or city. By then the blindfold was off again, and I started to see signs saying DAMAS. 'Jesus,' I though. 'Can this really be Damascus?' As I saw more and more signs saying DAMAS, I began daring to hope that it was the Syrian capital.

My escorts started to smarten themselves up. They put out

170

their cigarettes, turned off the radio, slid their ties tight, and straightened their clothes, as if preparing to meet somebody important. All that alarmed me. What were they getting ready for? Then, on a piece of waste ground, we pulled into the kerb, behind yet another Mercedes, and my front passenger got out. His place was taken by a much older guy, of maybe fifty, well dressed, and balding a little. His dark suit gave him a sombre appearance, but at least he looked cool and calm. The other two characters in my car were obviously in awe of him; as he walked towards us they stopped chattering, and more or less sat to attention, hardly daring to breathe.

The new man got it, closed his door and gave one curt instruction, hardly more than a grunt. We moved off towards the city centre. Every now and then he snapped a direction at the driver, very abrupt: 'Left . . . right,' and that was all. After about five minutes he turned round and asked in English, 'Are you OK?'

I nodded and said, 'Yep.'

'Won't be long now.'

Then he picked up all the things they'd taken off me – watch, ID discs, bootlaces and so on – handed them back and said, 'These are yours.'

I thought, 'What the hell's going on? What was the point of taking it all off me in the first place?' There'd been so many changes of mood. First there'd been the farm boy, definitely friendly. Then the driver of the truck had turned hostile, telling me I had no business to be in Syria. Then the policeman on duty had saved me from the mob. Next the twats inside the station had tried to steal all my kit – hostility again. Then the guy who made me write down my details seemed to be back on side. A few minutes later my escorts were giving me apples to eat. Then it was into the mock-execution, and more sick jokes about going to Baghdad. No wonder I felt confused.

Anyway, I started getting my kit back in place. I put away the maps and knife, and got the ID discs back round my neck; but by then my feet had swollen up so much that I couldn't get my boots on, so I didn't bother threading the laces.

All this time we were driving through the city, and I could tell how scared the driver was of our new passenger, purely from his reactions. He kept glancing fearfully sideways, looking for new instructions, and always at the last possible instant the man would bark at him, 'Left!' or 'Right!'

At last we came to a big modern building, probably ten storeys high. There were guards in green uniforms and armed with AK 47s on the gates, on the walls, everywhere: not the sort of place you could break into, or out of, in a hurry. Before I had time to wonder what it was, the gates swung open in front of us, and we drove into a courtyard.

Chapter Nine

Guest Of The Government

All my escorts got out. For a moment I was left sitting in the back. When I went to move, I found that my knees and ankles had locked solid. The older guy saw me struggling and clicked his fingers, whereupon the other two more or less lifted me out of the car, propped me up, and helped me – practically carried me – up a long flight of steps to the glass doors. They can't have enjoyed it much, because I was stinking like that three-week-old corpse I once saw and smelt in London.

After a few steps my legs began to function again, more or less. We shuffled into a big reception area, where everything looked efficient and well-guarded. Sitting at the desk was a man in uniform, with a peaked cap with a red band round it, who came to attention as we entered. Then it was into a lift, up a few floors, and out again. As the doors opened, we were met by a smartly-dressed, clean-shaven man in a dark-blue blazer, stripy tie and blue shirt. Beside him, hovering deferentially, stood another man, about the same age, but chubbier and less smart.

The boss-figure was an impressive character: in his mid-forties, he had a smart haircut, looked crisp and effective, and possessed obvious authority. I hadn't a clue who he was – and he did not bother to enlighten me. Only later did I discover that he was head of the Mukhabarrat, the Syrian Secret Police. For the moment I felt screwed up, unable to decide what the hell was happening.

The boss smiled, reached out, took my hand, and said in English, 'Welcome to Damascus. Welcome to Syria.'

The interpreter said, 'Come in, please,' and ushered me in.

Where was the catch? What were these buggers up to? It was horrible to be so unsure. I was desperately trying to think of all my options, and bloody fast, so that I didn't get caught out.

I followed them through into some kind of office and sat down on a Chesterfield. I could see the boss sniffing, and not liking what he was getting. Suddenly being in a clean environment, I could see what shit order I was in: my hair was matted, my hands and face were filthy. There was brown, dried blood on my DPMs. The boss himself took off the shamag, which was still wrapped round my head, and spoke sharply to the interpreter, clearly saying, 'Get this stuff off.' Someone else helped me out of the dishdash. Another guy brought in my bag and put it under a table. Then, through the interpreter, the boss said, 'Would you like to get cleaned up?'

'Yeah,' I said. 'Good idea.'

'Come with me.'

The interpreter's English was first-class, and he seemed very friendly. I thought, 'You'd better start playing a game, here,' and tried to appear grateful; but I still had no idea what was going on, and I expect I looked shell-shocked. Part of my mind was wondering what was going to happen, part trying *not* to anticipate, for fear of being disappointed. I had time to glance round the walls and noticed a gold-plated AK 47, as well as pictures of Assad, the Syrian President. A large, leather-topped desk stood in one corner, covered in ornaments and paperweights. Two or three settees were set out round a coffee-table. The whole room spoke of money and good organisation.

With the boss leading the way, followed by the interpreter, we walked out of the office, through a living room and into the bedroom, where some exercise machines were set out. Then we went into the bathroom, which had a big corner bath, a shower, a toilet, a pedestal basin with a mirror on the wall above it, and shelves full of toiletries. Everything was clean and glitzy, in an Arab way, with gold-plated taps and cupboard handles.

The boss walked around, fitting a new blade into a safety razor, putting some shampoo ready. Someone turned on the bath, and through the interpreter he said, 'This is all my stuff. Just use it, please.'

He went out and left me alone. There I was, in this luxury bathroom, with hot water running . . . It was then that I looked in a mirror and saw my face. Jesus Christ – what a sight! I was gaunt as a skeleton; under ten days' growth of beard my cheeks were hollow, and my eyes seemed to have sunk into their sockets. My hair was matted with every kind of filth.

I felt stunned, unable to make out what was happening. One minute I'd been gearing myself for prison; now I was being cosseted in a high-class apartment. But whatever else lay ahead, there was no reason not to have a bath. I started slowly undressing, and took off my shirt.

Looking in two mirrors at once (one in front, one behind), I caught sight of my back, and I could hardly believe it. My ribs and spine and hip-bones were all sticking out, as though I'd been starved for weeks. I could see every rib going round and joining my backbone. It was a shock to realise that I'd been living on my own body. In walking nearly 300 kilometres, and shuddering with cold for countless hours, I'd burnt away all the muscle which I'd built up during my time on the SP team.

In the mirror I saw a young boy coming in holding a tape-measure, and the interpreter behind him.

'What's going on now?' I demanded.

'We'll just take your sizes,' said the interpreter, and the boy started measuring me, round the waist, down the leg, under the arms, with the interpreter writing down whatever he called out.

'What the hell's this?' I was thinking. 'For a fucking coffin?' But I didn't ask – partly out of fear that I would find out something bad. Then the man who'd met me with the car also appeared, and asked what my shoe-size was. When I told him, 'Eight, eight and a half,' he said to the interpreter, 'He looks like a 42.' He then left, and I didn't see him again.

The boy soon legged it, and as I was getting my trousers off, in came another guy with a cup of Turkish coffee. I drank a mouthful of it, but it tasted like cough medicine and made me gag. 'Water!' I croaked, and made drinking motions.

I edged myself over the bath and lowered myself in carefully, backside first, keeping my feet out of the water. Then I gradually submerged them. As the heat hit the cuts, the pain was horrendous. After a few seconds I lifted them out again, then tried to lower them back into the water. I lay there with my legs elevated as I washed myself and shampooed my hair. Soon the water was absolutely black, so I got out, pulled out the plug, and started to fill the bath again. As I was doing that, the interpreter came back, and when he saw me, he said, 'Oh – excuse me. We have a shower, if you'd like to use it.'

'It's OK, thanks. I'm going to have another bath.'

I got back into clean water, and again the pain in my feet was terrific, as if needles were being driven into them. Apart from the cuts along the sides, they were discoloured, with red and blue patches. All I could do was lie there and bite my tongue. Then the burning ache seemed to subside, and I started to enjoy the hot water.

The interpreter sat down by the bath with his note-pad. 'Right,' he said, 'can you tell me what happened?'

'Play it like you're frightened,' I thought. 'Well,' I said, 'I'm a medic. I was brought in from the TA, and I was on board a helicopter going in to retrieve – '

'The TA?'

'The Territorial Army. The reserves. As I said, I was going in to retrieve a downed pilot, and something happened. There was a big bang, the helicopter crashed, and I just ran for it. We came down, and I was really scared. I didn't wait for anybody else . . .'

'Keep it light,' I was thinking. 'Pretend to be nervous.'

'How long ago?'

'Three days, I think.'

'Whereabouts was the crash?'

'I don't know. I just ran. I had no idea where we were. I ended up with a goatherd.'

'What sort of helicopter was it?'

'A Sea King.'

'What did it look like?'

'Just a helicopter . . . Single engine.'

The interpreter had been watching me closely, and now he just said, 'OK,' and left the room. I had the strong impression that he hadn't believed a word of what I'd told him. Too bad. I climbed out of the bath and got my beard off with a couple of shaves. Without the stubble, I looked very thin and tired. My lips were cracked and broken, but no more than if I'd been in the sun too long.

As I was drying myself, the boy who'd measured me brought in a set of clean white underpants and vest and laid them on the toilet seat. Also, he picked up my own stinking kit, and took it out.

Spotting a pair of scales, I stood on them. At first I thought the needle had jammed, so I shook the platform about – but no:

it stayed steady on 63.5 kilograms. I knew exactly what my weight was when I'd left Saudi, and I could hardly believe it. Ten days earlier I'd been 12 stone 8, or 176 lbs. Now I was 10 stone, or 140 lbs. I'd lost thirty-six pounds.

I pulled on the clean underwear and walked out into the bedroom, and there – for Christ's sake – was a brand-new dark-blue pin-striped suit, together with a white shirt and tie. By then it was 11 o'clock at night, but I realised they must have knocked up some tailor, and he'd run the suit together in half an hour. There was also a pair of black slip-on shoes. I put on the shirt and the trousers, but they were inches too big round the waist. The boss was watching me, and when he saw that something was wrong he went berserk, yelling at the young guy who'd taken the measurements. The boy was crestfallen and cowering, not daring to look up.

Anyway, as I took off the trousers and handed them back, the boss noticed the state of my feet. He telephoned for a medical orderly, while I sat on the edge of the bed and waited. Soon a medic appeared. He cleaned out the cuts with a lotion that stung, and put plasters on, but he made such a mess of the job that I reckoned I could have done better on my own. If they'd had any zinc oxide tape, I'd have taped my feet right up. Also, I knew I needed some antibiotics. By then my ankles as well as my feet were swollen, and the new pair of shoes wouldn't go on.

By the time the medic had finished, the trousers reappeared with the waist taken in. So I put them on, and the tie. The boss kept asking, 'D'you like the tie?' and I said, 'Yes, thank you. It's fine.'

'I think it's great,' he said. 'I picked it out myself.'

In fact it was a horrible mess of grey and red. The jacket of the suit fitted quite well, but because I couldn't get the shoes on I stayed in stockinged feet. Then suddenly I thought: 'Jesus – I know. It's a press conference. They're dressing me up for a staged press do. I'm going to walk into a room full of lights and reporters and cameramen. They'll all be asking questions. What the hell am I going to tell them?'

I hadn't a clue what was happening in Iraq. I presumed that the air-war was still in progress – but whether or not the ground-war had started I couldn't tell. I didn't even know what had become of the rest of my patrol. If I said the wrong thing now, I might blow the whole SAS operation in the Gulf. I might blow the fact that the Regiment was in Saudi. Did the Syrians realise I was in the SAS? Maybe I should tell them the truth, in the hope that they'd keep it quiet. One way or another, I could be in trouble.

Before I had time to worry too much, they ushered me back into the sitting room and the boss told the interpreter to switch on the TV. He tuned to CNN, and I soon saw that the air-war was still on – allied aircraft bombing Baghdad, and so on – but there appeared to have been no major action on the ground. Then the interpreter began to recap on what I'd told him.

'So you were a medic on board a helicopter.'

'That's right.'

After a bit of chit-chat he asked, 'Are you hungry?'

Hungry! In the past eight days I'd eaten two packets of biscuits and two apples. 'Yes,' I said, 'I am.'

'Just a minute, then.'

He let me watch CNN for a while, then led me through to the other lounge. I could move slowly without too much discomfort; my feet felt quite easy on the carpet, but I was sore and stiff all over. In my brief absence someone had set out a feast on a table. There were kebabs, steaks, rice, salads, bread, fruit. The interpreter kept saying, 'You must be starving,' and he heaped a pile of food on to my plate. The smell was fantastic, but when I cut into a steak and took one bite of it, it seemed to stick in my throat and I couldn't eat any more.

I just sat there drinking pints of water, until the boss asked, 'Is the food bad?'

'No,' I said. 'It's just that I'm not as hungry as I thought. More thirsty. I'm sorry.'

The other two had been eating, but I got the impression they were only doing it to be polite, and as soon as I gave up, they did too. Back in the other room, the interpreter asked, 'Well – what would you like to do now?'

I knew that a British Embassy had been hastily set up in Damascus when the Gulf War looked likely to break out, and I was on the point of asking to be taken there when the interpreter suggested, 'How about seeing some Syrian night life?'

'What?' I was astounded. Didn't these guys realise what a state I was in? I was making sense to them, but only just.

'No thanks,' I muttered. 'I can't walk.'

'Well – d'you need anything? D'you need to spend time with anybody?'

It was incredible: here the interpreter was, apparently offering me a woman. By then I'd seen the hand of God, and I was in no mood to muck around. I thought, 'Go for it,' and asked, 'Can you take me to the British Embassy?'

'Oh?' he seemed rather surprised. 'You want to go there?'

'Yes, if it's possible.'

'OK.' He began making phone calls. While he was doing that, I was led across to a table – and there was all my kit which had been taken away in the police station, and which I thought had been stolen piecemeal.

'Well,' said the interpreter, coming over, 'is everything there?'

I made a check, and found everything present – weapon, ammunition, kite-sight, even the white phos grenades.

'Yeah,' I said. 'It's all there.'

'This is interesting.' He picked up the kite-sight. 'What's this?'

'Oh – just a thing they gave us so that we could see in the dark.' I felt sure he knew what it was, so I showed him how to turn it on, and he stood there looking out of the window with it, down into the courtyard.

'Brilliant!' he said. 'I'll have everything packed away for you.'

I believe they knew exactly who I was, but they were playing along with my story. Then the interpreter asked whether I wanted my clothes washed, but I said, 'No thanks – just put them back in the bag.' So the young guy pushed everything back in, and I sat down again.

'You know,' said the interpreter keenly, 'I've always wanted to come to England for a holiday. Where do you live?'

'In Newcastle,' I said. 'With my parents.'

'Oh, I'd love to come there. Can you give me your telephone number and address? Maybe you could show us the sights and return our hospitality sometime? Could I give you a ring?'

I made up a number, giving the Rowlands Gill code with changed digits, and a dicky address. I thought, 'Jesus – you're digging yourself in deep here. If he asks you to repeat that number, you're going to be in the shit.' But once again, they didn't seem to question what I said.

'By the way,' the interpreter added, as we were waiting. 'Did you see anyone as you crossed the border? Did anyone meet you?'

That made me think they must have had people out on their own side of the frontier, watching, and waiting to receive escapers. But I replied, 'No. I didn't see anybody.'

'So you found the police station yourself?'

'That's right.' I told them more or less what had happened at the farmhouse.

'And this young boy who took you in – where was his house?'

I tried to describe the location, and the boss promised to send someone to thank the people there. Then he said, 'How was your journey after that?'

I thought, 'If I start saying what the bastards did to me in the desert, he may keep me here for days, until he's had the guys dragged in.' So I just said, 'Oh, it was fine, thanks. No problem.'

There was a knock at the door, and in came the driver of the car, actually cowering, dry-washing his hands in front of him, with his head hanging down. Until then, I'd only seen orientals do that, and it made me wonder, 'Who *is* this boss guy? What does he do to people to make them behave like that?'

The interpreter gave me a piece of paper with a telephone number on it, and said, 'If you have any problems in Damascus, ring this number and ask to speak to me.' I put the note in my pocket and tucked my new shoes under one arm. Then I shook hands with the boss, who patted me on the back. 'The car will take you to the British Embassy,' he said, 'and staff of the Embassy will meet you there.'

I limped downstairs and found a Mercedes waiting. In we climbed, and the driver set off.

The Embassy was a disappointment. Instead of the grand house in a walled garden which I'd visualised, thinking of Abu Dhabi, it turned out to be an undistinguished office building in a row on a street, with guards on duty in pillar boxes along the pavements. There seemed to be a heavy presence of men with weapons, dotted all over the place in ones and twos. As we pulled up, I grabbed my bag, thanked the driver and got out.

A young man was standing on the steps, waiting to meet me. He introduced himself as the Second Secretary, and I soon saw that he was a switched-on lad – tall, dark-haired, wearing glasses, in his early thirties, and quite smart-looking. With him was the Defence Attaché, older, clearly a Rupert of sorts, and a bit of a stuffed shirt – fortyish, short, dark-haired as well.

'Who are you?' he asked.

'Sergeant Ryan from 22 SAS,' I told him.

'OK – upstairs.'

I dragged myself up one flight and sat down in a room. What with the state of my hands, and blood oozing out of my stockinged feet, you might have thought the DA would dispense with formalities. Not at all.

'Right,' he said, 'I'm just going to ask you a few questions, to verify who you are – make sure you're not a plant. What's your parent unit? Who's the commanding officer?'

I stared at the guy and said, 'Listen – don't start this fucking shit with me. I'm from 22 SAS, and I've been on the run for eight days. Just get a message back to High Wycombe.'

That woke him up. He gave a kind of choke, and the Second Secretary told him, 'Look, cool it.' The DA seemed to have no inkling of what had been going on behind the scenes in Iraq, but I got the impression that the Second Secretary had a pretty acute idea.

'There's nobody else come out, then?' I asked.

The DA stared at me. 'No – you're the first we've seen.'

By then it was 1 a.m. I gathered that the diplomats were living in a hotel just down the road, and that they'd been out at some function, but had been recalled by a message from the secret police.

The Second Secretary asked, 'Can you tell us what happened?'

So I gave them a broad outline of the story: how the patrol had been deployed and had a contact, how we'd legged it through the desert, split up, lost Vince, moved to here, had another contact, and so on.

The DA seemed amazed that anyone should have walked out into Syria. 'Nobody had told us you were anywhere near the border,' he said. But then he let on that, a few days before, he'd had a visit from two British guys doing some sort of a recce. When I heard their names, I realised they were from the Regiment, and that they'd been making a security assessment. When I said I knew both of them, things began to make more sense to him. He warned me that the building was probably bugged, so that the Syrians were listening to every word we said. I just hoped they'd packed up for the night. Otherwise they'd immediately know that I'd been lying an hour or two earlier.

The DA wrote down some details of what I'd told him and brought in one of the communications clerks, a girl, who encoded a message and sent it off to the UK command centre at High Wycombe.

Things were getting a bit ridiculous. The DA kept calling me 'Sergeant Ryan'. I was calling the Second Secretary 'John', and he was calling me 'Chris'. Anyway, with the message sent off, I reassembled my weapon and secured it, together with my ammunition, grenades, TACBE and kite-sight, in the strong room, and saw everything locked up safely. Then they told me that I could spend the rest of the night in the Meridien Hotel, just down the road, and said they'd put me on the British Airways flight to London the next day. They evidently felt that the hotel would be secure enough, but they told me to stay in my room, and to order meals through room-service.

London! That wasn't what I wanted at all. My only concern was to get back to Saudi and find out what had become of the rest of the patrol. But before I could protest they were asking if there was anyone I'd like to phone. I thought, 'If I'm going back to UK, I'll let Jan know.' So I said I'd call my wife.

I realised that if I did fly in to London, I'd only have a very short time there – the Regiment would want me straight back in Saudi, for debriefing; if I got to Hereford at all, it would be for just one night. But Jan didn't even know that we'd been deployed over the border, and I didn't want anyone else to know it either. So I thought things through a bit, working out what I could say and what I couldn't, and put in the call, with the Second Secretary sitting beside me.

Jan sounded quite surprised to hear my voice.

'Hi, Jan,' I said, forcing myself to sound casual. 'I might be coming home tomorrow.'

'Great! How's it going?'

'Fine. No problem.'

'Why are you coming back, then?'

'Just to pick up a bit of kit, you know, and escort it back across. I might only be there half the night. A couple of hours, even.'

'Oh, great!' she said. 'Great! So – that's it.'

'Everything fine there?' I asked.

'Yeah – everything's boring. You doing anything?'

'No,' I said. 'Everything here's cool. The only thing is – don't tell anyone I've rung. Just don't tell anybody I've been in contact.'

The Embassy guys offered to get a taxi down to the hotel, but as it was only a couple of hundred metres away, I said I could walk. Yet when the DA set off at a normal pace, I couldn't keep up with him. I padded slowly along the pavement, and anyone I passed looked down at my stockinged feet in some surprise. As we arrived at the hotel, the porters standing around in the lobby also glared at my feet in disdain. The Second Secretary said, 'We may have a bit of trouble here, as you haven't got a passport; they don't normally let anybody book in without identification. But I'll see if I can square it away.'

The guy on the desk wasn't amused. 'No, no,' he kept saying. 'No passport, no room! He cannot book in.'

The Second Secretary began muttering about going back to the Embassy and spending the night there. He said that to get a passport made out he'd have to contact the chargé d'affaires. A photo would have to be taken, and it couldn't be done until next morning.

Then I said, 'Listen – I've got a telephone number from the police. The boss guy said if I had any trouble, I was to ring them.'

'No, no,' said the Defence Attaché hurriedly. 'You can't do that. Don't ring them. Don't involve them any more. In fact we've got a cellar bedroom in the Embassy, and you can sleep down there.'

'No,' said the Second Secretary. 'The place is filthy. He can't go in there.'

'Nonsense!' barked the DA. 'He's just roughed it for eight days. He'll be all right.' Then he added, 'At a pinch, he can have my bed.'

What I didn't realise until later was that the man had two double beds in his hotel room – but of course, because he was an officer and I was an other rank, he didn't fancy having me sleeping in there.

We didn't seem to be getting far, so the Second Secretary said,

'Where's that telephone number?' He got on the phone to my friend in the secret police, and within five minutes two Mercedes screeched to a halt outside. A swarm of men ran in. It looked like a raid by the SS; some of them were wearing long black leather trench-coats. With them was the interpreter. He came running up to me, grabbed me by the arm and moved me to one side. 'Chris,' he said quietly, 'in two minutes you're going to sign the book. Sign with a name that you can remember, and give any address you can remember. Everything will be all right. If you get any more trouble, ring me again.' He then had a word with the Second Secretary.

I turned round, and there were three blokes giving the piss to the hotel manager behind the desk. His eyes were going round in circles, and he was nodding like a robot. Then the secret police party walked out. 'I'll see you later,' said the interpreter, and he was gone.

I went back up to the desk.

'Yes, yes. Sign here, please. Anything I can do for you, sir?' I gave my surname as Black, and made up some address near Newcastle. The man snapped his fingers for a porter, and two guys grabbed my bags. The diplomats said, 'We'll see you in the morning,' and up I went.

By then it was after 2a.m. and the past twenty-four hours had been the longest of my life. I'd really been looking forward to getting into that room. Once I closed the door, I thought, I'd be free of worry and danger for the first time in ten days. I'd be able to lie down, chill out, and go to sleep. But it didn't work out like that. As soon as I was alone, I started worrying about the rest of the patrol. I'd hoped that some of the guys would have escaped into Syria ahead of me. Either that, or they would have been lifted out by chopper, back into Saudi; but now this possibility seemed unlikely. If the five had been rescued, and three guys were still missing, the Regiment would surely have alerted the Syrians to look out for us, and warned the Damascus Embassy. I'd come up like a bad penny, but nobody else. What had happened to the others? Were they dead, or hiding up somewhere? Were they still on the move? If they were, they must be in a bad way by now.

I was so wound up that I felt I was still on the run. I got out my notebook and began scribbling reminders about what I'd done. I'd brought the book with me in case I had to take down a radio message or compose one, but in fact, until then, I hadn't made a single entry, for fear that I might be captured. But now I went back one day at a time, logging details to refresh my memory, and working out where I'd been at various times.

The DA had warned me not to go downstairs for breakfast, in case press reporters had come into the hotel overnight. Instead, he said, I should get anything I wanted on room service.

So I lay on the bed, my feet propped up on pillows to help bring the swelling down – and all I wanted to do was drink. I had a craving for sweet drinks, particularly. When I looked at the room-service menu and found that they did ten different kinds of fruit-juice cocktail, I phoned down to a waiter and asked for one of each. 'Can you send them up?' I asked.

'Yes,' said the guy, 'but how many for?'

'For one person.'

'So which one do you want?'

'I want every single one. I want numbers one, two, three – '

'For how many people?'

'For one person.'

'Yes, but which one do you want?'

'SEND THEM ALL!' I yelled.

What do you think? The waiter came up with one drink! So I said, 'Fucking hell!', swilled this thing down, phoned up again and said, 'I want every single cocktail.'

'For how many people?'

'For ten people.'

This time the guy came up with ten glasses, and I went *whack, whack, whack* – straight down with the lot.

Then, lying in bed, I thought, 'Jesus, I need a piss.' But when I put my legs over the side of the bed, the pain in my feet was outrageous. I felt that they were going to split open – I really thought that the skin would rip, and flesh would burst out. I even considered slitting them to relieve the agony. I was nearly crying with it. As I crawled across the floor on hands and knees, I thought, 'This is bloody degrading! How much lower can you get? You're on your hands and knees in the shithouse!' But there was no other way.

I reached the bog and dragged myself up on to the seat. But immediately it happened again: the pain in my feet was so intense that I lost all feeling in my bladder, and couldn't pee. On the floor again, I crawled back to my bed and lay down. As soon as my feet stopped hurting, after about a minute, I wanted to pee again. Then I saw a metal wastepaper bin on the floor beside the bed, so I pulled it over and leaned over and pissed in that, and at last I could get my head down. But still I was tossing and turning, tossing and turning, my mind full of disturbing images – of my comrades wandering in the desert, or, worse still, being killed.

In the end, though, I fell asleep – only to be dragged back by the phone ringing. By then it was after three, and here was the Defence Attaché on the line, sounding ridiculously conspiratorial.

'What happened to the Charlie Oscar Delta Echo Sierra?' he breathed.

I said 'What?'

He repeated himself.

'What the fuck are you on about?'

'What happened to the *codes*?'

Suddenly I ralised that he was trying to be covert, spelling out 'codes' like that. Also I realised that it must be High Wycombe who were asking for the information; whenever we encrypt a message, we put it into code, then burn the cipher and smash the encryption device. In fact, Legs had carried our cipher equipment. He had burnt the codes and smashed the Emu.

'One of the other lads had them,' I said. 'He burned them. I never had them at all.'

'OK,' he said, and rang off.

That was when I knew for sure that nobody else had come out.

In the morning I ordered breakfast from room-service, and ate some fruit salad and a roll. I still didn't want anything subsetantial, but I drank pints of fruit juice and tea. Compared with the day before, I felt quite good. Then the Brits came to collect me, and I hobbled back to the Embassy, shuffling along the pavement in my stockinged feet, with my shoes under my arm.

By the time we arrived, the place seemed to be full of people. The chargé d'affaires had appeared, and there were two British girls on duty, one dealing with communications, the other a typist. I chatted to them for a while, then they put me up against a wall in my shirt and tie to take a black-and-white passport photograph with a Polaroid camera. 'Better be careful,' somebody said. 'We've only got two frames left.' But the first shot came out well, so they trimmed it, stuck it into a blank passport and stamped it. There I was, fixed up with a ten-year passport. The whole thing seemed so amateurish that I felt I was being given a Second World War escape kit.

During the morning some questions came back from High Wycombe about the locations I'd mentioned, and the fact that I couldn't even work out the latitude and longitude showed what poor shape I was in. The DA had to do it for me. When I mentioned to him that I'd walked through some installation which looked like a signals complex, the Second Secretary said, 'No, no: that's the yellow cake processing facility at Al Qaim.' He knew everything about the place – even the number of the Iraqi regiment guarding it. The latticework towers I'd seen on the high ground were for defence, not communication: apparently what I'd thought were cables slung between them were in fact chains, to prevent attacks from low-flying aircraft.

'What's going on there?' I asked.

'We don't know exactly. Some sort of nuclear processing.'

'Bloody hell! I drank some water coming out of that place, and it tasted terrible.'

'Effluent,' he said. 'Nuclear effluent.'

I felt my insides go cold. Had I swallowed some radioactive waste and contaminated myself, maybe with fatal consequences?

During the morning a fax came in from High Wycombe saying: 'Has Ryan spoken to anybody? Has he had contact with anyone?' The Second Secretary asked if I wanted him to record the call I'd made to Jan. I said, 'Well, yeah. I've got nothing to hide,' and I gave him Jan's name and telephone number. Within an hour of that fax going back to High Wycombe, the regimental Families' Officer was round at our house in Hereford, banging on the door.

Of course Jan was upset, because if he comes round like that, it usually means your husband's dead.

'What do you want?' she demanded, immediately deciding to cover up.

'Have you just spoken to your husband?'

'No.'

'He's been on the phone to you.'

'No he hasn't.'

'I know he has. He's phoned you.'

'Well, yes. He's said he's coming back to get some kit.'

'What else did he say?'

'Nothing.'

But the officer kept on with his questions, until Jan wondered what the hell was going on, and began to feel sure that something bad had happened to me.

In Damascus, I knew nothing of this, and we headed down to the airport to buy a ticket and get me on the flight to London. I'd bent in the heels of my shoes, so that they were like slippers, and occasionally I put them on; but my feet were still very painful, and mostly I was padding around in my socks. I got as far as the check-in desk, but there the guy stopped me because I didn't have a stamped visa showing when I'd entered the country. That was it; there was no arguing with him, and I ended up back at the Embassy.

The chargé d'affaires said, 'Right, it looks as though you'll be here for a couple of days. I'll give you some Syrian money, so that you can go and do a bit of shopping.' First, though, I went off with the Defence Attaché to see about a visa. We visited a building which was like a honeycomb of little offices, dozens of them, some with room for little more than a six-foot table, a chair and space for one person to stand up. Everyone was in military uniform. We went from one room to another, and one official after another said, 'Oh, no – it's the other one,' and directed us to somebody else. The DA showed tremendous patience, and in all we saw about twenty people. The last official said, 'Well, if you haven't got an entry visa, you can't leave.'

So we'd wasted the whole morning. I said to the DA, 'Why not phone my friend in the police again?'

'Oh no,' he said, 'We can't do that.' So I waited till I was away from him, and asked the Second Secretary the same question. He put through a call, and very soon a message was on its way from the police to the visa building. When we next went down, I collected my exit visa without difficulty.

The next flight out was in two days' time – but now things had changed. Instead of returning to the UK, I was told I'd be flying to Cyprus, where I'd be put on to a Hercules that was coming across from Riyadh. From Cyprus I was to fly to the Saudi capital, spend one night there, and then return to the squadron at Al Jouf. That suited me much better; there was nothing particular on at home, and I wasn't interested in going there. All I wanted was to get back to the squadron, so that I could find out about the rest of the patrol, and brief any other guys who might be going in.

That evening, back in the hotel, I had a meal in my room and went to bed. But still I couldn't relax: the missing guys were too much on my mind. It felt really bad to be sitting in Damascus, unable to contribute any information which might help with their recovery.

Back in the Embassy next day, I was shooting shit with the two girls. One of them, who was quite good looking, said, 'I've got a Walkman in the flat. Why not come down and listen to some music?' I said, 'Oh – great!' and we went downstairs into her living room. I wasn't sure what her interest in me might be, so I started talking about Jan and Sarah, to show her how the land lay. As we sat there chatting, I said, 'D'you mind if I take off my shoes and socks, and have another look at my feet?'

By then the cuts had dried up a good bit, but they still weren't a pretty sight, and when I stripped my feet off, she was horrified. Until then, I don't think either of the girls quite realised what I'd been through. They imagined I'd just been for a bit of a walk. Anyway, they were full of sympathy – and it was good just to sit there and let my feet breathe.

My fingers were nearly as bad as my feet. I still had no feeling in the tips, and when I squeezed my nails, pus kept oozing out. So I asked if she'd got a scrubbing brush, and went to the basin and scrubbed my fingers really hard. It was total agony, but I got the dirt out from under the nails, and all the pus, until blood was running freely. Then I rinsed my hands off, and from that moment the ends of my fingers began to heal up well. Obviously I should have seen a doctor, but the Embassy had no medic in residence, and a message from High Wycombe had specifically forbidden me to make contact with anyone outside.

The Embassy people did their best to entertain me. The DA's assistant, a sergeant, took me out for a drive round the heights of Damascus and showed me some of the military installations. Chatting about my escape, he said, 'God – you're going to get a medal for this.'

'Why?' I said. 'It was nothing special.'

Until that moment it hadn't occurred to me that I'd done anything exceptional. I'd just been for rather a long walk. The job we'd been tasked to do had proved rather more arduous than expected – but I'd had to go through with it all the same.

Back in the Embassy, one of the girls said, 'Would you like to go down the Street called Straight?'

'What's that?'

'You must have heard of it. It's mentioned in the Bible, and runs right through the city from east to west.'

I said, 'Yeah, OK.' So we walked down there and wandered through the casbah. I wasn't particularly interested, but the girls were all excited by the place's history. They started telling how, when the king died, and a new one succeeded, everyone squeezed off their old guns into the air, through the roofs of the covered market, and how one day after a heavy blast-off seven or eight people were killed by rounds falling back to earth. Certainly there were plenty of holes in the curved glass panels of the roofs.

I felt I was becoming a tourist, and to complete the picture I bought some clothes – a set of dark blue cords, a shirt, sweatshirt and track-suit bottoms. I also bought a bag to put my spare clothes in. We went for a couple of meals; at one I put away three helpings of chocolate ice cream in quick time. The girls kept looking at me as I got the stuff down my neck. Now that my appetite was returning, I had a craving for anything sweet and sloppy.

When the time came to leave, my weapon and ammunition obviously had to stay behind, but I wanted to take the TACBE and the kite-sight, because I knew that those things were in short supply back at the squadron. But the Second Secretary made me leave them, in case they aroused suspicion and got me pulled in for questioning at the airport.

When I went to board the Syrian Airlines aircraft I kept my bag with me, but as I reached the top of the steps, the steward said something aggressive to me in Arabic and threw it back down to the ground. As I went in through the door, I could only hope that someone would put it on board. On the plane, my seat was right at the back. As soon as we were airborne, with the no-smoking lights still on, everyone lit up. I've never been on an aircraft so full of smoke; you couldn't see from one end of the cabin to the other. But the relief of leaving Syria made up for everything. Even in the hands of the Embassy people, I'd never felt entirely safe. Damascus had a volatile, feverish air about it, and memories of the mock-execution out in the desert kept me on edge.

It seemed crazy to be flying to Cyprus, for the island lies more or less due west of Damascus, and it was east that I wanted to be heading. But the flight lasted less than a couple of hours, and soon we were coming in to land at Larnaca, with my mind racked by anxiety about what the score was in the squadron.

Chapter Ten

Back To Base

One good move the Defence Attaché had made was to jack up someone to meet me. He'd spoken to a friend in the RAF who was stationed in Cyprus, and arranged a pick-up. He hadn't said who I was, just that someone was on his way through.

When my bag came off the conveyer belt it had crosses of tape stuck all over it, and I was pulled to one side in the Customs. 'Open your luggage, please,' said the officer, and then it was, 'Why have you got all this army equipment? Where've you come from? What have you been doing?'

I said, 'I'm a British soldier, and I've been in Syria, working for the British Embassy in Damascus. Now I'm coming back to the base at Akrotiri.'

'Is anybody meeting you here?'

'Yes. There's a guy outside from the Joint Intelligence Company.'

The customs man looked into my waterbottles, little knowing they could well be radioactive. Then he searched my kit, handling everything. I began to think it was just as well I didn't have the kite-sight and TACBE after all.

As I came out, I spotted a guy wearing a Barbour jacket, and I thought, 'You're obviously a Brit.' So I walked up to him and he immediately said, 'Chris?'

'Yeah. Hello.'

'Good. I'm Brian.'

As he led me across to a car, he said he was taking me down to a family who'd agreed to put me up, and once we were rolling he asked if I needed to see anybody.

'Yes,' I said. 'I need to see a doctor.'

'What's wrong?'

'Well, for starters, I think I drank some poisonous water. Also, my feet are in bits. Look at that.'

I held out my hand to show him my fingers, which had not only lost all feeling in the tips, but now seemed to be turning blue. I saw him looking at me strangely, but I didn't enlighten him about where I'd been.

We drove into a nice-looking housing estate, with guards on the entrance, and I was met by an RAF officer, who introduced me to his Scottish wife and their two young kids. No questions were asked; obviously they'd been briefed. They just welcomed me and sat me down, and the wife said, 'Can I make you something to eat for tea?'

'Well, thanks.'

'Right,' she said. 'It won't take a minute. *EastEnders* is on the telly.'

So there I sat watching *EastEnders*, and eating eggs, beans and chips, and thinking, 'This is outrageous!' It was really weird. Then a doctor turned up, the wife sent the children out, and the doctor took a look at me, asking what was wrong.

'It's my fingers,' I told him. 'I can't feel them much, and they keep going blue.'

He did the squeeze test a few times and said, 'Well, the colour seems to be coming back. I think you've got a bit of frost nip, that's all.' Then he looked at my feet, cleaned them up as much as he could, put zinc oxide tape on them, left me some spare tape, and said, 'There's not a lot I can do for you. Is there anything else wrong?'

'Well, I was round a chemical plant, and drank some of the effluent. Could that be having an effect on my hands?'

'I don't see how it could. But you ought to have blood tests and other checks when you get back.'

When he'd gone, the woman gave me a beer, which went down well, and we sat around chatting. Then, just before eight, the husband said, 'Right, I'm off to work. I'll be back at four in the morning to pick you up.'

I thought, 'Jesus, you're trusting – disappearing like this, leaving a stranger in your house with your wife and kids!' Anyway, off he went, and because I knew I wasn't going back to the UK after all, I thought I'd better call Jan to say that plans had changed. I asked the wife if I could use their phone, and she said, 'Carry on – as long as you like.'

So I dialled through and said, 'Jan, I'm not coming home after all.'

'Oh, God!' she exclaimed. 'What's happened?'

'Nothing. It's just that they don't need the kit fetching.'

'Listen,' she said, 'the Families' Officer's been round here asking questions. What the hell's going on?'

'Nothing. Everything's all right.'

'There's things *not* all right, I know.'

'Everything's all right,' I repeated – but still she wasn't satisfied.

'Are you injured?'

'No, no. Not injured. Listen. There's been some trouble, but I'm all right. You remember the place we were talking about?'

'You mean the river?'

'Yes, but keep quiet.'

'Well?'

'I was along there.'

'How many?'

'Seven others.'

'What are their names?'

'I can't tell you. I'm the only one that's left. But I'm fine. Whatever you do, don't tell anybody I've been on the phone again. Everything's cool. It's just that I'm not coming home now. I'm going back across there.'

That was when the old tears started. She kept saying, 'Something's gone wrong, I know,' and I was repeating, 'No, no. Everything's fine, I promise you. I'll phone again in a couple of weeks.'

I rang off feeling pretty shattered, and took a minute to get myself together. Then my hostess said, 'You can sleep in that bedroom there. Would you like to get your head down?'

'Great,' I said. But first I went to have a bath, because I'd got so sticky on the aircraft. When I stripped off, what should I find but that my legs had gone blue as well, worse than my hands! For a few seconds I was horrified – then I realised what the problem was. The dye had been coming out of my new Syrian cords, on to my hands as well. What a dick I felt, after that scene with the doctor. At least I knew why I kept turning blue. But no matter the colour, my hands weren't right; my fingers were still feeling woody.

I got my head down, and the next thing I knew, my host was knocking on my door at 4 a.m. His wife was already up and had made a cup of tea; she was waiting for us downstairs, and as we went out I thanked her for her hospitality.

At Akrotiri airbase we were confronted by the inevitable stroppy little RAF corporal, who sat there saying, 'Where's your ID card?'

'I haven't got one.'

'Passport?'

'Haven't got one.' (I had the passport which they'd made out for me in Damascus, but I wasn't going to show it to this prick.)

'Name?'

'There's no name.'

'Well, who are you?'

'I'm a person that's getting on this flight.'

Behind me was the squadron leader who'd been looking after me. He was carrying my bags, and now he said, 'It's all right. He's going on this flight. I'll vouch for him.'

'OK, Sir,' said the corporal, and we walked through.

By then the flight crew had assembled, and the chief loadie – the flight sergeant in charge of the back of the Hercules – had heard all this. He was quite a big half-caste lad, and he stood there watching.

The squadron leader came in, put my bags down and said, 'You'll be going aboard with this flight crew. Soon as they go, you get on too.' He went across to them and said, 'That's some extra luggage you've got.' Then he shook hands with me, and I thanked him, and he left.

The flight crew were all laughing and joking together. I sat by myself across the room, and after a few minutes the flight sergeant came across and said, 'Who are you, then?'

'I'm not telling you.'

'What?'

'Mind your own business,' I said, and looked down.

'Who the fuck d'you think you are?'

'What the fuck's it got to do with you?'

'Uh,' went the flight sergeant, 'if you don't tell me who you are, you're not getting on my aircraft.'

'If I don't get on,' I told him, 'I guarantee your career will fucking *end* when this aircraft touches down in Riyadh. Now stop asking questions.'

It was out of character for me to be so aggressive, but I'd had enough of all these dickheads, and someone like that wasn't going to stop me getting back. I felt I'd been through so much that I wasn't going to bow down to anybody.

I could see he was annoyed, but he was a bit rattled too. He just said, 'OK,' and walked away. These exchanges weren't bantering, there was needle in them – but they were typical of what happens if someone tries to push an SAS guy. It's a privilege, a sort of power for people in the Regiment – they don't have to tell outsiders anything. With officers, obviously, you're polite, and if they ask for your identity, you just say, 'Sorry, sir, I can't tell you.' Most people have the sense to back off if you tell them in a civil way that they don't need to know, and suggest they leave it at that. But there are always one or two who push and push, until it comes to the point when you're saying, 'Hey, fucking sling your hook.'

The back of the Herc was packed full of equipment, netted and strapped down on pallets. As I sat on one of the web seats, the first person I saw was Mel, a young signaller from 22 SAS. I thought, 'Great – the first friendly face, the first person I know,' and sat down next to him. It turned out that he was escorting some equipment across, so that he'd had to stay on board during the stop-over.

The flight sergeant knew where Mel came from – so when he saw us together, he realised that I was SAS and that he'd put his foot in it.

Anyway, Mel and I got talking. 'Have you heard anything about what's going on over here?' I asked, and he said, 'No, not a thing.' So I told him a bit about what had happened. It was a terrific relief to be able to talk to someone I knew.

Presently we took off, and four hours later I landed in Riyadh for the second time. The airport terminal was in complete disarray, full of military personnel, with areas hessianed off, control points set up, and people buzzing in all directions. I was puzzled to find that no one had come to meet me. The other passengers disappeared, and I was left sitting in the reception lounge on my own. Then at last a young man, in uniform but wearing no badges, came up and said, 'Are you Chris Ryan?'

'That's right. Who are you?'

'I'm taking you somewhere.'

'No you're not. Who *are* you?'

At last he gave me his name – Corporal Smith.

'And who are you working for?'

'Taff,' he said, naming the acting quartermaster.

'OK,' I said. 'That's fair enough.'

As we drove off in a white land-cruiser, I asked him if there'd been any news about the patrol.

'Not a word,' he said.

'Jesus Christ!'

I asked about Scuds coming in, and he said that one had landed close to the airport a couple of nights back. He took me to a big, plush, modern hotel, where a room had been reserved for me. The place was full of RAF aircrew in their flight-suits, with pistols showing in holsters underneath. They didn't realise how well off they were, fighting the war from such a luxurious base.

I went up to my room and lay down. I was still feeling weak, and lacking in decision. I only had to walk a hundred metres before I was out of breath, and felt like an old man. Within half an hour there came a knock on the door, and there was the former sergeant major, newly commissioned as Quartermaster. I'd hardly come across him before, but I knew he was a fairly unapproachable character, and he greeted me with a typically gruff, "'Ullo, Chris.'

He sat down and said, 'Right – I know everything's secret. But are you all right?'

'Yeah,' I said, 'I'm fine.'

'Are the rest of the lads OK?'

'I don't know, Taff. It's more than a week since I saw them.'

He told me that the Director and Assistant Director – the brigadier and colonel in command of Special Forces – wanted to debrief me. But before they arrived, he suggested I went downtown and got a brew, so he sent an assistant round with the equivalent of a couple of hundred pounds in local currency. Filling in time, I went out and bought a Walkman, some music tapes, including one by Eric Clapton, and a small radio. We then went to a burger bar, where we found a gang of young Americans wearing T-shirts with motifs on them like DEATH BEFORE DISHONOR, and that sort of crap. They were in high spirits, and going on about the war, but I couldn't help thinking, 'What a bunch of dickheads! They haven't a clue what's going on out there.'

I heard that the two guys from 'B' Squadron who'd done the recce in Syria were back in Riyadh; so I went round to see them, and immediately asked for news. All they'd heard was that I'd come out; they couldn't even discover the names of the people who were missing, such was the secrecy that had been clamped on everything. It was great to talk to them, and after some chat they suggested we should go out for a meal.

'Why not have it at my place?' I said. 'I can get it on the room.'

So all three of us came back to my room and ordered mixed grills. Just as we'd finished eating, a message came to say that the Assistant Director was downstairs, on his way to see me. Ignoring my pleas for them to stay, the other two promptly scarpered.

After a brief opening chat, the Colonel said, 'I don't really want to know what happened. But have a good long think, because you're going to be questioned about why you ran away.'

I thought he was implying that we'd all been cowards. I was too stunned to say anything except, 'Yeah – OK.'

Only when he'd gone did I start to burn with resentment. That seemed to me a very strange thing for anyone to have said, let alone a senior Special Forces officer who didn't yet know exactly what had happened. Anyway, he told me that the Director was on his way to see me, so I waited up, and it wasn't until about one in the morning that the Brigadier came rolling in. He said nothing about us having run away. On the contrary, having been a 'B' Squadron man himself, he saw my escape as a feather in the squadron's cap, and congratulated me. First thing next morning, he said, I was to fly up to Al Jouf on a Hercules.

I couldn't come to terms with the fact that there was no news of the others. Because the Iraqis had not announced the capture of any prisoners behind the lines, it seemed more and more likely that they were all dead. The worst thing was that people kept coming up to me and asking, 'Well, what do you think happened to them?' I had no idea: all I could do was repeat the story of the contact and the break, and I told it so often that I was starting to do it parrot-fashion. Beyond that, I wanted someone to tell *me* what the score was.

In the morning I dressed in my clean uniform, which had been through the washing-machine at the embassy in Damascus, and I felt fresh and good to have it on again. My feet were still pretty sore, but I got my boots back on, and so looked quite presentable.

As the aircraft landed at Al Jouf I was so excited by the thought of seeing the guys again that I went and stood on the tailgate as it was dropping down, all teed-up to rush out and greet them. But to my surprise there was only one man there – Geordie, the SSM. It turned out that he had told everyone else to keep away, in case I was overwhelmed by emotion. In fact three of the guys had ignored his instructions and were hovering in the background. As I walked out, they came racing across and surrounded me, hammering me on the back, and calling out, 'Well done!' For a minute or two I couldn't really speak. Bob Shepherd was so shattered by my appearance that he burst into tears. In place of the fit, bouncing young fellow he'd seen off a couple of weeks earlier, here was a prematurely aged cripple, broken, bent and shuffling; as he graphically put it, a bag of bones. He was so upset that, instead of driving back to 'B' Squadron's location, he took a solitary walk round the airfield to sort himself out.

Geordie thinned the guys out, took me to one side, and said, 'Right. We've got to go in for the debriefing.'

The head-shed was housed in tents alongside the permanent control-tower buildings. Before we went in, the SSM asked if there was anything I wanted to tell him. I said, 'Yeah, there's quite a bit. I'll tell you what actually happened, but I'm not going to tell the CO.' So I told him about Vince losing heart. 'If Andy or any of the others come out, they'll confirm it,' I said. 'Until then, we'll just leave it. There's no need to say it was his fault.' The Sergeant Major said, 'Fine,' and so we went in.

We went down with a sergeant from the Int section, a nice guy, who asked me to tell the story while he wrote it down. I was a bit put out by the sight of the CO, sitting on a chair and reading *The Times* at the other side of the tent, but paying no attention to me. Then the Ops officer walked past, and he didn't say anything either. I became more and more convinced that in their view I'd done something wrong.

Anyway, I got on with the debriefing, and in the middle of it half the squadron came back from the ranges, together with the OC. His behaviour was entirely different. He grabbed me, shook hands, and said, 'It's really great to see you! Terrific that you're back! Is there anything I can get you?'

I said, 'No thanks – I'm just talking to this Int guy.'

'Right – as soon as you've finished here, we'll get you across the squadron, because everyone's dying to hear what happened.'

The debrief lasted two hours. Once it was over, Geordie drove me round the airfield to the squadron location, pointing out how all the light assault vehicles had been written off in training. On the way he asked, 'First things first: d'you want to go home?'

'No,' I said, 'I want to stay here and find out what's happened.' The last thing I wanted to do was desert the team.

Geordie also gave me amazing news about the other two Bravo patrols: they'd both come straight back. When Bravo Three Zero took stock of their location, the commander immediately decided that the area was impossibly dangerous. There wasn't enough cover to conceal the vehicles, and without further ado they began to drive back towards the Saudi border – a journey which took them two nights. Afterwards the commander was fiercely criticised, not least because he ignored an instruction to RV with 'D' Squadron – who were already in Iraq and needing reinforcement – not far off his route.

Bravo One Zero stayed an even shorter time. When the Chinook landed at their drop-off point, the pilot said to the leader, 'Pete – d'you want to have a look around while I hang on a minute? We crossed a road about fifteen miles back, and I can still see the lights of vehicles along it, the desert's that fucking flat. I can't see any depressions or wadis for miles. It's like a billiard table.' To prove his point, the pilot flew twenty kilometres up and down, trying to find some broken ground into which he could drop the patrol, but the desert remained horribly bare.

Pete took a decision which struck me as immensely courageous. 'Right,' he said, 'we're not staying here. We're flying out.'

Back at Al Jouf he was ridiculed and accused of being a coward – the word was actually used. But I and many others reckoned that of all the decisions taken by the three patrol commanders, his needed the most balls. To have stayed where he was would have been suicide – a replica of what had happened to us, if not worse. A year later people would start to say: 'Well, maybe he did the right thing after all' – but at the time he suffered.

Anyway, it was a big surprise for me to hear that all three OPs had been eliminated, for one reason or another. With Bravo Two Zero, it turned out that the comms failure had been due mainly to the fact that we'd been given the wrong radio frequencies. This was not the fault of anyone in the Regiment, but of the signal unit attached to us. The result was that although three of Legs' messages got through in garbled form, no reply ever reached us. I also found that we'd been seriously misled about the performance of our TACBEs; their effective range was only about 120 kilometres, and the closest most coalition aircraft were flying was 500 kilometres to the east. During the night of 24 January – our first on the run – one American F-15 pilot did pick up a call from Andy, and he passed it on to an AWACS aircraft. But because the call originated from a location which our head-shed was not expecting, it only caused confusion.

When the patrol went missing, tremendous pressure built up among the rank-and-file of the squadron to mount a rescue mission; volunteers were determined to make a box-search. When the CO refused to commit one of his few precious helicopters immediately to the task, some of the guys were on the verge of mutiny. But middle and senior management saw that, in the circumstances, the CO was right to delay a search until the patrol's situation became clearer.

The main problem was that the regimental head-shed was expecting us to strike back for the Saudi border in case of trouble, whereas after our initial feint we had set off in exactly the opposite direction. By 26 January, even though no explicit message had been received from us, it was clear that something had gone seriously wrong. At 1745 that evening a Chinook took off from Arar, with five members of the squadron on board, in an attempt to pull us out. That mission was aborted when the weather closed down. Another took off the next day – a joint Anglo-American team on board an MH-53 – which completed its planned route and approached to within five or six kilometres of our original emergency rendezvous before flying down what seemed the most likely escape-and-evasion route to the Saudi border, and almost running out of fuel in the process. A third search-and-rescue mission was mounted on 30 January, but this was also aborted when the pilot fell ill. The CO continued trying to arrange further searches until, in the early hours of 1 February, he heard that I had turned up in Damascus – whereupon it became obvious that none of the patrol could still be trying to return to Saudi.

More cheerful news was that 'A' and 'D' Squadrons had crossed the border in force just one night after our insertion, and that with their heavily-armed Pinkies they were creating havoc among mobile Scud launchers and communications towers. Their key weapon was the M19 – in effect, a machine-gun firing bombs at the rate of three or four per second. The ammunition was the same as in our 203s, except that the rounds contained more high-explosive – and when volleys of those things began bursting all round them, the Iraqis turned and ran. Details of the marauding operations had yet to emerge, but the squadrons' communications were working well, and from their operational reports it was clear that everyone was having a ball.

By the time I returned to Al Jouf, 'B' Squadron had tents, and life was much more organised. The OC and the SSM had organised a camp-bed for me – an American cot – in their own tent, which had a heater. I was amazed by the care with which Geordie was looking after me: before our deployment he'd seemed out of his depth, but now he was well in control, and really mothering me. He put my kit on the bed and said, 'Right, d'you mind speaking to the guys?'

'No, no,' I said. 'That'll be fine.'

An hour later they had a big map set up at the back of one of the tents. I stood at the front, and twenty of the guys came in to sit on the ground and listen. As I told them the story they kept perfectly still, absorbed, and remained almost totally silent – but I could tell from the occasional muttered curse that they felt what it had been like. When I described how it had snowed, and how cutting the wind had been, they knew I wasn't exaggerating, because at Al Jouf the weather had grown even colder since I left.

Afterwards the OC and the SSM made me dinner out of ration packs. Then we had to go back across to the headquarters, because the CO wanted to see me at 2300. I thought, 'Oh, God! Not again! Why the hell didn't he listen in while I was being debriefed?' But across we went to one of the control rooms, and I was there until two in the morning. At the end he asked, 'Is there anything you think you should have done?'

That nearly cracked me up. I almost burst into tears as I said, 'I should have tied Vince to me.'

'Listen,' said the CO. 'It wasn't your fault.' Then he asked if I'd mind going up to Arar, to talk to 'A' Squadron of Delta Force, the American Special Forces unit, which was about to deploy behind the lines. It meant leaving at 0530 – in about three hours' time – so we went straight back to our tent and got our heads down.

As I climbed into my sleeping bag, the CO draped a big goatherd's coat over me. I felt like a little kid.

Apart from my night in Cyprus, that was the first time since the contact that I slept soundly. I don't know whether it was because I felt secure at last; for whatever reason, I went out like a light, and the next thing I knew, Geordie was shaking my shoulder. He'd already cooked a fried breakfast with the light on, but I'd been out for the count and hadn't noticed a thing. So we had sausages and bacon and a cup of tea, and set out at 0530 in a Land-Rover, accompanied by Gus, an American liaison officer.

All the way up, as it got lighter, Gus was picking information out of me. We'd met in Hereford, when he'd come to the UK to command one of the squadrons. At that time I was Sniper Team Commander, in charge of all the high-rise options – climbing and abseiling on the outsides of buildings, inside lift-wells, or ascending glass buildings on suckers. We were hosting the Delta Squadron, and Gus and I seemed to spend all our time together in the backs of vehicles. Now we were in a vehicle again – but at least this time we could have a useful conversation. Delta's target was the area round the nuclear refinery, and whenever we came to a new kind of terrain during our drive, he asked if the ground where they were heading resembled what we could see. I told him, 'At X it's *that* colour exactly,' and, 'at Y it's like *that*.'

The journey took nearly three hours. Then, in the control room at Arar, I met Major General Wayne Downing, commander of US Special Forces, who'd recently flown in to supervise operations. Slim, fit-looking, with a crew-cut, he was the epitome of a successful American soldier. He shook my hand and introduced me to four or five other officers. Then we sat down on Chesterfields round a coffee table. Downing thanked me for coming up, and I told them what had happened. Again, at the end, there was silence. Then Downing said, 'That's the most amazing story I've heard in years.' There was a pause, and he asked, 'What have the doctors said?'

'Well – I haven't seen a doctor yet.'

He seemed shocked. With a look of worry and embarrassment, he said, 'I sure am sorry to have dragged you up here. You ought to have seen a doctor before you came. Tell you what, though: we've got some go-faster surgeons on the base. I'll have one of them look at you.'

I wasn't quite sure what he meant by a 'go-faster' surgeon, but I went to see one of them willingly enough. A quick examination confirmed that I had frost-nip in my fingers and toes. The doctor said that my feet would heal up in time, but that I needed some dental work done. When I told him about the nuclear effluent, he said I certainly should have a blood-test.

When I got back to Downing, he said, 'I know I'm asking a lot, but will you talk to 'A' Squadron? They're deploying tonight, and I know they'd appreciate it. You could probably give them a load of help.' Of course I agreed. So I told the story yet again, this time to about forty guys, and at the end they burst into applause, with everyone wanting to shake my hand.

Before I left, I went to see Downing once more, and he asked, 'Is there anything you need?'

'Well, yes,' I said. 'Have you got any of those large waterbottles, and a rucksack and stuff like that?'

'Sure have. You'd better go see the quartermaster.' So I did – and I came away with a vehicle nearly full of new kit, an embarrassing amount. Finally Downing sent me into a command room, full of signals equipment, where I found an SAS officer who'd been attached to the American Special Forces. I got talking to him about our patrol, and he said the mission had been sent off without proper briefing. His point was that the Americans could call up satellite imagery of any particular area within twenty-four hours of any request. When I asked why we hadn't done that, he could only attribute the failure to rivalry between Brits and Americans, or a reluctance on the part of the Brits to tell the Americans what they were doing.

Back at Al Jouf, I found myself endlessly speculating with other guys in the squadron about what could have happened to the rest of our patrol. I said I believed in my heart of hearts that Vince was dead, and Stan the same – or possibly captured. But I couldn't understand why the other five hadn't come out, or why there was no news of them. My own emotions were barely under control. On one occasion we were talking in a tent, and I found it was getting too much. I suddenly felt choked and said, 'Ah, listen: I'm off,' and went out. One of the others ran after me and put his arm round my shoulders. 'Don't worry,' he said, 'just get it off your chest.'

People began to assume that the rest of the patrol had been written off, and I heard that I would probably have to go on a tour of New Zealand, Australia and all round England to talk to the families of the guys we'd lost. The OC told me to stand by for the trip as soon as I got back to the UK. He said I wasn't to worry about it because the CO, the adjutant, the Families Officer and OC of the squadron would all be there; I wouldn't have to do it by myself.

In spite of emotional swings, I felt reasonably well – so much so that, when 'B' Squadron began getting ready to drive into Iraq as the security force on a major re-supply for 'A' and 'D', I asked the CO if I could go with them. Luckily he realised that I was a long way from being fit, and said, 'Not a chance.'

The re-supply proved a memorable expedition, and when I heard how it went I was sorry to have missed it. 'B' Squadron provided security for a column of 10 three-ton trucks, and this gave about a dozen of our guys a chance to take part in the war. The party included specialists such as REME fitters and a Royal Engineer who was expert in the repair of Magellans.

The column was commanded by a major called Bill – a really strong character, much respected, with a wealth of experience going back to the Oman campaign of the 1970s. The final briefing which he gave in the middle of the night, in a wadi just short of the border, will never be forgotten by those who heard it. With everyone gathered round in a huddle on the ground, muffled in the long Arab coats they'd bought in the souk, he put over his objectives with inspiring vigour and precision.

'We stop for nothing,' he announced. 'Effective enemy fire is when rounds are coming through your windscreens.'

The SSM of 'B' Squadron, who was driving a Land-Rover, and thought he could score a point, said, 'I don't have a windscreen.'

'OK, then,' replied Bill instantly. 'When you've got rounds coming through your goggles.' After that, there were no more questions, and the column crossed the frontier at 0300, with a couple of Land-Rovers leading the way, four motorbikes behind them to relay messages back if need be, and the trucks following at twenty-metre intervals. During the hours of darkness they made slow progress, as the terrain was rough and difficult; they were driving without lights, and the lorries bounced around violently over the rocks. But with the advent of daylight they forged ahead, sometimes reaching 80 or 90 k.p.h. over smooth stretches.

Their route lay up two main wadis which, on previous days, had been swept by Jaguar or Tornado aircraft making low-level passes to confirm that Iraqi troops had not moved in. On its way the convoy passed numerous little Bedouin encampments. A few of the goat-herders still had camels, but most were motorised, and some owned big Mercedes trucks. Bob Shepherd, who had learned to speak Arabic for the Oman campaign in the 1970s, several times stopped to pass the time of day, and generally found the people friendly. Stan, whom he knew well, was much on his mind, and he kept hoping that one of the herdsmen might have news of him.

The rendezvous with elements of 'D' Squadron was at a Y junction, where two wadis ran together. After a run of 180 kilometres, the column reached it at about 1530. The scouts took them forward to a deep, steep-sided wadi, and for the next twenty-four hours the trucks lay up there out of sight, while everyone else came in off the ground in small parties to collect supplies of food, water and ammunition. There was plenty of fresh food – meat, bread and fruit – but most of the guys were happy with the boil-in-the-bag rations. There were also numerous broken vehicles for the REME mechanics to repair.

When the time came for the column to return, Bob jumped

ship, unilaterally transferring himself to 'D' Squadron for the remainder of the operation. Back at Al Jouf he'd been told that if he did this he would risk being RTU'd, but he was determined to take part in the war. As he said, 'This was what I joined the regiment for. This is my big chance.'

On only his second day with his new unit, 'D' Squadron had a major success. It was a bright morning, and by noon the desert was shimmering under a heat-haze as eight SAS vehicles cruised forward on the lookout for targets. The raiders saw what they thought was an enemy convoy. As they crept closer, they managed to convince themselves that they could identify two tanks and one other vehicle, all moving very slowly. Then, at a range of only two kilometres, they realised that what they could see was a couple of tarmac-laying trucks which were not moving at all; they had been working on a road, but had been abandoned for the time being.

Later that day the marauders came on the real thing: two TELs – transporter elevator launchers – with their Scud missiles in the horizontal attitude. They were about twelve kilometres off, but by then the shimmer had gone, and with their telescopes and binoculars the SAS were able to identify them clearly. A quick radio call whipped the coordinates back to base, and a pair of F-16s were scrambled. The TELs looked as though they had just come out to firing positions, and were about to set up for a launch at last light, so that they could run away in the dark if anyone spotted them. A number of smaller vehicles were active round them, but after the SAS had observed them for about forty minutes, moving slowly closer, they all suddenly began to drive away. Clearly they had spotted the dust cloud raised by the approaching enemy, and they were off. For the Scuds, however, it was too late. At last light, before their crews could get them moving, the F-16s came in to hit them with missiles and 1,000-lb bombs.

For the onlookers, who by then had moved up to within about four kilometres, it was a phenomenal firework display. Evening haze obscured details on the ground, but the sky lit up with giant flashes, the impact of the bombs made the ground shudder, and the heat from the explosions could be felt. The SAS, talking to the pilots, told them that other Iraqi vehicles had pulled off in a particular direction, and sent them in pursuit. Yet it was not until the next day that they realised the full success of the operation. Only then did they hear that the total bag of Scuds in that one place had been seven or eight. The two they'd seen had been the outliers of the group.

That was just one of many successes. Whenever our guys put in an attack, the Iraqis almost always held or ran away; they hardly ever pushed out. The sight of a dust-cloud approaching, and the knowledge that it contained formidable fire-power, was generally enough to send them running. The SAS tactics were to hit hard and disappear quickly. A typical attack would begin with a salvo of 81mm. mortars. As the bombs were falling, the assault party would be creeping in to open up with .50 machine guns and M19s, as well as twin and single gympis. Once, because of the lie of the ground, they had to dismount and take out bunkers on foot.

Much of the terrain in which the squadrons operated was exactly what I had gone through: a moonscape of black or dark-grey rock and rubble, with large boulders dotted about. At night the units would run back and take up a defensive position, either in a wadi or in the open. If it was the latter, they would make what's known as a fish-hook, driving round in a big loop and coming back almost to the point at which they had swung off their original course, so that they could ambush anyone following up their tracks.

Each unit had been allocated a block of territory which it was to search, and gradually, as the guys developed a feel for the ground and for the behaviour of the Iraqis when under attack, they evolved an effective pattern of activity. Generally they would lie up for most of the day, and then, in the afternoon, push out a couple of recces to see what they could find. If they came on to anything, they would take it on just before last light, so that they had time to destroy it, defend themselves and pull out.

Their main targets were the towers designed for reporting air movement. Made of wood and steel, about ten metres high, they reminded everyone of World War Two goon towers set round prison camps. They were defended by forces of no more than platoon strength – about thirty men – most of whom ran away as the vehicles approached. At one, eight Iraqis were taken prisoner. When Bob questioned them, they said exactly what they were doing. They also said that their officer had run away with the radio set, an event that was more or less an SOP for them. They were very frightened, and wanted to go with the British. When they asked where the Brits were going, Bob told them, 'Baghdad.'

'Why?'

'To kill Saddam Hussein.'

'Good!'

Because the guys were low-level squaddies, there was nothing to be gained from sending them back to Saudi. Therefore, after the towers had been blown up, and the weapons and communications equipment destroyed, the SAS walked the prisoners about a kilometre out into the desert and left them there with a bucket of water, confident that their own people would come and rescue them before they suffered any serious hardship. Only once did our forces come up against hardened troops, defending a permanent signals outpost. The place had been hit at night by Coalition aircraft, and a request came for close-up damage assessment. For once the SAS pushed their luck too hard: they found themselves facing a large force of troops who were determined not to move.

At about 2200 a gang of four left their vehicle and went in on foot, trying to establish how big the station was. Much of it turned out to be underground, in bunkers, with the defenders in slit trenches. Challenged in Arabic, the intruders replied in kind, but immediately came under fire, and the sergeant major was hit in the back. A round went in just beside his spine and came out through his stomach, luckily without hitting any bone. He was carried out of immediate danger by a small lad called Ben (who later won the Military Medal for his gallantry), while their two colleagues gave covering fire. The four of them pepper-potted back to the vehicle, the Land-Rover returned to the rest of the formation, and the whole lot moved off about five kilometres before taking up a position for the night.

That same night, further north, the American Delta Force had a big shoot-out and sustained a couple of casualties. Next day a helicopter came in to pick them up. The Americans offered to collect the British sergeant major also, but he declined the lift because, along with the OC, he was leading his gang and wanted to stay on the ground. His sense of duty saved his life –

for as the helicopter which would have taken him came back into Arar, it crashed just short of the base's perimeter, killing everyone on board, including some of the guys I myself had briefed.

The SSM claimed that his wound was not too bad, but by the time two more days had gone by, he was exhausted and glad to be evacuated. The chopper which recovered him also took out the body of the only member of 'A' Squadron to be killed in the entire six-week operation.

When the Iraqi ground forces surrendered, on 28 February, 'A' Squadron immediately returned to Saudi territory, but 'D' stayed on for a few more days, lying low and keeping abreast of events by listening to the BBC World Service. For them, the ceasefire was something of a disappointment, because they had been planning a joint operation against a number of towers with Delta's Minibugs, their small strike helicopters. With the end of the ground war, this was called off. After three days they pulled back and drove, union jacks flying, down the wadi which they had used as their route in, with A-10s doing rolls and somersaults overhead.

Much as I would have liked to take part in all this, I knew I was still a long way from being fit. So when the CO suggested that I should go down to the rear base for three days' R & R and then maybe be deployed again, I was staggered. I looked at him and nodded, but I was thinking, 'Not a chance! There's no way I'm going back over there.'

Anyway, I went and packed, and as we were driving towards the control tower the OC suddenly said, 'I think that's your aircraft!' A Hercules was already taxiing into position for take-off, but he screamed across and scorched the Land-Rover to a halt right under its nose. When I got on board, who should I find in charge but the big loadie I'd encountered at Akrotiri airbase. This time he knew all about me, and apologised for his surly behaviour in Cyprus.

Back in the hangar where we'd lived when we reached the Gulf, I got myself a bed-space and went in search of the kit I'd left behind – only to find that in my absence someone had been through it. I'd lost a bivvy bag, an American poncho liner, and a few other things. I felt certain that none of the badged SAS guys had done it, and blamed one of the men attached from other units. I had a brief panic when I thought that my original escape map, with the names of the patrol written on it, was among the things that had been stolen; but then I found it, and kept it secured.

The cookhouse at Victor was about 200 metres from our hangar, and by the time I had covered that short distance, I felt knackered and had to sit down. I was still eating small amounts of food, and putting weight back on very slowly. As soon as I started chewing anything at all hard, my gums would bleed, so that I always had the taste of blood in my mouth – and as I hate raw meat, it made me feel sick. Observing myself in the mirror, I thought, 'You look like a fucking vampire!'

Altogether I spent two weeks with them, not doing much: eating, sunbathing, listening to music, trying to recover. I felt dazed, and I was shocked at how long it took me to regain strength. When I went to a gym and got on the bench, trying to lift some weights, I realised how weak I had become. I couldn't even do a dip. It was soul-destroying to have become so feeble.

A young troop officer who was running an anti-terrorist team told me I could take charge of the sniper team.

'No way,' I told him. 'I'm going into town for a couple of weeks to recuperate.'

'No, you can't.'

'Bollocks. I'm going. I'm not fit to work at the minute.'

Next morning two of the guys gave me a lift down, and as we went into a shopping centre, out came a man called Kev, with whom I'd passed selection. Somehow the sight of him was too much for me. I burst into tears. He grabbed me, pulled me to one side, and took me round to his accommodation in an army camp on the outskirts of the city, where I stayed for the next few days. That first night I went downtown with him to a disco. Life here didn't seem to make sense: with the air-war still in full swing, and the ground campaign coming up, everyone was drinking and dancing.

After a few days I felt stronger, and went back to Victor to take over the sniper team. We started work, living in a tented camp, but I found that the Arab food didn't agree with me. It began to go straight through me, and I started losing weight again. At the same time, preparations were in hand for a body-guard team job in South America, and I was told to learn Spanish. I was given a one-to-one tutor from the Army Education Corps, but I found it impossible to concentrate. In Bavaria I had had no trouble learning German, and I thought I was quite good at languages; but now I couldn't remember a thing, or even string a simple phrase like 'Good morning' together. My head felt numb; words went in one ear and out the other. I did so badly that my instructor soon got annoyed. 'Listen,' he said, 'have you got the slightest interest in what you're doing?'

'*You* fucking listen,' I answered – and I told him what had happened to me. He immediately apologised, and said, 'You shouldn't be doing this. You can't concentrate.' He got hold of a young Rupert and told him to have me taken off the course.

Because my teeth were still so slack, I made arrangements to see a dentist. Before my appointment, I was warned that I mustn't under any circumstances tell him where I'd been. But when I got into the surgery, the dentist proved a really sensible, nice guy. A New Zealander, he asked me to fill in a form confirming that I'd never had AIDS, and so on. Then he asked his assistant to leave the room, and said, 'There's obviously something wrong.'

'Yes,' I said, 'I've had a bad eight days.'

'I should say so. What do you do for a living?'

'I test Land-Rovers.'

'OK. I'm not interested in what you've done. But your mouth's in a serious state. Your gums show signs of malnutrition; they're receding – that's why they're bleeding. I can see the roots of your teeth. There's a chance you'll lose a few. I'll have to take two out, anyway. Meanwhile, rub this paste in.'

Noticing that I wore a diver's watch, and that the rubber strap was loose on my shrunken wrist, he said, 'Oh, by the way: I've got a watch like that, and if you like I can cut the straps down with one of my files.' It seemed funny that the instruments he used on people's teeth were equally good for fixing watches.

To this day my gums haven't fully recovered; some teeth are still loose. Otherwise, I made a full physical recovery. It took six weeks for feeling to come back into my fingers and toes. A blood test taken in a makeshift hospital on an American airbase revealed nothing wrong – but evidently the doctor who did it missed something, because another test, carried out in the UK, showed that I had a blood disorder, caused by drinking dirty water from the Euphrates, as well as an abnormal amount of enzymes in my liver produced in reaction to poisoning. I was also tested for radioactive poisoning, but there appeared to be no contamination. One doctor, talking about weight loss, told me that it was safe to shed one pound of meat a week. When I told him I'd lost thirty-six in a week, he said, 'It's impossible.' I said, 'It bloody well happened.' To which he replied, 'Well, that's not good.'

The psychological scars took far longer to heal. In the Gulf I began to suffer from a recurrent nightmare, in which I walk through the dark along a road. Ahead of me I see two hooded figures, dressed in black, on top of a mound. I know they're the two men I killed in the nuclear complex, but still I go up to them to ask directions. The night is very dark, and it's as if black rain is falling. As I come close, I see the eyes of the second man, wide with fright, and at the last second a knife-blade flashes as he makes a lunge at me. At that point I wake up, sweating with terror.

When the dream began, I realised that it was caused by feelings of guilt. I phoned Jan and said, 'I've done something terrible.' She understood exactly, and said, 'Forget it, forget it. Don't say anything.' But I was also plagued by worries about Vince. There was I, a fully trained mountain guide, thrown into a situation where we were all going down with exposure, and I'd failed to do the obvious thing of tethering him to me and dragging him on a leash. Even if I'd just held him by the hand, or kept him in front of me where I could see him, I might have saved him. I knew the reason was that I had been suffering from exposure, too – but that couldn't bring him back. On the other hand, he might have slowed us down so much that the cold would have got the better of us all. Again, if we'd stayed together as a group, I think we'd probably have been captured, because you tend to talk each other into actions which you wouldn't take on your own.

On 24 February, the ground war was launched at last. I spent the time glued to CNN television. There was one big set in the corridor between the hangars, with a few settees and chairs in front of it, and guys were watching at all hours of the day and night, often falling asleep where they sat. When the Coalition began taking prisoners, we couldn't believe the numbers: 20,000, 40,000, 50,000 – we kept a scoreboard.

In five days, unbelievably, it was all over. The squadron came back from Al Jouf to Victor, getting ready to go home. Moves were being made to bring 'A' and 'D' Squadrons back as well. Then the OC said that as soon as an aircraft to the UK became available, I would be on it.

Just after the ceasefire I was in one of the hangars when somebody rushed in, shouting, 'Hey! We've seen Dinger on the telly!'

Electrified, I ran back with him to see if I could catch a glimpse. There'd been shots of the Iraqis handing over allied prisoners.

'Are you sure it was him?'

'Yeah, yeah, it was Dinger all right.'

We sat there waiting for the next news programme. When it came on, someone shouted, 'There he is!' Sure enough, it was Dinger – and a moment later we saw Stan as well. Both were in Baghdad. They were wearing orange prison overalls, sitting at a table, on their way to being handed over to the Red Crescent. It was easy enough to spot Dinger, but Stan was harder to pick out, because he had lost a lot of weight and had become quite gaunt.

Just to see them was intensely exciting. We knew those two were safe – but what about the others? We were pretty sure that one man in 'A' Squadron, Jack, had been killed, because he had been seriously wounded and left for dead – but from Bravo Two Zero there were still five to account for: Bob, Vince, Legs, Mark and Andy. We asked the sergeant major what was happening, but he wouldn't tell us anything; then we heard through the regiment that the Iraqis had four more prisoners to release. We reckoned that meant one of our guys must have died.

Details trickled out slowly. The first to reach us, via Dinger, was that Legs had died from hypothermia after trying to cross the Euphrates. We therefore presumed that the other four would be coming out. Then, to our amazement, we heard that Jack had survived, and was about to be released. That meant that another of our own lot must have gone down. Rumours flew about, but there was no official information. Then some guys were detailed

214

to pack their kit and stand by to fly into Riyadh, so that friendly faces would be there to greet the prisoners when they returned, and sit with them in the aircraft when they flew on to hospital in Cyprus.

'D' Squadron was still inside Iraq, in case anything cracked off again, but 'A' Squadron arrived back at Victor, and there was a lot of in-fighting in their hangar as scores were settled and frustrations worked off – something that occurs a good deal in a unit full of very strong characters. The guys are so well trained that during operations they keep control of themselves, whatever happens – but once they are back at base they're quick to vent their displeasure on anyone who's done something stupid or unnecessarily dangerous. When I went in to see my friend John, I found three or four guys lining up to kick the shit out of one of their mates. I let them get on with it, keen to hear John's amazing story.

Together with two mates, John had been going forward in a Pinkie at night to recce an enemy camp, when their wheels became entangled in barbed wire. In the dark, they had motored right into a defensive position among slit trenches. When a man popped out, John shot him at point-blank range – but at the noise the whole place erupted. When soldiers popped up out of the ground, he despatched them straight away; but as the driver tried to move off, the wire caught up round their axles and gave off such a shower of sparks that it made them an illuminated target and attracted a hail of Iraqi fire. The Land-Rover was riddled with bullets. The big Mira sight on top of it came off and hit the driver on the back of the head, and he was driving semiconscious. In the end he stopped, so that two of the crew could get down and try to cut the wire away, while Jack gave covering fire from the vehicle.

While doing this, he was badly wounded by a rifle bullet, which travelled nearly the length of his leg, through ankle, calf and thigh. The other two abandoned the stricken vehicle. The driver was still semi-conscious, so John carried Jack as far as he could, stopping every now and then to pick off a couple of the Iraqis who were following up. Soon Jack had lost so much blood that he was convinced he was going to die, and since the Iraqis were pursuing them with vehicles, using their headlights, John decided to leave him. He got out his pistol and said, 'Jack – if you want, I'll shoot you.' But the wounded man, with his mind wandering, said, 'No, no, no – the squadron will come and get me. You carry on.' So John left him with a 66 and ran off.

All night, on and off, Jack struggled to pull the 66 out to its cocked position, so that he could take out any vehicle approaching him; but in his weakened state, he lacked the strength to manage even that simple operation. In the morning the Iraqis swept the whole area with a search-party and found him lying in the desert, saved by the tourniquets which he himself had bound on as he slipped in and out of consciousness. The surgeon who operated on him had left London just before the war started, and did a brilliant job. His leg was saved, and British doctors later said they couldn't have treated it better. John and his friend were picked up by their own colleagues next day, when they made radio contact with an A-10 circling overhead. By giving a sequences of bearings, they enabled the pilot to pinpoint their position, and he in turn guided the squadron on to them.

'B' Squadron were the next to return to Victor, and we had a couple of nights on the town. We were told to be back in camp by 2300 hours, but since things didn't liven up until then, John and I decided to ignore the minibus when it came to collect us. Instead, I asked a nurse whom we'd befriended, Annie, if we could get our heads down in her flat, rather than go to the expense of a hotel. She said, 'Fine,' so we got ourselves shitfaced, and some time in the early hours collapsed on to her settees. When we came round at 9.00 the next morning, we knew there'd be trouble in store; but when we walked round the corner to the pick-up point, there stood a troop staff sergeant and a sergeant from 'A' Squadron. We felt a lot better, finding we weren't the only offenders, and in fact when we got back to camp, nobody said a thing.

Very soon after that, a message came telling us to pack. I would be on the first aircraft going home, together with the OC, SSM, and a couple of people needed for team jobs. So we left Arabia. When the Hercules landed at Cyprus and we walked into the terminal, someone said, 'Oh – we've just had some of your guys come into the hospital.' Immediately the OC got on the phone, but – quite rightly – security was tight and nobody was being allowed to speak to the released prisoners, so he had some trouble getting through. In the end he managed it, and I spoke to both Dinger and Stan.

Their voices sounded a bit flat, and I could tell they'd been through a lot; they weren't their normal bouncy selves. But Dinger said, 'Look – I owe you a pint for making me keep my jacket. I reckon it saved my life.'

'That's all right,' I said. 'But what happened? How did we split?'

'We heard an aircraft and went to ground. But I can't say much now. We'll see you when we get to the UK.'

Obviously he didn't want to talk on the phone, but I asked, 'Who else is coming back?'

'Andy and Mark.'

That was all he said. But it meant that, besides Legs, Bob Consiglio had gone. I felt very sad about Bob, good, tough little guy that he was – and immediately I wanted to know what had happened to him.

I also had a brief word with Stan. 'Ey,' I told him. 'You dropped a bollock there.'

'I know,' he agreed. 'I owe you a few pints on that. I should have stayed with you. I bloody well should have stayed.'

Chapter Eleven

Counting The Cost

As we came in to land at Lyneham, the OC was worried that the Press might be waiting for us. With our suntanned faces, we were obvious targets. He asked if I had a hood on my jacket. 'You may have to lie on the floor,' he said. But in fact there was nobody waiting for us. My main worry was that the Customs man would drop on my aluminium trunk, which contained a good deal of music equipment.

'Right,' he said. 'I know all the squadrons from your regiment are coming back. You're the first man through. Do you have anything to declare? And remember – if I find you're not telling the truth, I'm going to strip all the squadrons.' I looked him in the eye and said, 'No – I've nothing,' and he let me through.

At the guardroom in Hereford I found a message telling me to go straight to the doctor. I went round the corner on to the quadrangle, and there was Janet. It wasn't the moment for an emotional meeting; it could have been an ordinary weekend. She ran over, greeted me briefly, and came with me to see the doctor, who had arranged an appointment for me that same day at the Queen Elizabeth Hospital in Woolwich.

First, though, we drove home for my reunion with Sarah, who was being looked after by Jan's parents. It was a terrific moment. I'd been away two months, and was worried that my daughter might not remember me. But Jan told me that every night when she went to bed, she'd kissed a photograph of me and said, 'Goodnight, Daddy.' Now as we reached home she shouted, 'Hello, Daddy!' and jumped into my arms.

Once we'd got sorted out, we drove up to London, and reached Woolwich about 5p.m. I don't know what people had been expecting, but they'd scrubbed out an isolation ward for my sole benefit, and when I stuck my head round a pair of double doors, someone shouted, 'Get out! Get out!' as though I was going to contaminate the whole building. When I said I was from Hereford, they replied they'd been expecting someone to turn up in an NBC suit, glowing all over. By then the surgeon had got fed up with waiting for me, and had left; when I spoke to him on the telephone, he was not very polite. 'I've been waiting for you since nine o'clock this morning,' he griped.

'Well,' I said, 'I'm here now.'

'All right, then – I'll come back in.'

Even in the flesh he wasn't very happy at first. But when I told him I'd gone eight days without food, and might have been contaminated in a nuclear refinery, he became a different man, and asked me to report for tests in the morning.

We booked in for the night in a hotel on Blackheath Common. It was the first chance we'd had to be alone and talk the whole thing through. We went for a walk, and then, as we lay in bed, I told Jan the story.

Next day, the tests lasted all morning and into the afternoon. At the end, I went back into the isolation ward, and the doctor came in and said, 'You'd better take a seat.' His face was sombre – as if he had really bad news. Jan was outside, looking in through a glass screen.

'You've got a viral infection,' he said – but I thought he'd said 'a *venereal* infection', and nearly died. Naturally Janet and I had slept together the night before, and I thought, 'My God, surely I can't have given her a dose?' I prepared to defend myself hotly, saying I must have caught it off a toilet seat, but he saw me looking worried and asked, 'What's wrong?'

'Did you say *venereal*?'

'No, no – *viral*. I said *viral*.' he laughed and said, 'It's just a viral infection which will work its way through your body.'

He also found that I had a blood disorder, and enzymes in my liver. On the nuclear front, he did mention leukaemia, but brushed aside the possibility. Naturally that worried me, as I thought the army might be sweeping the subject under the carpet, rather than facing the truth.

After that we returned home, and 'B' Squadron went on three weeks' leave. For me, the prospect of the Everest expedition suddenly revived when Harry Taylor, who was still making his preparations, turned up at the house.

219

'You still on?' he asked.

'Damn right I am.'

I was feeling better every day, and couldn't turn the offer down. Harry said he would make special arrangements whereby I would stay at the base-camp for as long as possible and, as he put it, fatten myself up for a walk straight through all the intermediate stops – an opportunity most people never get. Usually on that kind of expedition you're sherpaing all the time, feeding the camps, building platforms for the real climbers, and then at the end the leader picks the two fittest guys to walk through. But now Harry said, 'It'll be a hell of a thing, after what you've just done, to walk straight through to the top.'

The temptation was tremendous. A glamorous adventure like that seemed just what I needed to take my mind off the Gulf and its aftermath. After a chat, we went down to a bar in Hereford to discuss things further. One reason he particularly wanted me to go was that I had medical training, and could act as expedition doctor.

As Harry and I returned home, we found the OC there. He said the army had decided to give all the survivors of the patrol a thousand pounds each, so that we could go on holiday. It was the first time the Regiment had ever done such a thing.

'Oh, great!' I said, without thinking. 'We can use that money for the expedition.'

'No way!' said Jan.

An argument set in between her, me, Harry and the OC – Harry and myself against the other two – and in the end I lost. At the end the OC said, 'I'll tell you something now. You're not getting permission from the Regiment to go on this expedition.'

'OK,' I agreed. 'Fair enough.' So instead of going to the Himalayas, I went with Jan for two weeks' holiday in Tenerife, the only place where we could book up at short notice.

In retrospect, I can see it was a mercy that I didn't go to Everest, as I simply wasn't fit enough. The party went up the North-East Ridge as planned, but Russell Bryce fell ill with altitude sickness and a stomach complaint, so that they had to return. The guy who took my place, an Australian, tried to climb the North Ridge, but turned back just short of the North Col with frostbite in his nose and fingers. The weather was horrendous. When I heard all that, I thought maybe I was well out of it.

All the same, lying by the pool in Tenerife wasn't quite the same thing, and after a short time I began counting the days till we got back. Jan and I realised we had made a mistake in not taking Sarah with us; if she'd been there, she'd have entertained us both, and stopped us from getting bored. In purely physical terms I was making a good recovery, but the psychological damage I had suffered ran deeper than I realised.

Bit by bit, we pieced together what had happened to the rest of the patrol. I'd only been home about three days when Stan phoned and came round to our house. He said the worst thing he'd ever done in his life was to ignore my warnings in the wadi. He apologised for having been an idiot, and promised that if ever we found ourselves in a tight corner again, he'd do what I told him.

After he had left me, he told me now, he walked for about four hours with the goat-herd. Towards evening they sighted a small group of buildings, with vehicles outside them. The Arab pointed to them, and Stan went down on his own. As he arrived, an Arab in a fine-looking white dishdash came out of the building, heading for a Toyota land-cruiser. Stan tried to engage him in friendly chat, but the man made a dive for the vehicle. Thinking he might have a gun there, Stan fired a single shot through the window and dropped him. The report brought about eight militiamen, armed with AK 47s, hurtling out of the building, and a firefight broke out. Stan dropped the first, and the second, but then his ammunition ran out, so he leaped into the vehicle. The key was on the floor, under the body of the first Arab, but before he could start the engine the windscreen smashed in on him and a weapon was stuck into his face. Guys dragged him out and were immediately on top of him – so that was him captured.

After what he described as 'an incredible display of uncontrolled firing into the air', the militiamen bundled him into another car and drove him into the nearest town. At first he was treated well, given tea, and questioned by relatively civilised officers who spoke good English; but later he was kept blindfolded, starved, and beaten so badly that he sustained a depressed fracture of the skull.

His cover-story, about being a medic on board a chopper on a rescue mission, held longer than anybody else's. In particular, he said he was a dentist – which he was – so that when the Iraqis actually brought patients in to him, he was able to look at their mouths and give a diagnosis that was completely plausible. One of the interrogators then asked him where he had worked in London – and when he gave the number of some orderly room, the Iraqis went so far as to ring it to find out if the details were genuine. Early in February he was moved to a base camp near Baghdad and reunited in a cell with Andy and Dinger.

Of course Stan and I indulged in a lot of speculation: if we'd done this, if we'd done that; if we'd stayed together; if we'd walked down the railway line. In fact, if there'd been two of us, I think we'd both have been captured. Lonely as it was to be on my own, I was probably better off. Psychologically it was bad, but physically it was safer. There was only one person to hide, one made less noise than two, and there was no chance that the pair of us would talk ourselves into doing something stupid. On my own, I was more careful than I might have been with a partner. If there'd been two of us, we probably would have broken into a house in search of food, and that might have led to our capture. Being alone was what saved me. That said, I would have given anything for a companion.

Happily, Stan made a full recovery. He'd had a hell of a battering, but his equable character seemed to enable him to bounce quickly back to normal. Thinking over his final firefight, he realised it had been Vince's weapon that he was using, and Vince could never have reloaded with a full magazine – which would have held up to thirty rounds – after the initial contact. We assumed that after he had been captured, the goat-herd must have come down to the buildings where the firefight took place, told the militia that there was a second runaway out in the wadi, and directed the party that came in search of me.

After our return to the UK, Stan and I remained on close terms. Andy was a different matter. When he got back, he didn't seem to want to make contact. Several times I phoned his house in Hereford, but I always spoke to his girlfriend, and he never returned my calls. That seemed strange to me. I couldn't make out why he was being so stand-offish. It was as if he didn't want to come round and face me.

It was inevitable that we would meet sooner or later. Sure

enough, on one of our first days back at work, we bumped into each other in the OC's office on the squadron. When I saw him, I went, 'Hey!' and he just looked up and nodded. There was no handshake, no 'Glad to see you back' or anything like that. I was disappointed that a mate of mine could behave in that way, and I could only put it down to jealousy and the fact that I'd got away while he was caught. Thereafter, we'd talk about it if we were thrown together, but we never met for a drink to shoot the shit. To me it was pretty sad that anyone could carry on in a way so alien to the spirit of the Regiment, which values companionship and loyalty above everything. A psychiatrist who had us all in for a talk told us that after what we'd been through together, we'd remain very close to each other – and indeed his words applied to everyone except Andy.

As to the reason why the patrol originally broke in two – that was never satisfactorily explained. What happened, unbeknown to me, was that Andy, who was four back down the column, heard a jet overhead, and immediately went down on one knee in an attempt to contact the pilot on his TACBE, calling out to Vince ahead of him, 'Go to ground!' He was so busy trying to raise the pilot that he didn't realise Vince had never heard his call, and had carried on. The rest of the guys, who had gone down behind Andy, were all watching their arcs, as they should have been, so that they noticed nothing either.

Up front, I'd heard nothing. How I missed the sound of an aircraft, I can't imagine – it was the one noise we were all longing to hear. Whatever the reason, I'd gone on walking as hard as I could. Whenever I glanced over my shoulder, I saw Stan behind me, and Vince behind him, and I never had an inkling that anything was amiss. Then again, how we became so widely separated we've never managed to work out. Andy told me that after trying to contact the aircraft he'd heard, his party saw movement up ahead. As they went to ground and watched, three figures came walking across their front. His own guys weren't sure if the men were friend or foe, but they assumed they were an Iraqi patrol and didn't challenge them, letting them disappear into the night.

In any case, the five picked themselves up and started walking to the north-west, and when dawn came they laid up for the day in the lee of a mound, where they destroyed the encrypting unit for the radio – no easy task, as it was in a soldier-proof metal casing. They also burnt their code book. Because they had no use for Stan's Minimi, they stripped it into pieces and scattered the parts over a wide area of desert. Luckily for them, they had ignored the orders for maintaining hard routine – no cooking or smoking – and they'd all brought brew kits, so that they were able to make themselves hot drinks. Even so, because of the snow, rain, wind and bitter cold, Mark began going down with exposure, so the group decided to risk a daylight move. They got up and made good progress until they reached a main road, where they planned to hijack a vehicle.

With Bob playing the part of a wounded man, and leaning on Andy's shoulder, they flagged down a car which turned out to be a taxi. As it stopped, the other three came up out of cover and surrounded it. Evicting the driver and two other passengers, they took one man with them, because he looked so scared that they thought he might help, and set off westwards along the highway.

All went well until they reached a VCP. Some way short of it they got out of the car, having – as they thought – arranged with their driver that he would drive through the control and pick them up on the other side. In fact he shopped them, and they had to take to the desert, boxing the VCP on foot.

Back on the MSR further west, they tried to pull the same wounded-man dodge again, but all the drivers were going, as Andy put it, 'like madmen', and three successive attempts failed. Leaving the road again, and moving north towards the Euphrates, they found themselves in an area of habitation. By then they reckoned they were only ten kilometres from the river; but behind them military vehicles began to pull up on the highway, and troops poured out and opened fire. The rounds went well over them, but then three or four anti-aircraft guns opened up as well. On the whole this was helpful, as it made locals think an air-raid was in progress, and put them into shelter.

From a high point the patrol saw that the town of Krabilah was in fact joined up with Abu Kamal, and that the built-up area extended right across the border. Reaching the bank of the Euphrates, they took a fix with their Magellan, and this confirmed that they were only ten kilometres from the frontier. By then it was dark. They considered trying to cross the river, but concluded that the risk of going down with exposure was too high. In the end they decided to keep heading west, with the hope of reaching the border that night.

Inevitably, they came on enemy positions; contacts ensued, and the firing brought all the defenders to a high state of alert. Creeping, crawling, working their way forward through ploughed fields and along hedges, they made slow progress. Andy, Mark and Bob had a contact during which Bob got split off and ended up in a contact of his own, when he held the Iraqis off for thirty minutes, single handed, before he was shot and killed outright. To have defended himself like that for half an hour, against a force of maybe a dozen Iraqis, was one hell of a feat. At the end, I feel certain, he must have run out of rounds. God knows how many Iraqis he took out: a lot, I know. After the war he was awarded a posthumous Military Medal.

With Bob cut off on his own, Mark got shot in the arm and ankle, and he and Andy split up. In the end Andy was captured only a couple of kilometres from the border – and he must have been somewhere very close to the line of my own route.

Legs and Dinger, on their own now, went towards the Euphrates, but soon ran on to another enemy position. Suddenly they heard a weapon cocked, and something shouted in Iraqi, from only ten metres ahead. They let fly a hail of automatic fire from the 203 and Minimi, and received only half a dozen rounds in return. Pulling back, they retreated to the river bank. By then enemy were closing on them from the east, firing occasional bursts. Finding a canoe moored to the bank, they tried to release its chain but could not manage it, and slipped into the water, planning to swim across. Soon they came to land again, only to find that they were on a spit or island, with the main channel still to cross. Only 200 metres upstream, a big road-bridge spanned the whole Euphrates. They could see several vehicles parked on it, and numerous people, some shining flashlights down on to the water. Elsewhere, intermittent firing kept breaking out.

After waiting an hour, during which they became increasingly cold, they decided their only option was to swim the second channel. Luckily Legs had found a polystyrene box, and they broke this into pieces, which they stuffed into the fronts of their smocks to increase their buoyancy. Then they waded out and swam.

The water was icy, the current strong; they found it hard to make progress, and had to let go their weapons. Legs, who was going down with hypothermia, began to fail. When he fell back, Dinger got hold of him and towed him on. Reaching the far bank, Dinger dragged him out, only to realise that he had become incoherent, and could not walk.

Daylight revealed a small tin pumphouse some fifteen metres from the shore. Dinger pulled Legs into it, but he was so far gone that he kept trying to crawl back into the river. Inside the shelter Dinger lit his remaining hexi-block and brewed up a cup of hot water, hoping it would revive his companion. Legs, however, was making no sense, and instead of drinking the hot water, he hit the mug away. When the sun rose, Dinger dragged him out into it, in the hope that it would warm and dry him, but he was too far gone; his skin remained cold, and his eyes flickered meaninglessly back and forth.

When farmers appeared and started to work in the fields, Dinger pulled him back into the hut. Then at mid-morning a man with some children in tow came within ten metres of the pumphouse. Seeing that he was about to be compromised, Dinger showed himself to the farmer, whose response was to lock the two fugitives in and run off shouting. By that time Legs' smock was dry, but he was slipping into unconsciousness. Clearly he could not move, so Dinger burst his way through the roof of the hut and made off towards the north, away from the river, in the hope that he'd pull the enemy away from Legs and give him a chance to recover. Almost immediately he was spotted and followed by a posse of locals, who soon swelled into a crowd. He tried to do a runner, but was caught by the mob, one of whom proposed to cut off one of his ears. The guy was actually holding his ear when he managed to bring out one of his sovereigns. The people fought over that, but then realised he had more, and he started handing them out, which cooled them down. Then they walked him into a village, where the people went wild and beat him to the ground before he was handed over to the police. While in the police station, Dinger saw Legs being brought in on a stretcher. He was quickly cross-loaded into an ambulance and driven away, but although Dinger watched closely, he saw no movement, and feared that his companion was already dead. So ended a gallant escape attempt.

By the next night, when I had my own contact and made the Euphrates, the survivors were in gaol, and being questioned by officers who'd been through Sandhurst. But the Iraqis had evolved their own kind of interrogation techniques. All the survivors were brutally beaten for several days, partly in the course of interrogation, partly by their guards, who hit them casually whenever they saw a chance. Even Mark was beaten between operations on his wounded ankle. The Iraqis were greatly agitated by their belief that the prisoners were Israelis, and when Andy tried to convince them that he was not by showing them his foreskin, they were astonished. Our guys stuck to their story of being a medical team for as long as possible, and then fell back on controlled release of real information.

Back in the UK, I was glad that I had been tortured by weather, thirst and hunger rather than by human beings. But all of us had suffered, and all reacted in different ways. Stan bounced back quickly. So did Andy. The worst affected was Dinger. I believe he felt exactly as I felt – that all he wanted was to be back with the guys, working among them. But because he'd appeared on CNN television news, the head-shed decided that his security was blown, and sent him off to a safe house in the middle of Wales.

That was the last thing he wanted. It was as if he'd been transferred from one prison straight to another, and soon he was desperate for company. He phoned me and said, 'Chris – for Christ's sake come up and see me, or get the guys over. I'm cracking up here.' I went into the Squadron and asked if we could go, but they said, 'No visitors. No one's to go up.' So I had some long chats with Dinger on the phone, and got his version of events.

It took him a long time to recover. For a year, at least, he remained very emotional, and to me he looked like a lost boy, on the point of panic. Because the Press found out where he lived, and took to hanging about outside, he had to move to a less nice house. But eventually he settled down again.

As for me – I tried to persuade myself that all was well, and when the psychiatrist asked if everything was all right, I just said, 'Fine.'

'Sleeping all right?'

'Fine.'

In fact I was still being troubled by the same recurrent night-mare. But if I wanted to talk about it to anyone, I preferred to talk to Jan, to my mother, my father or my brother, rather than to someone who didn't know me.

One day I was lying in bed at about eleven in the morning, when I got a telephone call from the guy who had been Vince's next-door neighbour. 'Chris,' he said, 'the family's all here wait-ing for you to come round. They've asked me to make contact with you. I'll come and pick you up.'

'Is the CO and everybody there?' I asked him.

'I think so, yes.'

'OK,' I said. 'I'll get ready.'

A few minutes later I was there, but I found that the only other outsider present was the CO's wife. As soon as I walked into the room, she stood up and legged it. I was left with Vince's Mum, his Dad, his widow and three of his brothers. Everybody was looking at me, and I was looking at them. It was a horrible feeling, to have to sit and tell them the story.

The father said, 'You've come round to tell us what hap-pened.'

'Yeah, OK. D'you want me to tell you, and then you tell the family – because it's quite distressing?'

The man went, 'No – just tell us all together.'

Until then the Regiment had said, 'You don't tell anyone any-thing about what happened on this patrol. There's nothing to come out.' Well – I was there, and I thought, 'Bollocks – I'm going to start from the beginning.' So I sat down with them and told the story.

I left out some details about Vince not wanting to be there, and just said he had died of exposure during our second night on the run. The family were pretty stunned. I hardly knew what to say, because I was in a difficult position.

One of the brothers turned round and said, 'How come *you* didn't die, then?'

I said, 'Well, I was lucky. Exposure can take you at different times.'

'But my brother was really strong,' he protested. 'He'd worked in the snow loads of times and survived.'

I don't blame them for wanting an explanation. But I legged it as soon as I could.

The Iraqis had returned the bodies of all the dead men, and five or six days later we had the funerals. It was a harrowing occasion for everyone, as we'd all lost close friends or relatives. The survivors of the patrol gathered together – and then Vince's father and brothers came across towards us. When one of the brothers accused me of not telling the truth about Vince, I took a deep breath and walked away. Andy McNab grabbed the man and said, 'Just watch your mouth. That's enough.' I knew why the brother had thought that: some newspaper had reported that Vince had been captured and tortured by Iraqis, so that everything had become confused. I think the family had had this image of a super-hero – someone who could never be taken, who was indestructible. It was difficult for them to believe that two of the patrol had frozen to death in the desert.

Then everything died down until about three months later. One evening I was in a bar with my wife and I saw this man come in. I said to Jan, 'Jesus, I know that guy, but I can't think who he is.' The fellow kept staring across at me. I thought he looked like an old-time Regiment guy. Then I realised: it was Vince's father, together with the brother who had challenged me.

By then the inquest had taken place. We'd all had to go to Oxford and give evidence from behind a screen. A pathologist had given his report – but the family had never seen Vince's body. So anyway the father came up to us in this bar and said, 'Chris, I need to talk to you.'

I thought, 'If the brother says anything, I'm going to drop him.' For a moment I stood there looking – but Jan must have seen my reaction, because she came straight over.

The father said, 'Listen – did you tell me the truth about Vince?'

'Yes,' I said. 'I've nothing to hide. In my heart of hearts, I know he died that night.'

'Well – you said Vince died on 25 January. I've just been up to the Regimental graveyard, and on his plaque they've got him dying a month later.'

'That's got to be wrong, then,' I said. 'I can give you my word it was that second night.'

I could see that the father was really distressed. As far as he was concerned, things didn't add up. No wonder he thought a cover-up had been staged. I knew 'A' Squadron was having a party up in the camp, and knew there would be someone there who could confirm my story – so I offered to take father and son straight up. Jan came with us. We jumped into a taxi and legged it up towards the camp. On the way I made the driver stop at the regimental plot and wait while I ran in and looked at the stone. Sure enough, the dates were wrong, not just for Vince, but for all three of them, Bob and Legs as well. Someone had made a terrible cock-up.

I took Vince's people into the club, got hold of the sergeant major and told him what had happened. He promised to sort it out, confirmed the real dates, and apologised to Vince's family. Next morning I went in and told the Families' Officer – and in due course they got new gravestones and changed the plaques.

Some aspects of the aftermath were less gloomy. As I was walking through the camp one day, the Quartermaster – who'd been the RSM when I passed Selection – shouted across at me, 'Hey, Chris – come 'ere!'

In his office he said, 'What happened to your sovereigns?'

'Oh,' I said, 'I lost them during the contact.'

'Well – I've got a list of the kit you lost during the contact, and you must have had a bergen the size of a bloody caravan.'

'Why?'

'Look at this.'

The list was a mile long, a complete farce. It included things like mountaineering boots and a Lacon box – a big metal container. What I didn't realise was that the SQMS had written off mountains of stuff without telling me.

'This includes everything I took to the Gulf when we went out,' I said. 'Not what I had in my bergen. When I got back to Victor, the Lacon box had gone missing and I'd lost the lot.'

'All right,' he said. 'Write me a note saying how you lost your sovereigns, and we'll forget about the rest.' In fact I had distributed the remaining sovereigns to those who I thought most deserved them – the other survivors of the patrol and members of my family.

With 'B' Squadron settled back in Hereford, Jan and I threw a party at home. Somehow 110 people crammed themselves into the house, and at one point the OC sighted my escape map, by then framed on the wall, with three sovereigns mounted in the surround.

'Chris,' he said. 'I thought you'd lost them all.'

'Yes,' I said.

'Well – you've got three up there. You shouldn't do that . . .'

'Yeah – right!' And that was the end of it.

Chapter Twelve

Wash-Up

Only six weeks after the squadrons returned to Hereford, there took place the Regiment's 50th anniversary celebrations. Unfortunately the founder, David Stirling, had recently died, but many veterans of the Second World War took part in the festivities, and everyone said how strange but also satisfactory it was that in Iraq the SAS had reverted to its original role as a long-range desert group, operating heavily-armed, motorised patrols in enemy-held territory.

We owed the fact that the patrols were deployed to General de la Billière's enthusiasm for Special Forces, and to his understanding of their capabilities. But it was largely luck that the SAS played such a crucial role. DLB had been advocating their insertion for general intelligence-gathering purposes, but as it turned out, their arrival in the Western Desert abruptly cut off the stream of Scud missiles which Saddam Hussein was directing at Israel, and so, by a hair's breadth, kept Israel out of the war. If she had come in, the results would almost certainly have been disastrous, because some or all of the Arab nations would have refused to fight alongside Israeli forces, and the Coalition would have disintegrated before the ground war began.

The role Special Forces played in the war was, therefore, outstanding. All the same, to lose three out of eight men in one patrol was a severe blow to the Regiment, and the disaster led to various internal reforms. Oddly enough, the survivors of Bravo Two Zero were never brought together for a formal debriefing: instead, we were all asked to write reports of what had happened, and these were collated at regimental level. I also had to give a five-minute talk to the Regiment as a whole.

In retrospect, it was clear that shortages of ammunition and equipment had had little material effect on the outcome of

232

events. They had worried us, certainly, but they had not contributed to the patrol being compromised. The most serious deficiency lay in our maps, which were totally inadequate, and in the lack of accurate intelligence about the physical nature of the area into which we were deployed. If we'd known there was no sand, we would obviously have made some alternative plan.

Another fact which became clear was that we should have compiled a formal written E & E plan before we deployed. If we'd done that, and made it clear that in the event of trouble we were going to head for Syria, we'd have had a much better chance of being picked up by the searching helicopters. It was also clear that we seriously over estimated the capabilities of our TACBEs – and the fact that we were given the wrong radio frequencies was simply a mistake, probably due to the speed at which we had to prepare. As to the way the patrol split, I see no point in blaming anyone. It was just something that happened, at a moment when we were all under maximum stress.

In Hereford, together with the Int Officer and a decent map, I worked out the exact distances I had walked. On the first night, before and after the split, we covered 70 kilometres. On the second night Stan and I made forty, losing Vince in the middle. On the third I walked another forty to reach the Euphrates. The fourth night was the most frustrating, as I had to cover forty kilometres in zig-zags and boxes to make only ten towards the border. On the fifth night I advanced thirty kilometres and then did another five or six during the day, up into the wadis. The sixth night took me into and out of the nuclear refinery – another thirty. The last and most terrible night I did between forty and fifty – most of them unnecessarily. The total came to 290, or just under 200 miles.

I found that people were beginning to compare my escape with that of Jack Sillito, who trekked for more than 100 miles through the Western Desert of North Africa in 1942, having been stranded behind German lines. In spite of the fact that all members of the SAS are supposed to know their regimental history, I must confess that I had never heard of Sillito until somebody pointed out his name in a 50th-anniversary account of the Regiment by the cartoonist Jak. Without realising it, I had easily beaten Sillito's distance, walking nearly twice as far. But in fact the two escapes were made in widely different circumstances.

Whereas my main enemy was cold, his was heat, and he had no river to give him water or guide him. Instead, he navigated by sun and stars, and scrounged liquid from condensation in abandoned jerricans.

At the end of June I heard the good news that in the Gulf War honours list I had been awarded the Military Medal. Many of my SAS colleagues also received decorations, and the tributes to the Regiment which flowed in were enough to make anyone feel proud. In a personal letter to General de la Billière, General Norman Schwarzkopf described the performance of 22nd SAS as 'courageous and highly professional'. He recorded that the activities of 'A' and 'D' Squadrons, combined with those of Delta Force 'A' Squadron, had convinced the enemy that in Western Iraq they were facing forces more than ten times the size of the units actually on the ground. He also stressed the very high value of the briefings which SAS personnel gave to the US Special Forces before they were deployed, and said that if it had not been for these 'thorough indoctrinations', the Americans would have suffered many more casualties.

I myself received several flattering letters from senior officers. 'Your personal bravery, sound judgement and quite outstanding resolve were an example to all SAS soldiers,' wrote Field Marshal Lord Bramall, former Chief of the Defence Staff, and by then Colonel Commandant of the SAS. 'Your escape is a classic of its kind, and worthy of national recognition.' At the end of the typewritten letter the Field Marshal added in his own hand: 'What a feat of courage and endurance. Well done indeed.'

The Director of the SAS wrote in similar terms, saying that my escape 'more than proves that our E & E training is fully justified'. Another stirring tribute came from Colonel J.A. McGregor, who wrote on behalf of the Parachute Regiment to say that 'undoubtedly Airborne Forces are very proud of your dedication and professionalism, and you will certainly inspire others to follow in your footsteps'. Yet for me the most pleasing of all was a note from General de la Billière, thanking me for my 'personal support' while under his command, and saying how delighted he was that my operational work had been recognised by the Queen.

Later, in a presentation copy of *Storm Command*, his book about the Gulf War, he wrote, 'You have personally made SAS history.' For us survivors, a particularly memorable day was the one on which he brought General Schwarzkopf to Hereford. The big American couldn't have been more friendly or informal: he shook hands with each of us, sat down for a debrief, signed our escape maps, and was exceptionally generous in his praise of what the Regiment had achieved.

My involvement with American Special Forces was renewed when Major General Wayne Downing asked me to go across and give a talk to their Training Wing about lessons learnt in the war. The guy who picked me up at the airport didn't know what I'd done, and began talking big about some escape-and-evasions in which his people had been involved. 'We had one of three, and one of seven,' he told me proudly.

'Seven what?' I asked.

'Seven hours – it was quite something.'

'Great!' I said. 'I've just done one of seven *days*.'

After that initial hiccup, the Americans looked after me magnificently. Among other facilities, they showed me a big interrogation centre out in the middle of Fort Bragg, built to look like a Vietnamese camp. When my guide said casually, 'By the way, we've arranged for you to spend a couple of days going through it,' I nearly died. 'There's no way I'm entering that place,' I told him. 'I'll walk round it, but that's all.'

More to my liking was a vertical wind-tunnel, designed to teach free-falling techniques. I'd never done any free-falling, but the Americans soon had me in the tunnel, where a powerful rising column of air, created by a jet engine, enables you to learn how to become stable and manoeuvre before you jump out of an aircraft. My hosts were hell-bent on arranging a full course for me, and actually did so – but unfortunately my own training commitments prevented me taking up the offer. When I came to learn free-falling proper, I found that my half-hour in the tunnel had given me a tremendous advantage over other beginners, and that on only my second jump, from 12,000 feet, I was immediately stable.

My trip to America was good fun, but I was amazed to learn that an F-15 E fighter-bomber had been shot down by a surface-to-air missile over northern Iraq on 19 January – three days before Bravo Two Zero had been deployed. The target had been the nuclear refinery at Al Qaim, and the pilot and navigator had landed by parachute next to the very power cables which I had followed. The downed air-crew had managed to contact another pilot with their TACBEs, but in trying to escape, they walked up to three buildings which they thought were houses – only to find that they were bunkers housing the troops from the nearby anti-aircraft position. It was extraordinary to realise that these were the buildings which I myself had approached, and had sheared off in the nick of time. I also learnt that Al Qaim had been one of Iraq's main Scud-holding areas.

I found all this fascinating – but also it was disturbing that none of the information had been passed to us in Special Forces, before we were sent across the border. We had not even been told the refinery at Al Qaim was one of the Americans' main targets. Looking back, it seemed all the more incredible that I had come through unscathed. First, the Americans had repeatedly bombed the plant. Then the aircrew had been captured near it. Then Andy and the rest of our patrol had been picked up or killed close by. The very night I passed through the complex, the Americans bombed it again.

Had I known how hot the area was, I would never gone near it.

For a while after our holiday in Tenerife, my relationship with Jan was all right. I was kept busy on exercises, and seemed to be more my old self. Then in August 1991 I and one other guy were detailed at short notice to go out to a central African country, where the political situation was deteriorating fast and people were needed to guard the British Embassy and evacuate the ambassador, together with his remaining staff.

Jan was furious that I, out of everyone available, had been selected for what was obviously a dangerous task. But in fact the team grew from two to four, and then to eight.

By the time we flew out, things had become so bad that there was a strong possibility that we might have to stage a fighting withdrawal across a large river into the friendly state next door – but the limitations on our equipment raised uncomfortable echoes of Bravo Two Zero. We decided we would need anti-personnel mines, 66s, a 7.62 gympi, claymores . . . and the Government turned round and said, 'We can't send you with all that; you'll take pistols and 9mm. sub-machine guns.'

Those would be little good against a crowd on the rampage. We arrived in Africa to find the atmosphere highly volatile; riots and looting were being orchestrated by the military, but things seemed to cool down as quickly as they heated up, and it was impossible to tell what would happen next. An operation that was supposed to be over in three days ended up lasting three months – and three very long months they seemed.

One by one the other nations pulled out – first the French, then the Belgians, then the Americans, leaving us on our own. The British Ambassador was constantly talking over a satellite telephone to Douglas Hurd and other leading figures at the Foreign and Commonwealth Office in London, but the message didn't seem to sink in at the other end. Even when we'd reported a major riot within 200 metres of the Embassy, London kept asking, 'Yes – but what's the atmosphere like?' The straight answer was 'Bloody dangerous!' and we felt like saying, 'For Christ's sake get us out of here.'

The reason we stayed so long was that the diplomatic complex was brand-new – a £5 million building which dealt with five of the surrounding African countries. Outside it, the place was in chaos, with inflation raging, and food running out. Outside, the hospital lepers were carrying off the bodies of patients who'd died, to eat them, and they were even scrounging the limbs of amputees.

One night things seemed so edgy that we told the staff to collect their possessions, leave their houses, and gather in the embassy itself. The Manager heard that people were raiding his home, and came running for help. Gary, who was in charge, got the team together, but I said, 'What's the point of going up there, just to save a load of crap? There's nothing worth having.'

But Gary said, 'No – we've got to do it.' So we put on our ops waistcoats, collected our MP5s and pistols, with night-sights, and drove down a back-alley between whitewashed buildings. We could hear the rumble of the crowd in the distance; when the vehicle stopped, and I lifted my kite-sight, I could see several hundred people, all looking at us.

'If they've got weapons, we're knackered,' I said. But we got out and started walking down towards them. At our approach they fell back, tripping over each other. The noise of so many people moving was enough to scare the pants off you. Then the manager went running into his house, and back out again with a single pair of trousers in his hand. As he jumped into the vehicle, he was yelling, 'Let's go! Let's go!' The second we moved off, the crowd erupted. They poured over his house, into it, through it, like ants, and ripped the place to shreds.

Back in the embassy I was furious with Gary, effing and blinding. 'Cunt!' I stormed. 'We could all have been killed, just for a pair of trousers!' Poor Gary did his best to soothe me down, but I stormed off to my room still in a rage.

The situation was frightening by any standards – there are few more alarming sights than that of an African mob on the rampage – but on a personal level I was becoming worried, because my own behaviour had grown noticeably erratic. The other SAS guys noticed that I wasn't my normal self; I would refuse to carry out quite reasonable requests, and often gave way to outbursts of anger.

In the end, in November, the Ambassador heard that I had been summoned to go to Buckingham Palace to collect my Military Medal. Because a young secretary needed escorting home, he asked me to go with her.

At the airport check-in, the official told me to open my suitcase, and also my Lacon box, in which I had several native clay masks which I'd bought in the market. He started unwrapping the masks, and said, 'These are works of art, which you're taking out of the country. I need money off you.'

'No, no,' I said. 'They're not worth anything. You can buy them everywhere.'

'I need money,' he repeated.

'Well – I haven't got any.'

For some reason I went into a deep panic, as if I was physically scared of the man. He became so upset that he threw my case off his desk, so that my things went all over the floor. If I'd been myself, I'd just have said, 'Sling it. You can have the lot,' and I'd have left everything where it lay. As it was, I behaved as if these things were all my worldly possessions, and grovelled about trying to get them re-packed. Behind me came some Japanese people with a television set packed in a wooden case. Again the man demanded money, and when they said they had none, he ripped the packing to bits and threw the television aside, so that it had to travel without protection. God knows what state it was in when it arrived at the other end.

Altogether, the atmosphere was horrible – and in the VIP lounge the security people were into my briefcase, demanding money again. (The girl I was supposed to escort had to fly economy, so that she was already checked in.) During the flight I was so wound-up that I spent a lot of time in the toilet, being physically sick. I couldn't eat or drink anything, but sat there feeling ashamed of myself at being so frightened.

Back home, my symptoms grew even worse. When I was under pressure at work, a rash like psoriasis came out on my face and chest, and the nightmares started recurring. Worst of all, I had changed emotionally – how, I don't know – but when I came back, all I wanted was to be by myself. Suddenly I didn't want to be married any more. I didn't want to be with Jan, or even to see Sarah.

I began behaving impossibly. Jan was destroyed; she couldn't make out what she had done wrong – and of course I couldn't explain, because she hadn't done anything. The trouble lay in me. All I could say was, 'I don't know what the matter is. I just don't want you around.'

Things became so bad that she decided she'd take Sarah to live with her parents in Ireland. I mortgaged our house as far as I could afford, to give her some money, and we agreed to try a separation. So she planned to move across, and I faced the prospect of living on my own.

Even as I was walking out, on the day she was leaving, I said, 'You know, this is probably a mistake.' We went through with it for the time being; but, almost as soon as she'd gone, I seemed to realise what I was throwing away. Three or four months later I rang her up and said, 'Listen, I'm off to the jungle for six weeks, but when I'm home again, will you come back?' Her response was guarded: she said she'd come across, because she wanted to talk, but she didn't commit herself.

While I was away she moved back in, so that I found her and Sarah in the house when I returned. Things remained up and down for a while, but then, I'm glad to say, we got back to the level we'd been on at the beginning.

At the time I just didn't know why I behaved as I did. Now I see that the trouble must have been post-traumatic stress, coming out months after the event. When I returned from the Gulf, I didn't feel any different from normal, but a few of the guys noticed that I wasn't myself, and it seems to have been the pressure of life in Africa that brought the problem to a head.

On the family front, my mother was pleased that, of her three sons, I was the one who had had that unnerving experience. 'I knew that if *anyone* would come back, you would,' she said.

My Dad had always maintained he would never forgive my cousin Billy for getting me involved with the SAS in the first place, and my reply had always been, 'Well – look at the good side. If I hadn't joined up, I'd never have met Jan, or had Sarah.' Now he wasn't going to change his tune, and he said very little about my long walk. But I think that he was secretly proud of me. Oddly enough, in the past few years he'd gone right back to where he had started in terms of shooting; having given it up, and frowned on me for wanting to kill birds and animals, he was once again as keen as ever.

As for our visit to Buckingham Palace: it was all very splendid going to London, and an honour to meet the Queen, but I would have much preferred to receive the Military Medal in front of the whole Regiment. My ideal would have been to have all the guys on parade, and for every man who had been decorated to be brought out of the ranks and get his award with all the rest watching. I knew that the medal-winners included some of the bravest soldiers in the world. In the SAS, no award is given away, and every one had been fully earned. When I came home, I pinned the medal on Sarah, and she wore it as a badge.

Lying in bed four years later, I still see incidents from the patrol, and hear the sounds, as clear as day. I see rounds flying between us during the first contact. I see Stan walking off down the wadi with the goat-herd. I see the two hooded Arabs waiting for me on top of the mound. I try to put the images from my mind, but they creep back in. More and more I realise how lucky I was not to be shot, not to be captured, not to be caught up in the barbed wire on the border. Sometimes I feel that I must have used up all my luck.

All in all, my experience taught me a good deal about myself. Most people, I think, don't know what they're capable of until they're put to the test. Before the Gulf War, if somebody had told me I could walk nearly 300 kilometres through enemy territory in seven nights, with no food and practically no water, with inadequate clothes, no proper sleep and no shelter, I wouldn't have believed him. When I had to, I did it. Whether I could do it a second time is another matter.

In 1991 I was at a peak of physical fitness, and armed with the skills, the endurance, the competitive instinct and the motivation which SAS training had instilled in me. In any event, I devoutly hope I'll never again be faced by such a challenge. With an ordeal of those dimensions, once in a lifetime is enough.

CPSIA information can be obtained
at www.ICGtesting.com
Printed in the USA
LVOW11s2114190517
535100LV00002B/2/P